Taxation and Ethics

An Introduction to Tax Policies for Voters

by Carl Simmons
© 2019 © 2026

Table of Contents

1

The Difficulties of the Discussion

Why Tax Policy and Ethics *should* Matter to Voters, but in Fact Don't

Theoretically, tax policy is very important to voters. After all, most individual voters do not like to pay taxes—but at the same time most want [at least some] of the government services that their taxes (or at least other people's taxes) pay for. In theory, this would result in voters having frank and informed discussions with each other regarding what government services they are actually willing to pay for, and at what price. Yet that is not at all what actually happens—and is in fact so far removed from reality as to be absurd. But why is this case? And must it be the case?

Many different factors and processes have contributed to the current situation, and it may not be possible (or even entirely useful) to detail them all; but one or two of the more significant factors warrant particular examination. One of the most significance is ignorance: most voters simply do not understand tax policy—either the economic or the political issues surrounding it—and are certainly not motivated to invest great amounts of time and energy in trying to understand it, as they themselves get no direct hand in building it, but rather only vote for representatives who enact policy. Meanwhile many elected representatives themselves do not understand it or even try to, but rather rely upon staffers, experts, and/or their party leadership to make judgment calls for them. What the elected politician is more concerned with understanding is how to get re-elected, and it pays them little dividend to develop a deep understanding of tax policy if that will not win them votes. The object of their understanding is to balance their voters' competing demands for lower taxes and greater government services—which they often resolve by simply promising both, and let future generations take the consequences. Which attitude the voters seem content to accept, insofar as they continue to elect these representatives instead of changing them out for better ones. Clearly, promising benefits now while deferring costs to future generations is a winning electoral strategy, at least most of the time; which brings us to the second great factor to consider: we, as a society, do not seem to be much concerned with the ethical matters relating to tax policy.

This book is an attempt to address both of these issues—the ignorance of the economics of taxation and the apathy towards ethics—upon which our current system(s) of taxation are managed. It aims to be a beginning step toward voters having those frank and informed discussions with each other regarding how much they are willing to pay for the government services they desire—and how much they are determined to make their fellow voters pay for them. (As for the scope of services desired, those conversations are so varied and numerous I leave it to others to address; I will confine myself to the taxation portion only, which we must consider whether we want larger or smaller government.)

Ignorance of the Economics of Taxation

To say that voters are ignorant here is to risk giving great offense; for no one enjoys being told they are ignorant, even when the statement is quite true. It might help if I pointed out that the people who pick up a book like this are more likely to be better informed about the topic, and therefore the problem is that *other* voters are ignorant—but while that strategy might mollify our pride, it is unfortunately not as true as we need it to be: yes, the majority of "other" voters lack economic knowledge, but even many (or most) intelligent, well-informed voters are ignorant (or at least uninformed) about important aspects of tax policy—or to be more accurate, tax poli*cies*. To tackle this issue, we will have to get over our offense, and instead adopt the wisdom of Socrates, who was wisest of all the Athenians because he understood that he was ignorant.

Ignorance (or more politely, the state of being uninformed) is our natural condition; and we cannot possibly become experts in every domain of knowledge. Now for most aspects of our lives, we do not have to become experts, but can rather entrust ourselves to those who are expert: so we trust our doctors with our medical treatment, and our mechanics with our automobiles, and our IT department with our computers—and our politicians with our economy. But this last bit of deference is not like the others, for while we have very good reasons to trust our doctors (who have degrees and very good reputations) and our mechanics (at least those who have built very good reputations) and our IT departments (who have fixed our computers before, and so built their reputations), we do *not* have very good reason at all to trust our politicians (who generally do *not* have very good reputations). Our doctors, mechanics, IT technicians, and other experts build their reputations through repeated successes; but our politicians build theirs through rhetoric and promises (which are often discovered to be false) and by passing legislation which might or might not have the effect(s) they intend (and other effects besides), but which economic effects we are never informed of (of misinformed of, as different politicians and analysts claim different effects).

Yet even while most Americans do not trust their politicians, they still vote for them (for at least they trust the ones they vote for more than they trust the opposing candidates)—and the fact that Americans vote makes the problem of ignorance even more significant, for as voters we get to have some little say about which economic policies we want, so we really ought to invest in developing enough knowledge and understanding to choose wisely. But making that investment is difficult, for a number of reasons:

1. To begin with, we are simply busy. A person who works 40 hours a week, and has other responsibilities besides, has many more pressing priorities which take up the scarce amount of time available. To say a voter is responsible for learning about a topic is one thing; but just how much time *ought* a voter invest in learning a topic which only seems to matter once every couple of years?

2. The average American has only had instruction in economics for one semester of school, during the 12th grade—and that class probably never specifically addressed tax policy. (Meanwhile the quality of economics classes is highly variable across the country, with some people getting a very helpful introduction to economics, and others getting very little insight into the subject at all).

3. We can look up expert opinion on economics, and specifically on the economics of tax policy—but many of the experts vehemently disagree, so who are we to trust? If acknowledged/accredited experts can be in such disagreement about the facts, what knowledge in this field is even possible?

4. While we can predict the impacts of different economic/tax policies, we cannot run multiple Earth experiments using different policies; so we are unavoidably ignorant of what would have happened had we tried another policy. Given the uncountable variables at work in any economy, there is always room for disagreement between people (experts or not) about the specific results of specific policies.

5. Sometimes, however, we get data that matches predictions very well, so we can be confident in our theories; but this means we have to be attentive not only to the debates before a policy is passed, but also to the effects after it has taken into effect, measure across significant time spans. But how do we review this data? Politicians are not to be trusted in their accounts; and our primary news sources do not track results of specific tax policies (for many reasons, not the least of which is that other stories sell better). Without having data to review, we remain ignorant of the consequences of our past policies.

6. Meanwhile we have tax policies enacted at not only the federal level, but also at the state and local levels—and these governments frequently enact such policies without much media attention. Even when there is media attention on a particular tax, there are just so many different options for taxation that even a vigilant media is hard-pressed to keep track of it all. So how do we keep informed?

Given these problems, it is no wonder voters are so disinclined to investigate the economics of tax policies. Yet each of the above can be answered with a little effort on our part, if we believe it important enough:

1. We are busy; but learning the basics of economics does not require so major an investment as to make it impossible. A college degree in economics is not required before you can draw some sensible economic conclusions; and we, as a country, will be at least marginally better off if enough voters made a marginal investment in their economic understanding, and began to vote that way. If you vote only once every other year (or every four years, if you only vote during presidential election cycles), you can find enough time to read a book or two.

2. Our 12th grade economics class was inadequate; but as adults responsible for our own learning—and with so many free resources available to us—we have within our power to redress the inadequacies of our public education.

3. The experts [on opposite sides of the political spectrum] disagree about a lot; yet there is a great deal about which they *do* agree. We can start there.

4. Difficulty #4—that we cannot run controlled economic experiments—is our biggest obstacle, and one which significantly separates the study of economics from the hard sciences. But this does not mean that we can know nothing; rather we need to acknowledge the limits of our empirical knowledge, and recognize the needfulness of careful *a priori* reasoning (more on this method later). Furthermore it is an important reminder to us to be more hesitant, more skeptical, and more humble in formulating our theories—and consequently, more careful in enacting government policy, and more reluctant to employ the use of force in implementing those policies.

5. Meanwhile we can be attentive to the empirical data available: for although the mainstream media may be busier reporting on political scandal and celebrity activity and the many other things that garner audiences, there are several research tanks that specifically track this type of information, and make it available online. The important thing is to refuse to forget; refuse to allow the politicians (who have their eyes mostly set on the short-term goal of re-election) and the news outlets (which are focused on the short-term goal of sales) to redirect our attention from actually investigating the results of past policies: just what *was* the result of such-and-such tax increase/decrease we just passed?

6. And finally, although politicians are so adept at confusing voters by distributing taxes among diverse sources so that no one can keep tabs on them all, we do not have to keep tabs on them all in order to begin to effect change. If voters were to attend only one issue, they could begin a marginal improvement; and if such attention could be generalized into a pattern which could be applied to all tax issues generally, they could make a significant change.

Apathy towards Ethics

Increasing our knowledge of economics is a great help, for it helps us avoid unintentional error, but avoiding error is only part of our political problem: a greater problem is when legislators (and voters) know well enough (or have the ability to know well enough, if they cared to make the effort), but are simply unconcerned with any ethical constraint on how to use that knowledge. For to many, tax policy is not even considered a matter for moral concern, but rather simply a tool for accomplishing some political end (which end may or may not itself be a matter of moral concern). For example:

Some legislature decides it good to create some new government program (and maybe this program is even to accomplish what they—or at least their constituents—perceive as a moral good); but how are they to fund such an endeavor? Ultimately, they do so through taxes (though in the immediate term, they fund it through debt-spending, this debt must be paid off by future revenues obtained through taxation). But having already committed to the necessity of funding the program (which, again, they and/or their constituents have decided is a Good program), they cannot stop now to consider if the means of funding it also must be good, for the program is to be funded regardless. So they pass some tax, not so much seeking to do right and avoid wrong in passing the tax, but rather seeking mostly to minimize negative voter reaction, so that they may safely be re-elected on the strength of their new program instead of being voted out on account of their new tax.

Is this a cynical depiction of policy-making, or a realistic one? Certainly it is possible that legislators, sometimes, do a little better than this, and perhaps they often intend to; but structurally, their political incentives motivate precisely this kind of behavior:

1. First, an elected representative's primary goal is to be re-elected—and if you object that some moral beings have more significant goals above this, you must still recognize that so long as accomplishing those significant goals depends upon them remaining in office, they must of necessity devote themselves first to the goal of being re-elected.

2. Since re-election depends not so much upon the reality of policy consequences as it does on the *voters' perceptions* of those consequences, their incentive is to be more concerned with the perception of their actions rather than their real effects.

3. Again, since it is *voters' perceptions* that matter for re-election, highly visible benefits (such as new programs) weigh more heavily than less-visible costs. It is in the politicians' best interests to make costs (such as taxes) as invisible as possible

(by spreading them out, delaying them, or obscuring their nature), rather than as ethical as possible.

4. Where new taxes cannot be made invisible, it is in the politicians' best interest to localize them to some smaller group of voters, who do not have the voting power to punish them. For example, if their district is made predominantly of non-smokers, they could levy a tax on the minority of cigarette-smokers. But more commonly, they can simply tax a subset of "the rich," who are by definition a minority of voters. (Note: there may be ethical reasons for targeting a particular tax on a particular group of people, and this will be considered later; for now I am pointing out that the incentive for the politicians is to do this whether it is ethical or not.)

5. Since re-election is always on the short-term horizon, the incentive is to prioritize short-term gains over long-terms gains, and to delay costs to the future.

6. And ultimately, voters tend to vote for them based upon what the voters perceive to be in their own interests, rather than based upon some narrow set of ethical concerns directly related to taxation. In short, *so long as voters fail to punish them for passing taxes in an unethical manner, they have no incentive to consider tax policy from an ethical perspective.*

Meanwhile voters, for their part, have their own reasons for being unconcerned with the ethical aspects of tax policy:

1. To begin with, people tend to find unimportant the things that do not concern their daily activity; and since they have no direct hand in creating tax policy, the ethics concerning that activity are naturally unimportant to them.

2. When it does become important to them, they may regard themselves as having no acceptable means of punishing their elected representatives, since doing so could mean handing power over to a representative of the opposing party, which they would like even less. If the cure would hurt worse than the disease, they'll accept the disease.

3. When the taxes do hurt badly enough, and they do act to remove the offending legislators, they do so not because the tax was unethical, but because it *hurt them personally.* For nearly any tax is endurable to a person, so long as someone else is paying for it.

And that is the crux of the problem: most voters are not as concerned with the ethics of tax policy as much as they are with *getting other people to pay the taxes.*

The Threatening Nature of Democracy

We might have frank and informed discussions with each other regarding what government services they are actually willing to pay for, and at what price; but instead, we have an environment wherein different blocs of voters dispute over what other people should pay. When we participate in this mindset, we can easily regard politics as a simple contest of power between groups, and in a power struggle one is continually tempted to prefer doing evil to receiving it. For how can a person abide by ethical limitations if it means conceding power to their opponent?

Not that we plan to be this way, or are even cognizant of it—but we *feel*, on a visceral level, the sense of threat. For both the raising and the lowering of taxes brings threat, to different groups of people: raising taxes threatens some by taking away their wealth, while lowering taxes threatens others who depend upon the government services that the taxes make possible. One person bristles under a taxation they perceive as theft, while another celebrates the taxation of other people as a legitimate weapon in an ongoing class struggle. And this enmity is not only between different socioeconomic classes, but also particularly felt on the borders of those classes also: for a person starting to move from one economic condition to another is like to find themselves subject to different levels of taxation, and in response to the new felt costs develop new opinions about who should pay and how much—opinions which may be taken as a betrayal of their former class. Now we have a natural drive to protect ourselves; but insofar as we assent to and participate in this conception of struggle, we repudiate the very ethics would should unite us—such ethics are simply not useful to us in our defensive, threatened, vulnerable state.

Yet it does not have to be this way. Or at the very least, it does not have to be this way *for you*. For even if we lack the power to restructure all the incentives for our politicians to pass self-serving policy, and even though we lack the power to change the hearts and minds of the whole of the voting population, we can nevertheless decide, on an individual level, to rise above the conception of taxes as power struggle and concern ourselves instead with, *what is Right?* What is right, even if it is unpleasant to me personally? What policies promote not only my personal good, but also Good itself? Given that any policy choice will distribute benefits and costs unevenly (threatening some and rewarding others), do I have appropriate justification for these costs? What policies can I advocate unashamedly, free from accusation from my conscience pointing out that I am really only pursuing my own self-interest?

The fact that you picked up this book indicates you are already willing to consider such questions—and to do so with a mind open to the possibility of changing your opinions. But many are not, which leads to our final obstacle:

The Need to Win

One may debate for the purpose of clarifying thought, and attempting to arrive at a better conclusion; or one may debate for the purpose of "winning"—of demonstrating the superiority of one side over another. Political debate naturally favors the latter option, with the consequence being that a debater who is in error cannot actually change their mind, since that would mean "losing" the debate. We may allow our politicians this type of debate, since we as the audience can personally choose to listen with an open mind; but if we are to truly consider investigating a topic, we must deny this option to ourselves. One cannot search for better conclusions if one has begun the search with the assumption that all their prior conclusions are already correct. If we do, our discussion of ethics becomes a farce.

Postmodern thinkers frequently make the claim that what we call ethics is in reality a disguised means of perpetuating a particular set of power relationships. If we argue without admitting the possibility of change, we make ourselves susceptible to this critique. This is dangerous not only to our own thinking, but also to the thinking of anyone who buys into the critique: for if "ethics" is merely a mask for power, then we are once again reduced to a political situation wherein all debate is simply a contest of power between groups of people—war carried on by other means.

On Political Parties

I do not expect to change anybody's party affiliation with this text—after all, we select our alliances for many reasons besides tax policy, and those reasons may be much more important to you, and worth keeping your alliance even if your chosen party has bad policy. But perhaps you may end up more motivated to participate more in your party's primary elections, where your vote and voice can incline them towards better policy and more ethical behavior—and then you can settle for the candidate that wins that contest, if you choose. Yet even here you must make a choice about cost, for you may believe that it is not worth selecting the more ethical policies in the primary if that makes your tribe less likely to win in the general election. For many, this is a genuine ethical conundrum of its own.

In the interest of pursuing genuine discussion, I declare all of the conclusions reached in this text to be tentative, open to further refinement and rebuttal. I will attempt to lay out the facts as clearly as I can perceive them, and make what suggestions of value I believe are most helpful; but I can only provide the beginning of the discussion, not the end. It is up to you, and all those with whom you discuss and debate important matters, to continue the investigation.

2

Framework for the Discussion

Tax Policy vs. Tax Policies

In general, when politicians discuss tax policy, they simplify to the most basic overarching concept—basically, either being in favor of lowering taxes, or raising them [on the rich, of course]. However, the devil is in the details: for it matters a great deal *which* taxes they wish to change, as different taxes have different economic effects. Getting into such detail may not be particularly effective as a rhetorical, vote-getting strategy; but it is necessary if voters are to be able to make informed decisions.

Therefore one goal of this text is to expand the concept to a discussion of tax poli*cies*, so that voters may more accurately consider the questions at hand, and begin to recognize that even if they prefer one overarching idea (like raising taxes on the rich), they may differentiate between different options for doing that (such as raising personal income taxes, or corporate income taxes, or inheritance taxes), and begin to recognize that each option has different effects—some of which they adamantly oppose. Indeed the very diversity of tax possibilities is part of the problem: for legislators have so many different options for taxing the population that not only is it difficult for voters to keep track of, but it is also difficult for them to keep track of it themselves, resulting sometimes in multiple tax policies that are even in conflict with one another (for example, when a city lowers one kind of tax in an attempt to entice an industry to move in while at the same time raising another tax which discourages that same industry from doing so).

In addition to considering many of the various options for taxation as separate policies, each with their own economic effects, we will also be considering some of various purposes for adjusting different tax policies—for it is not always about changing revenue. Some kinds of tax policies are pursued less for their revenue than they are for their other economic effects. In particular, tariffs (taxes on imports and exports) today now have very little to do with revenue and very much to do with trying to rectify perceived problems in international trade. Similarly, excise taxes (a.k.a. sin taxes) are another government tool to address perceived problems, generally levied for the explicit purpose of changing people's undesirable behavior (for example, to discourage them from driving so much, or eating too much unhealthy food), with the revenue generated being portrayed as just an additional bonus. Additionally, some politicians (and voters) are even so bold as to advocate taxes more for punitive purposes than for revenue-generating purposes, seeking to rectify inequality. In each of these cases, it is *social* policy which is the driving ideology, with tax policy taking a back seat. When this happens, the ethical component of the conversation takes on an additional and more significant dimension; and the questions of taxes become merely questions about tactics in promoting a greater goal; and the ends (the social goal) are treated as justification for whatever means (like tax policies) are required to get there.

How Much Economics do I Need to Know?

But in order to consider each kind of tax separately, does that return us to the problem of needing a college degree in economics just to get started? And from which college? For as noted before, economists themselves disagree on many things. Yet we also noted that there are some fundamental economic principles that are agreed upon by most; and fortunately for us, some of these are understood quite readily, even intuitively, needing only a little explanation for people to discover that they know them. Furthermore, such fundamental concepts underlie so much of economic activity that we can begin to get a handle on quite a variety of different tax applications if we just attend to their logical consequences.

For example, nearly everyone understands that when the price of an item they regularly purchase goes up, they tend to buy less of it than before (so long as they have alternatives). This fundamental economic concept (perhaps made more difficult in formal economic terms: "aggregate demand tends to go down as price goes up") can and should be readily applied to tax policies: for when the government taxes a specific product, it raises the price, which in turn tends to result in fewer sales of that particular product. Now while it may take an expert economist to be able to estimate exactly how much sales will be affected (though they can never be exact, or even nearly so, since there are always other variables acting upon the result), the common voter with just this simple understanding of the basic principle at work will still be able to anticipate the general result.

At least the voters can—meanwhile it is almost astounding that the government projections often do not bother with considering these effects (for reasons we will elaborate upon shortly): for when the government increases the price of an item through taxation, government accountants routinely overestimate the amount of tax revenue the new/increased tax will generate, since they do not adequately take into account how much less people will buy at the new price. California, for example, recently legalized—and taxed—marijuana; but the amount of tax revenue generated fell short of their budget predictions by more than one hundred million dollars, due to so many marijuana buyers making their purchases on the illegal (and untaxed) black market, where it is so much cheaper. (We will be examining this type of result in more depth shortly, when we describe the Laffer Curve.)

Another basic concept that most people already understand is that changes in prices affect different products differently: for example, a 10% change in the price of butter will have a bigger impact on sales than would a 10% change in the price of insulin—because buyers of butter have the freedom to choose an alternative (such as buying margarine, or simply the alternative of consuming less butter), whereas buyers of insulin do not have this same freedom (since an insulin-dependent person needs it to live). Now we do not need an economics degree and the ability to compute the exact price elasticity of demand for butter or insulin at a particular price in order to appreciate and apply the general concept here: it is enough that we recognize that taxing one class of items has a large impact upon the sale of those items, while taxing another class will have a smaller impact upon their sale. This is important to remember when considering tax incidence—that is, who actually bears the burden of a tax—since taxes are frequently passed from the seller to the buyer in the form of higher prices. Now a master's degree in economics may help us to estimate the exact proportion of a tax will be passed on to consumers, but we do not need that level of expertise to appreciate the fundamental concept that taxes on specific products or businesses are partially (or sometimes entirely) paid by consumers in the form of higher prices.

Basic Principles of Economics

Human action. People act to change their current circumstances for better ones. When their environment changes, and/or the incentives before them change, they change their behavior to accomplish their ends.

Scarcity. We have limited resources to achieve the results that we want. Consequently, each individual must choose/prioritize between different wants; to *economize* is to use one's limited resources to obtain the greatest amount of what is wanted.

Subjective value. Each individual chooses their priorities differently; we cannot expect all other people to value the same things that we value.

Trade. To reduce scarcity, humans engage in trade, a mutually beneficial exchange of goods and/or services (frequently, but not always, using money).

Prices as information. The price of a good or service communicates the value of that item to the seller—that is, the amount of money they want to part with that good or perform that service. Although each person values each good and service differently, the market price reflects a kind of aggregate of all individual subjective values in the market. The money price provides us with a common means of comparing the relative values of different items to a single standard.

Law of demand. As the price of a good or service goes up, demand goes down (people tend to buy less of that particular good or service).

Law of supply. As the price of a good or service goes up, supply goes up (people tend to perform more of that service or produce more of that good for sale).

Mutually Beneficial Trade and Deadweight Loss

No human being can meet all of their wants alone; in fact, few human being can meet even a few of their wants all by themselves. Consequently, humans engage in trade, in exchanging items they have but don't need/want for items they don't have but do want/need. A hunter may sell game and furs, a farmer may sell grain, a laborer may sell their time, an entertainer may sell a performance (another sale of time), and so on. In this way, people can get more of the things they want, without having to develop the separate expertise and means of producing all those things themselves; and the consequent ability to specialize (to focus on the production one or a few goods and services, instead of trying to develop and master the means of producing all of them), each individual can produce more total wealth, and the larger society becomes richer.

Each person involved in a freewill trade must benefit from the trade—otherwise they would not bother to trade. In a freewill trade, each participant exchanges something they deem to be of lesser value for something they deem to be of greater value. This would not be possible if all people valued everything exactly the same; but because different people place different values upon things, two people can each gain from an exchange. Such exchange does *not* take place at the expense of the other party, but in fact *benefits* the other party. Frequently, this takes the form of each person selling an item they have a surplus of (they have more than they need)—the farmer's grain, the shopkeeper's inventory, the laborer's free time—to buy something they have a shortage of (or more typically, to get money, which they in turn use to buy something they have a shortage of). Freewill trade make each person better off; and in addition to the immediate effect, it incentivizes every person to produce things that are valuable to other people, which in turn makes the larger community better off.

[Freewill] Trade creates wealth, and promotes the creation of more wealth.

Prices in a market reflect the relative values of all the things being traded, allowing us to compare all alternatives to a single unit (money) rather than trying to compare the relative values of each individual thing directly (apples to oranges to cell phones to cars to leisure time to dental work to everything else). Fundamentally, prices are information which buyers and sellers use to make decisions about how to devote their scarce time and resources.

It is unavoidable that taxes affect prices. While this is most obvious when examining taxes on goods and services, it is still true when examining taxes on income. Wherever a tax is levied, it changes the price of the thing being taxed, and therefore changes the relative value of that thing compared to available alternatives. Thus, a tax on beef increases the price of beef, making the alternatives of pork and chicken relatively more attractive to the consumer, who has only so much money (scare resources) to purchase food. Meanwhile a tax on income decreases the amount of money a laborer may take home from working overtime, making the alternative of enjoying their day off relatively more attractive to the laborer, who only has so much time (another scarce resource) to devote to all the things they want to do. In either case, a tax decreases the attractiveness of the taxed item. Consequently:

If a government wants less of something, then tax it.

How *much* less trade you get from taxing an item depends upon several factors, including the size/rate of the tax, the price sensitivity of the consumers who purchase the good/service, the availability of alternatives, and more. Teachers and students in economics classes frequently calculate the amount trade had been reduced—called deadweight loss—in sample exercises that describe simple systems with few variables; but no economist is capable of calculating the actual deadweight loss resulting from a tax in a complex economy with literally millions of variables (including the prices of every other item in the market, and the individual preferences of every consumer in the market). Consequently, there is a great deal of room for debate between economists regarding the extent of such loss; nevertheless, virtually all economists agree on the basic principle:

A tax on a specific good or service raises the price of that good or service, which in turn results in fewer transactions between people who were willing to trade. This reduction of trade—this effective cancellation of mutually beneficial exchanges which would have otherwise have increased the standard of living for those making such exchanges—is an additional cost of the tax itself. While the revenue collected from the tax may be positively spent, this additional [opportunity] cost remains as a "deadweight loss," resulting in a system that is less efficient—less wealth-producing—than without the tax.

This deadweight loss does not automatically mean that all taxes are bad; it simply represents an additional cost of the tax. Now if the deadweight loss is substantial, and the positive effects of the tax (that is, the positive effects of how the government spends the collected revenue) are low, *then* we may say that the tax is harmful; but if the deadweight loss is small, and the government spending is economically useful, then we may be quite willing to pay this cost (or in other words, we are willing to sacrifice some amount of trade opportunities in order to garner the benefits of the government spending). In either case, it is a cost-benefit analysis; and we need to make this analysis if we are to effectively evaluate the merits of a particular tax proposal, instead of simply counting the benefits and ignoring the costs, as is the wont of benefit-promising politicians seeking election and/or re-election.

And this is what politicians—and in turn, voters—must remember about the economics of taxation: tax policies create changes in human behavior. These changes are not absolutely predictable (in fact they often result in unforeseen effects), but neither are they entirely random; therefore to some imperfect extent they can, and ought to be, anticipated when considering the merits and demerits of new policy.

For fundamentally, economics is about human action, about human beings making choices about what to do with their limited resources because they prefer one state of affairs over another. Thinking economically about tax policy begins with taking such human action into account, asking how people are likely to respond to the policies in question. Now it may take a trained economist to gather all the data and parse all the many variables to determine how people actually did respond to a particular change; but even the untrained economist can begin thinking economically, applying their own knowledge of human behavior to ask questions and form theories about what humans are likely to do.

Throughout this text, as we consider different kinds of taxation and tax policy, we will start from this common ground, that all of the readers are human and therefore have some significant knowledge of human action already. We will add to this some more defined economic concepts, but will remain in the realm of general knowledge accessible to all voters, rather than trying to drill down to more specific and mathematical minutiae. With each kind of tax we will ask, what incentives and disincentives do people have to change their economic behavior (that is, how they choose to spend their limited resources to meet their practically unlimited desires), and how significant or they? (Though for some readers, the very act of identifying the different incentives and disincentives created by various tax policies will be new—for example, many people do not even consider that a higher tax rate on personal income provides a significant disincentive to earn money).

As we investigate each type of tax, one particular economic concept related to changing behavior will come up again and again, and it is misunderstood enough that it is better to offer a fuller explanation of it before proceeding. This is the idea that tax rates and tax revenues do not have a perfectly linear relationship, which today is commonly referred to as the Laffer Curve. Although a fairly simple idea, a great many politicians and ideologues seem to have some difficulty understanding it; but it should not be so difficult for you here.

The Laffer Curve

What happens when you double a tax rate? Does this result in a doubling of tax revenues? Well, if human behavior were entirely *un*affected by the change in tax rate (what is termed a static model), then a doubling of the tax rate would result in a doubling of revenue; but if human behavior is affected—that is, if human beings make different economic decisions as a result of the higher tax rate (as they do whenever they encounter higher prices elsewhere)—then the doubling of the rate would result in somewhat less than a doubling of the tax

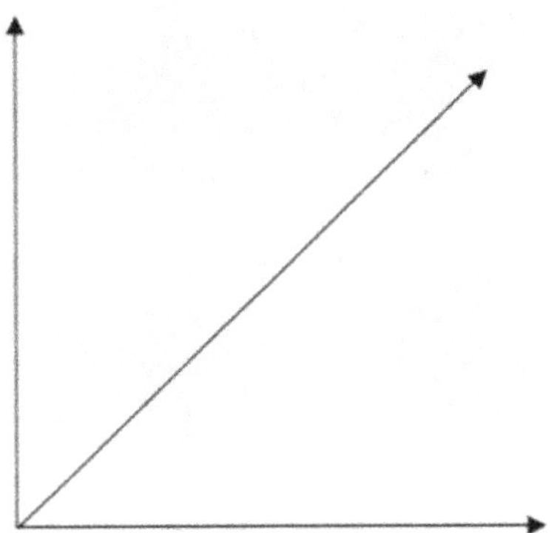

Figure 1: A Static model of tax revenues: Supposes that increases in the tax rate result in proportional increases in revenue

revenues. This simple observation is the fundamental reason for the Laffer Curve (named for economist Arthur Laffer, who popularized the concept in the United States), which postulates that tax rates and tax revenues do not have a simple linear relationship.

That a curve is a better model than a straight line for representing the relationship between tax rates and tax revenues should be self-evident: for the static model predicts that a 100% income tax rate would generate five times as much revenue as a 20% tax rate, whereas in reality it might well generate no revenue at all, as people choose to stop working or refuse to pay the tax. Or, consider a tax rate that may go higher than 100%, like the excise tax on cigarettes: again, the static model predicts that the state of New York could double the $4.35 excise tax it places on packs of cigarettes (note: New York City adds an additional $1.50 to this rate) and consequently produce double the tax revenues (or triple this rate to get triple the revenues); but in reality people buy fewer cigarettes as the price goes up, and eventually stop buying them altogether (on the legal market) when the price gets high enough— New Yorkers currently may be willing to pay $12 per pack of cigarettes (or not—many get them

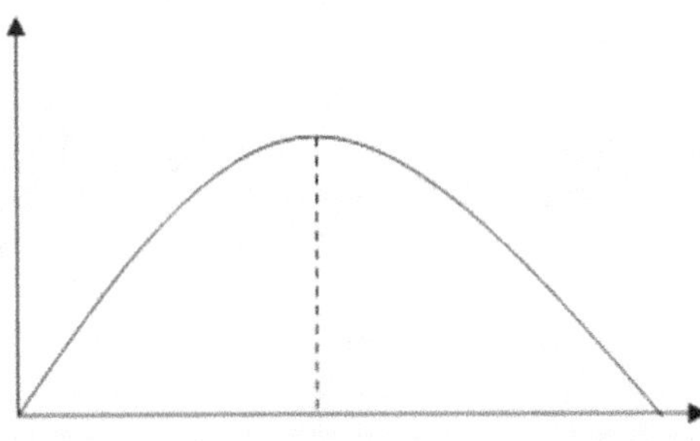

Figure 2: Sample Laffer Curve: Supposes that increases in the tax rate result in increases in tax revenue only to a certain point, after which any further increase in the tax rate actually results in lower tax revenues

on the black market instead, or purchase them out of state), but they probably wouldn't be buying any if the cost were $50.

That much is simple; but where it gets more difficult is in anticipating the *shape* of this curve. For while we may anticipate that a particularly high tax rate would generate no revenue, we may not know *exactly* at which point that occurs, nor do we know *exactly* at which point the line actually curves, and a further tax increase first results in lower revenues.

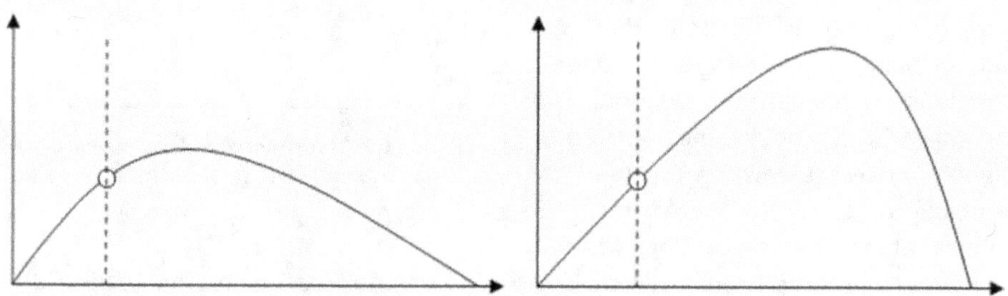

Figure 3: Possible Laffer Curve Shapes
For only a single point of data (the current tax rate), either of these two curves is possible. If the curve on the left more accurately reflects taxpayer behavior, then a tax increase would not generate much more revenue; but if the figure on the right more accurately reflects taxpayer behavior, then the tax rate may still be increased significantly before any negative revenue effects are realized.

In order to generate a perfectly accurate curve, we would need to create a computer simulation of all the participants in a market, and then run that simulation for every possible tax rate. However, it is quite impossible to program the cigarette-buying behavior of every New Yorker into a computer program, or the work choices of every individual subject to an income tax. But what we can do is model small portions of the curve based upon the data points that we do have—specifically, tax revenues immediately before and after a change in a particular tax rate—and extrapolate from there. Such projections will tend to be more accurate for the portion of the curve closest to the data points, and tend towards lower accuracy further away—but this is not so great a problem, since policy makers generally consider marginal changes to tax rates rather than drastic changes (few would propose raising an income or capital gains tax rate to the 60-100% range).

Typically, discussion of the Laffer Curve is centered around the federal tax rate; but it must be acknowledged that there is no single tax rate, for in addition to having a graduated income tax rate (wherein different portions of a person's income are taxed at different levels, with higher tax rates being applied as one's income increases), the federal government also has different rates for different kinds of income (capital gains, for example, is taxed at a different rate than wage earnings). It is therefore vitally important to note that the shape of the Laffer Curve is not the same for all kinds of taxes. Generally, when taxpayers have more control over their income (as with capital gains income, since people may choose when to realize their gains), the more the peak of the Laffer curve shifts left (and the lower the peak gets). In contrast, a change in income tax rates on lower-income families may not have much of a curve at all (until the rates near 100%), as those people are still likely to work just as many hours as before (they do not have as many options available in regards to changing the activity being taxed). Similarly, state income tax rates on the richest 10% of the population have greater Laffer Curve effects than do federal income tax rates on the same population, since it is generally much easier for a person to move to a different state than it is to emigrate to another country. Laffer Curve effects are even more evident on excise taxes (like that on cigarettes) since the change in tax rate results in a change in the price of cigarettes, and the buyers of cigarettes are highly price-sensitive, changing the amount they purchase with changes in price.

Anticipating the curve's shape for a particular tax—and identifying one's current position on that curve—can have significant impacts upon setting tax (and spending) policy. Suppose a tax rate is currently set at some point **A** (Figure 4); an increase in the rate might yield point **B** on the graph, but if you were using a static model, you would have anticipated **B'** instead—and if

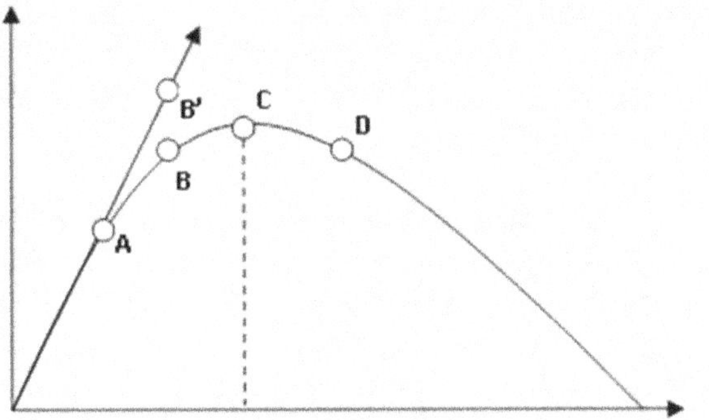

Figure 4: Tax policy implications:
Changes in the tax rate (up or down) will have different results depending upon where in the curve you are.

you had based your spending on that projection, you would have ended up with a budget shortfall. Meanwhile if you were at point **C** on the curve—the revenue-maximizing point—any increase in the tax rate would actually *decrease* the tax revenues collected (since there would be fewer economic transactions from which to collect the tax). Finally, if you already were at point **D**, then you might propose moving to point **C** to increase tax revenues—or better yet, even propose moving to point **B**: for even though this would not generate any further tax revenue, it would result in a greater number of economic transactions (in other words, more economic growth). In Figure 4 above, the reduction in economic activity between points **B** and **C** is much greater than between points **A** and **B** (there is a greater change in taxpayer behavior to avoid the tax); the tax revenue at point **C** may not be worth the corresponding loss of economic activity (that is, the decrease in national income).

This last point needs additional emphasis, as the effect of a tax rate upon economic productivity may be substantially more significant than its effect upon revenue generated. When taxpayers change their behavior to reduce their tax burden, this is a cost that must be considered. For example, when investors choose to realize their capital gains income less often and at higher thresholds, it results in less investment capital being available to new and growing businesses, and therefore less overall economic growth. And when wealthy taxpayers (both individuals and businesses) in one state move to another state in order to reduce their tax burdens, then the economy of the state with the higher tax rate loses both the economic activity of those taxpayers' consumption (they now buy their goods and services in another state) and production (the goods and services formerly produced by the businesses which relocated, including all the jobs those firms created). If policy makers are only concerned with maximizing immediate tax revenue, they will not count the costs of such reduction of economic activity. But when a policy maker is concerned with these greater economic effects, they may advocate a tax rate to be kept lower than the revenue-maximizing point (point **C** on Figure 4), at the growth-maximizing point instead (point **A**, where economic behavior has not been adversely impacted by the tax rate), acknowledging that this will result in lower immediate tax revenues ("immediate," because over time, more growth yields a larger tax base to draw revenues from).

Now because the Laffer Curve addresses tax policy, which is an inherently political issue, and because economic matters frequently get misrepresented in political discussion, a few points of further clarification are in order. This is particularly important because while politicians' distortion of this economic concept may be easily criticized, such criticism may not logically apply to the concept itself. Furthermore, we must not dismiss the facts upon which the Laffer Curve is based simply because we wish to reject the policy recommendations of some politicians: for whatever our preference for tax rates and whatever our purposes (e.g. to increase revenue to fund programs, to use tax policy to encourage or discourage certain behaviors, to make the economic system more fair, etc.), we still must grapple with the reality that taxpayers change their behavior in response to changes in the tax rate.

The simplest and most common distortion of the Laffer Curve concept is that decreases in tax rates pay for themselves. This is only true (in the short run) if the previous tax rate is on the right side of the curve's peak (the revenue-maximizing point); but for many taxes, this is not the case (or more fundamentally, it is not known if this is the case or not, as for any given tax rate, we do not have very many data points available to model the full curve). As stated before, the more responsive/reactive taxpayers are changes in a particular tax rate, the further left is the peak of the Laffer Curve for that tax; whereas the less responsive they are, the further the peak is to the right.

It is important to clarify between the short-term and long-term consequences here: for some reductions in particular tax rates may generate less immediate tax revenue, but more future tax revenue, *if* the foregone revenue promotes sufficient economic growth that the future tax base grows larger. This might happen in regards to capital gains, since money would more freely circulate for investment; but if increased deficits compete away that investment money through the sale of federal bonds, then that might not happen. Projecting such long-term effects is made difficult (if not impossible) by the fact that myriads of other variables are also operating, which themselves may have more significant consequences that variable you are concerned with.

Another common distortion is to generalize findings regarding one type of tax to all types of taxes. As discussed above, the shape of the Laffer Curve is different for different types of taxes, depending upon the alternative choices available to the taxpayers: for example, the curve for federal income tax on wages has a peak further to the right than the curve for capital gains tax, since taxpayers who have income based upon capital gains have more freedom to choose when to realize their income. Therefore if we were to find that current income tax rates for wage income is on the left side of the peak for wage income tax, this would provide us no useful information regarding the shape of the capital gains curve.

Meanwhile, on the opposite side of the political spectrum, the Laffer Curve is often dismissed as a tool to justify lower tax rates for the rich (particularly because the capital gains tax curve peaks at a much lower rate than taxation of wages), and anything with this effect must automatically be wrong from a values-perspective. But while a person may reject a particular policy based upon their particular values, their rejection does *not* alter the fact that people change their behavior in response to different incentives. Sometimes reality is not as we want it to be. Such people would be more honest to instead recognize the reality of the Laffer Curve, and then admit that they might prefer higher tax rates even when those rates result in reduced revenue. Meanwhile Laffer Curves remain present even for taxpayers who are poor, such as with the excise tax upon cigarettes.

Politicians on both the Left and the Right may distort the economics of the Laffer Curve (usually in different ways); meanwhile taxpayers continue to respond to new tax rates by altering their behavior, and tax revenues will be impacted by those decisions. For each of the more than twenty types of taxes discussed below, we will consider how and how much taxpayers are likely to change their behavior in response to changes in those taxes; and while we will not be able to exactly describe the different shapes of each separate Laffer Curve, we will be able to anticipate the general tendencies by examining the available alternatives people subject to each tax.

Ethical Framework

Any discussion of ethics is an invitation to debate, as there is no universally accepted ethical system. Yet we are better off debating the ethics of taxation than we are dismissing or ignoring them entirely, since that course inevitably leads to an increase of unethical behavior.

Yet while it is true that voters cannot be expected to perfectly agree on every ethical principal, it is also true that they nevertheless agree on quite a bit: indeed, we assume as much when we accept a statement like, "it is better to debate ethics than ignore them." Beyond this, the vast majority of us are likely to share many basic beliefs, such as the idea that the voters have a say in the tax policies, that being told the truth about tax policy is preferable to being lied to, that government is expected to use tax revenues to serve the people rather than to simply enrich politicians and their friends, and that politicians do not have unlimited authority to tax (though we might disagree about the extent of their limits, we likely will agree that some limit exists). Nearly every voter would assent to these basic ideas—even as all three are routinely violated by corrupt politicians. From such common ground, we could articulate the following ethical guidelines to begin our discussion:

Representation

Certainly no one likes to pay taxes; but it is even worse when citizens of a representative government are still given no say in the matter. In fact, one of the rallying cries during the American Revolution was, "No taxation without representation!" as British colonists in the Americas had no say in the elections of representatives in England who would create tax law governing the colonies. When an elected official has to answer to their constituency, they have some limitation upon how far they may increase taxes; but when they can pass taxes on other people who cannot take any action but revolt, they may tax with impunity (at least until they provoke a revolution).

Given that this is a founding American principle, and given that America is still a representative government with politicians answerable [at least in theory] to the electorate, I believe that the vast majority of voters can agree on the following ethical principle:

> *Any tax that is applied to people who can respond to the tax through the exercise of their voting rights (such as by electing new representatives) is more ethical than a tax applied to a people who cannot so respond.*

For example, if California legislators pass a tax on CA residents, those residents could then elect different legislators; but if California legislators ever managed to levy a tax on Nevada residents, we could agree that such a tax would be unethical, since Nevada voters could do nothing about it. A more complicated case—about which there is not universal agreement—is when California wishes to tax goods that Californians buy from Nevadans: here the California buyers can respond with their votes, but the Nevada sellers may not. This example has been made real by the US Supreme Court's decision in *South Dakota v. Wayfair* regarding sales made over the internet (overturning an earlier Supreme Court decision, *Quill Corp. v. North Dakota*): now, one state may demand that retailers in another state comply with their sales taxes, whereas before they could only demand that their own citizens could.

Colorado's TABOR

While taxation with representation is more ethical than taxation without representation, it is even better when voters get to respond directly to tax initiatives, instead of having to wait until an election cycle to express their approval or disapproval less directly (for there are many reasons besides tax policy which affect what representatives one votes for). Accordingly, the state of Colorado has had a Taxpayer Bill of Rights (TABOR) added to their constitution, which prevents the legislature from raising any tax rates without first getting permission from the people through a vote. They also are not allowed to spend surplus revenues, but must refund them back to the taxpayers. Requiring voter approval for new taxes quite restricts the ability of the legislature to do as it wills (or as some would insist, do as it needs); but any taxes which are passed have a much stronger ethical foundation.

But what about when a subset of the population technically has the ability to vote on their representation, but on account of being a minority within a larger population, has no effective power to do so? How are we to judge the ethicality of taxes in that situation? Fortunately, we have historical precedent for this type of decision as well: for one of the core principals of the founders of the United States government was to protect the rights of the minority against the potential tyranny of the majority. While today's America is much more democratic than the America of 1776, the vast majority of Americans today continue to acknowledge the importance of maintaining minority rights. From this ethical habit we may therefore extend the above rule regarding representation as follows:

> *Any tax applied to the whole of the voting population is* more *ethical than a tax applied to only a minority of the population.*

Note that this ethical principle does not assume that a tax upon the minority is automatically unethical, only that it is less ethical than one which applies to the whole of the population. There may indeed be compelling reasons for taxing a minority/subset of the population; but when those other compelling reasons are absent, we should find the minority tax to be ethically questionable indeed.

For example, most Americans acknowledge that there are compelling reasons to levy a tax on smokers (that is, on the sale of cigarettes), such as paying for the health costs of second-hand smoke. However, when smokers are a small minority of the population, it becomes tempting to increase the cigarette tax to pay for a variety of other things (schools, roads, promotion of literacy, homeless assistance, etc.) that might have nothing to do with smoking; the smokers (that is, the buyers of cigarettes), being a minority, may never be able to muster the voting power to oppose these further increases. In such a case as this, we ought to conclude that such tax increases would be decidedly unethical—unless we wish to acknowledge a right of any majority to impose unpopular costs upon any minority without consideration for their persons.

Honesty / Openness

While it is true that people generally don't like paying taxes, it does not follow from this that the only way to get them to pay taxes is to lie to them. Most people are actually willing to pay some [small] amount of taxes to fund the services they support; but rather than appealing to the voters' willingness to do this, politicians/legislators may find in expedient to simply deceive the voters into thinking that they are not paying so much—or that other voters are actually the ones paying for it (for many a voter is perfectly content with a tax so long as someone else is paying for it).

Throughout this text, we will assume that voters agree that it is unethical to be lied to. Sometimes, it will not be easy to evaluate a tax by this criteria: for the tax itself cannot lie, only the people who create the tax; so for some taxes, we will have to consider how they were actually passed. In such cases, we may apply the following:

> *If a tax was passed on deceitful premises, it will be regarded as less ethical than a tax passed honestly; if it was passed in secret, it will be regarded as less ethical than one passed openly.*

We can further expand upon this principle by examining if a tax, after it is passed, is easily visible to voters (such that they can, with little effort, be aware of how much it is costing them), or if it is hidden from voters (so that it takes a great deal of effort and investigation to discover how much it is actually costing them). When the costs of a tax are visible, the voters have greater ability to tell their representatives whether they are satisfied or dissatisfied with the tax; in this way, the ethical principle of Openness supports the ethical principal of Representation.

A hidden tax is less ethical than a tax which is visible.

Simplicity

When writing rules—whether for formal laws or for simple rules to govern a school classroom or social club—it is important to make those rules clear, so that the people governed by those rules don't end up violating them by accident. Similarly, when we devise tax regulations, we ought to make certain that those laws can be easily understood. For if a person is willing to abide by a law, and earnestly attempts to do so, yet transgresses the law on account of it being too difficult to understand, the fault seems to lie more in the writing of the law than in the citizen trying to obey it. Thus:

> *A tax law that is simple and understandable is more ethical than a tax law that is complex and confusing. Tax laws that can only be understood with the help of professionals are less ethical than tax laws which can be understood without such expense.*

Appropriateness

Many taxes are levied to meet the general needs of the budget; that is, they are passed without any specific spending in mind, but simply to raise overall revenue. Some taxes, however, are levied for explicit spending purposes: for example, a tax to fund improvement of roads, or to fund health programs, or to fund the Spanish American War. When taxes are passed for such specific reasons, most Americans recognize that it is better to collect them from matching sources: so the transportation funds may be collected from a gasoline tax, and the funds for certain health programs from a cigarette tax. Such appropriations are deemed appropriate, whereas collecting funds for transportation from a tax levied on, say, snack foods, would not be. From this we could declare the following:

> *When raising revenue for a particular service, it is more ethical to tax the population being benefited, than to tax a separate population.*

Sometimes the benefit applies to the whole population, but it may not be feasible to collect the revenue from the whole population: particularly, most Americans agree that it is not good to raise taxes among the poorest people. Consequently, it was considered appropriate to raise funds for the Spanish American War (1898) by passing a telephone tax, as telephones at that time were only owned by the wealthy. (This tax on telephone service has been repealed and reinstated many times since the end of that war; but as telephone use became more widespread, the tax no longer impacted only the wealthy, but nearly all Americans, and it was collected to serve general revenue needs, instead of for funding a specific military endeavor.)

For the purposes of this text, we will acknowledge that there is a reasonable debate regarding the virtues of a flat tax (taxing all people equally) versus a progressive tax system (taxing the wealthy at a greater rate than the poor); but we will assume a general agreement on the following principle:

> *It is less ethical to tax the poor to fund necessary government than it is to tax the rich to fund necessary government.*
> *It is even worse to tax the poor to serve the needs of the rich.*

(The ethical question regarding taxing the rich in order to serve the needs of the poor will be discussed later, since on that issue there is not the same general agreement.)

Minimizing Harms

Taxes can be painful; they can even be made high enough to shut down some economic activities, stopping trade and closing businesses. In some cases, voters might decide that some level of harm is justified by the positive benefits of the services funded by the tax; but virtually all voters agree that a tax which raises the same amount of revenue while inflicting less harm is generally preferable to the tax that inflicts more harm.

The extent of the harms inflicted by a tax is a debatable economic question; so voters who share the same ethical framework may nevertheless arrive at different conclusions about a tax depending upon their own economic assessments. Harms must be satisfactorily proved before they can be cited as evidence of a tax being unethical. Nevertheless, we may suggest that generally:

> *The greater the harms a tax inflicts, the more ethically suspect it is.*
> *Tax policy which seeks to minimize harms (economic costs) is more ethical than tax policy that does not even consider them.*

And when judging harms, it is important to note *who* bears the cost; for it does us no ethical good to justify the harms of a tax based upon net benefits, if all those benefits are enjoyed by one group of people while all those harms are suffered by another (in accordance with our principle of Appropriateness). Similarly, it does us no ethical good to consider only the intended targets of the tax, if the tax also inflicts additional unintended costs upon other people.

While all the ethical principles recommended so far should be generally agreeable to most voters despite the variety of political opinion, this next guideline relating to harms might face some opposition from certain political factions.

Sometimes a tax is explicitly levied to injure—to punish—some portion of the population. For example: class warfare taxes, advocated by some politicians specifically to punish the rich, are popular among some political factions—though they may prefer to couch their arguments in terms of "fairness" rather than "punishment." Significant politicians have gone on record stating that even if a tax increase were to bring in less revenue (in accordance with Laffer Curve effects discussed earlier), they would still advocate raising tax rates in the name of "fairness." In such cases, they are openly admitting a willingness to increase harm upon one segment of the population without any benefits to tax revenue; in this case, the [perceived] benefit is a reduction in wealth inequality (or more cynically, the real benefit is an increase in votes from those who are happy to inflict harm upon "the rich").

One of the problems with this philosophy is that it changes punishment from a criminal matter to a voting one, where a majority of elected representatives get to determine punishments in accordance with their personal ideas instead of a judge determining punishments according to an established body of law. The founders of the United States recognized that this could be a temptation for the legislature, and so explicitly built into the Constitution a prohibition against passing laws which declared people guilty (the Bill of Attainder, prohibited in Article I, Section 9 of the Constitution). Yet legislators can evade this prohibition if they seek to punish through their power to tax, and are only prohibited from doing this when the voters turn them out; but this means that punishment becomes subject to the popular will, rather than to an established Rule of Law. So throughout this text, I will advocate the following ethical principle:

It is unethical to use tax policy to administer punishments.

We may need a few further words of clarification here: for while there may be a general agreement that taxes should not be used to "punish," people will certainly disagree about what constitutes a punishment. For example, are smokers being "punished" for smoking when a cigarette tax is levied to pay for hospital costs associated with secondhand smoke, or are we simply collecting payment for a real cost that smokers impose upon hospitals? Throughout this text, we will *not* assume agreement when such situations arise, but rather will articulate and investigate the various ethical positions.

Peace

As noted earlier, most people are content to accept new taxes so long as it means that other people will be paying them. In a democratic culture, this becomes particularly problematic: for if we accept this attitude as normal, then we cannot avoid the corollary that other people directly threaten us with their votes. (Indeed, this applies not just to tax policy, but to all legislative action in a democratic society, as my neighbor's political power may result in laws that affect my freedom.) Consequently, it is all the more important that we seek to pursue tax policies which promote the common good, rather than good of some interest group individual (me) over the good of other groups or individuals (not me).

This last ethical principle overlaps with all of others previously identified; if we were to adhere to them, then we should be able to more easily adhere to this one:

> *Tax policy which pits groups of people against each other is* less *ethical than tax policy which unites the larger population.*

Further Ethical Guidelines

The principles articulated above are only a starting point for discussion; there are many more ethical guidelines which may be considered, which do not [currently] enjoy the same level of popular agreement. Several of these we will address later in this book, after having applied these more commonly accepted principles to a variety of tax policies. Indeed, one of the purposes of this book is to invite readers to consider some additional ethical principles; but we may need to start from a place of relatively common ground if we are to succeed in doing so.

And just in case it needs to be clarified: my selection of ethical principles based upon what [in my experience] the majority of people are likely to share does *not* imply that I believe ethics to be a matter of popular opinion. I quite believe that there are objective, universal ethical principles—but I recognize that not all people share this belief, and that among those who do share this belief we still may disagree about the content of those principles. Part of both the republican and democratic (not the parties, but the systems of government) challenges is devising a system of laws that matches the common ethical norms of the society being governed, while leaving certain protections in place for minority opinions, and inviting continued discussion about those norms. The areas where we share values, and the borders of those areas, where we are yet considering our values, are where we are like to have the most fruitful discussion.

Regarding Fairness—a Disputed Ethical Value

"Fair" is one of those words with multiple meanings, and a very strong emotional connotation. What one person calls "fair" is often very different from what another person calls "fair." Consequently, use of the word in a debate frequently makes matters less clear rather than more clear.

One sense of the word "fair" means nearly the same as "just;" but another sense instead means "even/equal"—and sometimes these senses overlap, but not always. In many cases, different people have equal claims to a particular resource or good, and in these cases, it is both fair and just to divide the resource or good equally among them. But in other cases, people do not have equal claims: and in these cases, it would be unjust to divide the good equally among all claimants.

For example, if working Bob earns more money that nonworking Andy, it is just (but certainly not equal/even) for Bob to get paid more than Andy. Or if both are working, it is just for each to get paid whatever they have freely agreed to—whether that is equal or not. This point can upset some people's idea of "fair," when they perceive—from their third-party perspective—that Bob and Andy did equal amounts of work. But if Bob agreed to work for Dan at \$20/hour, while Andy agreed to work for Zeke at \$15/hour, there is no justice to be found in forcing Dan and Zeke to pay exactly the same amount (do we force Dan to pay less, reducing Bob's income? or do we force Zeke to pay more, reducing his wealth, though he would never have freely contracted Andy's services at that price?). It does not matter if Bob and Andy worked the same: they do not have equal claims, since they have each contracted with different people on different terms.

Inequality is all around us, and that feels unfair—or it is unfair, in the sense of being uneven/unequal—but that does not necessarily mean that it is unjust. Sometimes it is unjust: when wealth is obtained through robbery, fraud, or the like, it is unjust; but when it is obtained through freewill transactions, it is just. Perhaps most people naturally agree with this principle in the abstract—but when this principle operates on a large scale, and as a consequence of freewill transactions some people accumulate more wealth that others, it often doesn't feel so just. Particularly when we know that some kinds of wealth accumulation are unjust—it is quite natural to wonder how much of what we see around us is the product of unjust dealings and how much is the product of just dealings. Of course, it does not follow that we can assume that the differences in wealth must be primarily the result of unjust dealings—none of us are omniscient, none of us have observed the billions of transactions that have yielded the end result. All we can observe—and this without perfect accuracy—is that the world around us is very unequal/uneven; and this may feel very unfair, insofar as we equate fairness with equality/evenness.

Sometimes it is more difficult to come to agreement in one context than it is in another, even when the same principle is discussed. So to help us see the abstract principle of freewill transaction leading to inequality, let us consider an example from relationships: here is another context wherein we observe great inequality/unevenness, as some people get many more dates and romantic interactions than others. (And again, some of this may be obtained unjustly, through deceit; but most of it is still achieved through freewill interaction.) Some people are perceived as more attractive than others. If this fair? Is this just? Again, "fair" is an emotionally fraught and inexact term: we can instead speak more exactly, that while this is unequal/uneven, it is not necessarily unjust; whereas in contrast, most people would agree that it would be absolutely unjust to attempt to force everyone to some equal distribution of romantic engagement. However, people do not have the same level of agreement on this principle when it comes to wealth (and this example will not "prove" the argument there—though perhaps it will at least illuminate the difficulty of the concept of "fairness").

Meanwhile, there are additional points where people disagree on what is in fact just when it comes to the distribution of wealth. Consider: is it just when Bob inherits millions of dollars and you do not? Of course—as it is just when you give a present to your child and not to every child. It's not "fair," in the sense of equality/evenness; but no injustice has been done. Yet not everybody feels that way—and some will insist upon making "just" mean "even/equal," even to the point of advocating or deploying violent force to make things more "fair:" These are the revolutionaries, and to a lesser but substantively similar extent, the voters and politicians who would use the force of the government—that is, taxation and the threat of imprisonment or death—to confiscate wealth from one group to give it to another. And this is a fundamental tension in our democratic society: if I believe that I have a just claim to your possessions, then I will behave and vote fundamentally differently than if I believe that I do not have any claim to your possessions. It is possibly this difference in belief, more than any other, which makes discussion of the ethics of taxation so difficult: for people who differ on this belief start on seemingly irreconcilable sides of the discussion.

My own position is that I do not have a claim/right to your possessions, and neither do you have any claim/right to mine. If we have common ground on this belief, then the remainder of this book may be an easier read; but if we do not have common ground on this belief, I exhort you to consider where we do have common ground—perhaps on many of those ethical principles enumerated earlier—and read on with an open mind, with the aim of clarifying both your ethical positions and your understanding of the ethical positions of others.

Initial Ethical Principles for the Discussion of Tax Policy

Representation. Any tax that is applied to people who can respond to the tax through the exercise of their voting rights (such as by electing new representatives) is more ethical than a tax applied to a people who cannot so respond.

Participation. Any tax applied to the whole of the voting population is more ethical than a tax applied to only a minority of the population.

Honesty. If a tax was passed on deceitful premises, it will be regarded as less ethical than a tax passed honestly; if it was passed in secret, it will be regarded as less ethical than one passed openly.

Openness. A hidden tax is less ethical than a tax which is visible.

Simplicity. A tax law that is simple and understandable is more ethical than a tax law that is complex and confusing. Tax laws that can only be understood with the help of professionals are less ethical than tax laws which can be understood without such expense.

Appropriateness. When raising revenue for a particular service, it is more ethical to tax the population being benefited, than to tax a separate population.

Consideration. It is less ethical to tax the poor to fund necessary government than it is to tax the rich to fund necessary government. It is even worse to tax the poor to serve the needs of the rich.

Minimizing harms. The greater the harms a tax inflicts, the more ethically suspect it is. Tax policy which seeks to minimize harms (economic costs) is more ethical than tax policy that does not even consider them.

Justice. It is unethical to use tax policy to administer punishments.

Peace. Tax policy which pits groups of people against each other is less ethical than tax policy which unites the larger population.

A Complicating Ethical Issue: Spending and Deficits

Ethical conclusions have very clear consequences: if an action is determined to be unethical/wrong, we should stop doing it. Unfortunately, when we stop doing something that we have been doing for some time, this often has additional consequences that we do not like—and which themselves may appear [to some] to be worse than continuing to commit the unethical act. This is a major obstacle to reasoned, public discussion of the ethics of taxation: for if any particular tax (or level of taxation) is determined to be unethical/immoral, then we would have an ethical/moral obligation to eliminate (or reduce) that tax, which would in turn reduce government revenues, resulting in greater budget deficits, greater debt, and/or loss of funding for important government programs.

Or, to put it in purposely emotional and more familiar terms, "If we cut taxes, hungry people will go unfed, sick people will go untreated, and children and old people will die." Some form of this argument gets deployed constantly in budget discussions; it got quite a bit of use during the government shutdown "crises." Although quite misleading—and logically fallacious at several points—it nevertheless resonated with many people who saw these consequences as worse than violating some abstract ethical principal regarding taxation. Therefore if we are to make any headway in considering the ethical principles of taxation, we must first dispel this fear, lest some readers find it morally objectionable—or even impossible—to even consider the possibility that [some particular] taxes may be unethical.

First, the argument that reduction in taxes must lead to the death of children and old people is not only hyperbole, it also commits the logical fallacy of the false dilemma (or false dichotomy): it arbitrarily assumes that we must choose between one of two options (either current government spending, or reduced spending with disastrous consequences, hyperbolically stated as the death of children and old people). But in fact we have many alternative choices available: to begin with, there are many kinds of government spending which are not as impactful upon people's lives, and we could theoretically begin reducing spending there, instead of where it is most harmful.

But, a person may reasonably object, once we have eliminated all less-important government spending, we are still left with an amount of important spending which we do not want to cut; so surely we must take that into consideration when discussing the ethics of tax cuts. After all, much of our current spending is financed through debt rather than through taxes, so it is even possible that we are already under-taxing for these more important services. This objection is much more reasonable than the first; yet it, too, is committing the false dilemma fallacy: in this case, presenting the artificial alternative between the government providing certain services, and nobody providing those services.

In fact, many important services currently provided by the government have not always been provided by the government: we have historical precedent for many alternatives to government as the provider of these services. Now, one might reasonably debate whether these alternatives are more effective or less effective than the current government programs—there is enough to consider here and dispute that it is by no means obvious to many people. Certainly this discussion would take a great deal of inconvenient mental work; but only after we have determined that all non-government alternatives are inferior to our current government programs can we legitimately press this dilemma as an objection to cutting taxes/spending.

Yet even if we did agree that all non-government alternatives to current government programs are inferior, and that therefore any cut in taxes/spending will inevitably have great negative consequences, we still are stuck in a false dichotomy: specifically, that a determination of a particular tax as unethical forces us to choose between keeping our current taxes or eliminating them entirely. But in truth we have another option: if we determine that a particular tax is unethical, but also determine that eliminating the tax entirely will have too sudden and disastrous a consequence to justify the change, we may at least argue for limiting the tax in the future—in other words, if we cannot eliminate an evil, we might at least mitigate it. Now such a compromise may not be entirely satisfactory to us (compromises rarely are; and yet we make them because the alternatives are worse); but it is at least a logical option, which could be honestly discussed—with perhaps different levels of compromise on different taxing/spending conundrums, according to all the negative consequences identified in each different situation.

Put another way, we are not required to take an all-or-nothing approach to implementing policy; and where it is unfeasible for moral and/or practical reasons to switch instantly from current behavior to a completely different behavior, we might at least take incremental steps in the right direction. So long as this option is available, we cannot pretend that all tax cuts are automatically so disastrous as to force us to accept the taxes' legitimacy.

But let us go further: suppose we acknowledge (for the moment) that any cut in taxes/spending whatsoever is certainly going to result in some identifiable harm—what then? Do we then decide that we have no choice but to accept all current levels of taxation—and future increases as well? Certainly not! For at least three reasons:

1. Not every kind of tax is the same: each type has different economic impacts, and different ethical considerations. Therefore if we determine that one particular tax

is unethical and ought to be reduced and/or eliminated, we may recover the lost revenue by increasing another tax that is less harmful/more ethical. If pursuing this option, it is *all the more important* to have a frank and thorough discussion of the ethics of taxation, so we might be able to identify which taxes and tax policies are better than others.

2. Although a reduction in spending might result in some identifiable harm, it is also true that the tax (or debt) which supports that spending also produces some identifiable harm: the proper course of action then is to weigh these harms against each other, rather than simply avoiding one without examining the other.

3. Even when reducing government spending produces results which are very unpleasant to us, we are still morally responsible to prefer enduring these unpleasant results to the alternative of committing evil. (If "evil" is too strong a term, substitute "injustice.") If you absolutely *must* commit some amount of evil/injustice/wrongdoing in order to protect some greater good—then you had better be clear about where you draw the line, lest you continue to justify ever greater levels of injustice (only a little at a time, of course, so that each individual increment does not seem too objectionable) in the pursuit of your greater good. Determining precisely where to draw that line requires frank and reasoned discussion of ethical principles.

Therefore we have an ethical responsibility to consider the ethical questions regarding our current and proposed tax policies; to neglect such consideration because we have determined *a priori* that taxation is necessary because we have already committed to spending is an abdication of that responsibility. Furthermore, abdication of this responsibility (and we, as an aggregate voting body, *have* abdicated it; we must now decide between continuing in this course or taking the responsibility up again) results in being kept forever hostage to further spending increases beyond authorized levels of funding, for every politician knows that they may spend as they please, and then afterwards claim we have an obligation to raise tax revenues in order to keep the "inviolable promises" made to the recipients of such profligacy.

Having said all this, we must note that so far no argument has been advanced in this section that any particular tax is unethical, or that taxation in general is unethical—only that a particular tax policy *might* be unethical, and we must admit this possibility. If we do not accept this as a possibility, then any further discussion is useless: for generally, people will not accept any premise which forces them to a conclusion that is intolerable to them. (Alas, some people—politicians particularly— count on this, and exploit it to their advantage whenever their preferred spending policies are threatened.)

> ### On Bureaucratic Evil
>
> It is a sad reality that some people in charge of bureaucratic agencies will purposely act unethically to further their own narrow self-interests, and this becomes particularly apparent whenever their budget is threatened. For example, imagine an agency with two mandates of differing levels of importance: the first is to provide medicine to the ill, and the second is to publish children's books which promote good health habits. If this agency's funding is reduced, what will be the result? Clearly, the moral thing to do would be to reduce efforts for the second, less important mandate; but if the person in charge of the agency makes that choice, then that agency's funding is likely to remain cut. So the agency instead reduces its efforts for the first mandate, resulting in more painful consequences— then they argue publicly that sick people are being harmed by the cut in funding, and so convince legislators to give them their funding back. While you might think that such a strategy is patently deceitful and would not work, the unfortunate fact of the matter is that this strategy often does work, for many legislators are more afraid of bad press which could cost them votes needed for re-election than they are afraid of doing wrong.
>
> The strategy of making budget cuts as painful as possible is business-as-usual in the American federal government—particularly during a shutdown "crisis." It is an ethical problem that needs to be addressed—and can only be addressed if the voting public takes the trouble to pay attention to such deceit and repudiate it, demanding the immediate replacement of such bureaucrats and the reduction of funding to their agencies (that is, demanding negative consequences for this unethical behavior). But so far, the American public has not made such a demand; so the false crises continue.
>
> In the meantime, voting Americans must recognize that many (and perhaps most) of the harms resulting from spending cuts are the artificial products of immoral bureaucrats and politicians, *not* the natural products of spending cuts.

Since the ethics of government spending is a separate discussion (or actually very many separate discussions), I will attempt in this text to first consider the ethics of taxation independently from it (as philosophers would say, "in a vacuum"), assuming that the related issues of spending have no weight. Of course in reality they do have weight; but before we consider that we ought to first be able to clearly identify the other ethical matters on their own. After we do so, then we can re-introduce this complicating matter and consider its impacts upon our selection of tax policy.

3

Tariffs

Tariffs, which are taxes on goods imported to or exported from a country, were one of the most significant sources of revenue (along with excise taxes) for the United States of America prior to the passing of the income tax; in 1912, for example, tariffs provided approximately 30% of the federal government's total revenue. Today, however, very little revenue is obtained through tariffs: today it accounts for only 1% or so of total revenues. But revenue is no longer the primary purpose of enacting them: today, tariffs are enacted to achieve other economic and political ends, such as to protect particular industries/jobs—and these purposes are so significant to the policy makers and voters that the separate matter of tax revenue generated is almost entirely disregarded as incidental and unimportant. Consequently, discussion of the economic effects upon tax revenue may be fairly easy, conducted without much disagreement; whereas discussion of the economic effects of tariffs upon jobs and the national economy is likely to be much more difficult, fraught with dispute.

Description and Purpose

A tariff (also referred to as a "duty" when discussing a tax on a particular import/export) is a tax passed on a product that travels across the national boundary, collected at the time of customs clearance at the border/port where the good enters the country. Administratively, it is one of the easiest taxes to collect ("easiest" referring both to the lower expenses involved in collecting and auditing the tax, and to the fewer difficulties to solve for in the implementation of the tax collection). In the United States, tariffs refer only to import duties: the US Constitution explicitly prohibits the federal government from levying any duty on exported goods (Article 1, Section 9: "No Tax or Duty shall be laid on Articles exported from any State.")

A tariff might be levied at a specific price per unit (known as the "specific" tariff; for example, $300/ton), or at a percentage rate (the "ad valorem" tariff; for example, 25% on imports of Chinese steel). It may be levied on a particular product regardless of origin; or upon a product only if its origin is from a specific country; or upon all products from a particular country; or not at all (about half of industrial goods imported to the United States have no tariff imposed upon them). Some industries are subject to a great many tariffs (about 4/5 of imported clothes have a duty upon them at an average rate above 15%, and nearly all imported shoes are taxed, at an average of more than 10%), while other industries are taxed little (only 1/6 of the computer equipment and industrial machinery is subject to import duties, and these average near 3%). The average tariff rate for all imports is actually quite low, around 2%. Consequently, while tariffs may not account for much of the total tax revenue for the United States, they make up a significant portion of the country's tax code: the Harmonized Tariff Schedule of the United States, listing all the of the various taxes upon goods imported to the US, is more than 3,700 pages long.

This long list of products subject to tariffs is not built with consistency in mind: for example, cross country skies are not taxed, but downhill skies are taxed at 2.6%, for... some historical reason that might be documented somewhere, but certainly not articulated in the tax code itself. Because when a government selects an import to tax, it frequently does so to protect some domestic production—but it does this because some domestic producer has lobbied for that protection, or some number of voters are clamoring for it. That means that tariffs get passed not out of some reasoned and internally-consistent set of principles, but rather through the same process of special-interest legislation that so many other laws go through, with those who clamor more and pay more getting the most benefits. Tariffs are not decided by economists after careful calculation (the majority of them would tend toward eliminating tariffs), but rather by politicians attempting to satisfy their constituent voters.

Economic Effects

The immediate effect of a tax upon an imported good is that it raises the seller's cost for supplying that good to market; in order to make the same amount of profit, the seller then needs to raise the price of that good for the consumer. However, when the price is raised on any good, consumers tend to buy less of it; so the overall sales of that good are reduced (this is the deadweight loss discussed earlier). The price change further results in several consequences:

1. Tariffs have very noticeable Laffer Curve effects: that is, raising the tax rate on an imported good past a certain point will actually result in less tax revenue, or even no tax revenue at all, if the tariff is made so high that it becomes unprofitable to trade that product. The fact that high tariff rates can result in less (or zero) revenue was actually observed by the founders of the Unites States. As Alexander Hamilton noted: "It is a signal advantage of tax on articles of consumption, that they contain in their own nature a security against excess. They prescribe their own limit; which cannot be exceeded without defeating the end proposed – that is an extension of the revenue."

    For example, the United States imposes a 25% duty on imported light trucks; consequently, the United States does not import any light trucks, as Americans won't pay so much more for this product when they can buy a light truck of similar quality produced inside the country.

2. Domestic businesses which compete with the imported goods experience reduced competition, since their competitors' costs have increased. If their competitors raise their prices, the domestic business has the option to either sell more cheaply to the customer (which will eventually drive the competitor out of the market, since they will not have enough sales—and at that point,

the domestic firm will be able to raise their own prices), or the domestic business may simply raise their own prices to match the competition, taking in a greater profit margin than their competition. The greater profit margin allows them to compete away better workers (through higher wages) or make greater investments in developing their firm—or [commonly] they may simply take the higher profits without changing/improving their business practices (since they are under no market pressure to do so).

In the short term, these domestic businesses experience a benefit from the tariff, as the reduced competition allows them to make more profit—which is touted as "saving" jobs in that industry. In the long run, however, reduced competitive pressures tend to result in less innovation: the protected industries become slower to invest in new technology or make other changes needed to stay competitive worldwide (so long as they are insulated from worldwide competition), and these industries become increasingly dependent upon the protective tariff to stay in business using their unchanged business model.

Meanwhile the effect upon consumers is that they invariably end up paying higher prices for the product, and frequently get a lower quality of product, than they would in a more competitive market.

3. Other domestic businesses which are themselves consumers of the taxed product experience an increase in their costs as well. For example, when a tariff is laid upon steel, all the domestic businesses which purchase steel to create their own products (cars, refrigerators, lockers, industrial machines, etc.) experience an increase in their own costs. Consequently, their consumers also end up paying more—and again, as prices go up on a product, sales tend to go down. Thus increasing the tax on imported steel increases the price and reduces the sales not only for steel, but also for everything made with steel.

Overall, the reduced sales in both the taxed good and all the products which are created from the taxed good mean less overall production—and fewer jobs—in multiple industries. Counting the loss of jobs in the various industries which purchase the taxed good is much more difficult than counting the number of jobs "saved" in the protected industry, as they are spread out; additionally, there is no way we can count the jobs that might have been created but weren't because of the drop in sales. Thus, politicians who promote tariffs are always more able to promote the benefits ("saving" jobs in an industry), since the real costs are less countable and less visible to the voters.

4. Higher prices for both the imported good and all products made from that imported good mean consumers will be left with less money to spend on other products (how much less depends upon how much of the taxed product they continue to buy). Consequently, the remaining sectors of the economy also experience a decline in demand (reduction in sales), which they then need to adjust to—possibly through innovation, but also possibly through layoffs or cancellation of plans to expand their business. Again, there is no way to count the number of jobs not created by a reduction in consumer demand (unless we could observe a parallel earth which did not institute the tariff in question), so these are largely invisible—but very real—costs.

In other words, the total wealth of the national economy is reduced by the foregone production of goods and services which cannot be afforded due to the higher prices of the taxed goods. The nation is left poorer than it otherwise would have been.

In summary: domestic producers of the taxed import reap the benefits of reduced competition, while the foreign sellers of the product and the domestic consumers of the product pay the costs (that is, experience the harms) in the form of higher prices and less wealth produced. Benefits are concentrated among the few, while costs/harms are distributed among the many.

Now it is important to note the effect upon foreign producers of the taxed good differs according to the buying power of the country passing the tariff. A tariff levied by a small country, which has very little purchasing power on the world market, may not affect the sellers' business significantly: for the producers of the taxed product can just sell in other countries. But a tariff levied by large country, which has significant buying power on the market (more accurately, had a significant number of consumers buying the product), may result in a crippling reduction in demand: for the foreign producers of the taxed good may not be able to find the same number of buyers in other countries. In some circumstances, this can result in entire industries in foreign countries shrinking or even collapsing. Consequently, a big enough country can attempt to threaten another country with a tariff (the operative word here is "attempt"), if it is confident that the other country will experience greater harms than its own.

Unfortunately, politicians in different countries (and voters within each country) cannot clearly see all these effects: as noted before, the full scope of the costs/harms cannot be counted, for we have no way of counting jobs created or lost in an alternative universe where the tariff was not passed. We can only anticipate the type of harms from a priori principles of supply and demand (fundamentally, that all other things being equal, when the price of an item goes up, people tend to buy less of that item; and that given a finite amount of buying power, and increase in price in one part of a budget results in a re-prioritization of other items in that budget). Consequently, many politicians argue—and have argued for hundreds of years—that the benefits of tariffs (the protection of domestic industries, or "saving jobs") outweigh the costs/harms (the higher prices paid by domestic consumers—the harms inflicted upon foreign producers tend to be utterly unimportant to politicians, since those people can't vote). Meanwhile the vast majority of economists have argued—for hundreds of years—that on the balance, tariffs cause more harm to the country levying them than they reap in benefits: by raising prices on their own consumers and business, they reduce their own economic growth overall.

When one country attempts to threaten another country with a tariff, the threatened country often responds with a counter-threat—a tariff of their own upon some product the first country produces. From one perspective (that of most economists), this seems like a self-immolation contest: because country A harmed itself by raising prices on their own consumers, country B responds by harming itself in the same way. Yet from another perspective (that of most politicians), this is a simple tool of diplomacy to deploy against another country to try to get them to change policy: country A harms its own consumers but harms country B's producers even more, in an attempt to get country B to adopt a policy more preferable to country A—only country B usually resents any attempt made by one nation to dictate policy terms, so frequently responds by trying to inflict the same kind of harm upon the country A. This is what is known as a trade war: a competition between politicians in two sovereign countries to impose their will (policy preferences) upon one another (that is, to usurp the other country's sovereignty) through impeding their own citizens' ability to buy products imported from the target country.

The effects of a trade war last far beyond the initial confrontation. For example, in the 1960's, France and West Germany imposed a tariff upon imports of American chicken, since they wanted their own citizens to buy chicken from European chicken farmers (promoting the European economy) instead of from American chicken farmers. Since this drastically reduced the sales of American chicken farmers, the American legislators felt compelled to respond to "protect" the American chicken farmers (their constituents)—this was so important to one senator that he actually interrupted a NATO debate on nuclear disarmament to discuss the "unfair" trade sanctions on US chicken. Eventually, the United States responded by imposing tariffs on light trucks (a major German product) and brandy (a major French product) in an attempt to force them to remove their chicken tariff—or at least to punish them for imposing it in the first place. That tax on light trucks (25%, referred to earlier) ended the import of light trucks from Germany (they could no longer be sold at a competitive price in American markets)—and it is still in place today. That is why Americans cannot buy VW light trucks in America; that is why Ford (an American company with a production plant in Turkey) built one of their light trucks in Turkey as a passenger vehicle (circumventing the import tariff), then converted it to a light truck after shipping it to the states (this process increased the production cost of each vehicle by several hundred dollars, but saved several thousand in taxes). Light trucks in America are more expensive, and American consumers have fewer choices available to them, than they would be in a more competitive environment.

Tax Incidence

While a tariff is nominally paid by the holder of the good when it is imported into the country, much of the actual tax is passed on to the end consumer. How much of the tax is passed to the consumer depends upon how sensitive the consumers are to any change in price: the more price-sensitive they are, the harder it is for the seller to raise their price, so they incur a greater portion of the cost by reducing their profits; but when the buyer is less price-sensitive, a greater portion of the tax can be passed to the consumer in the form of higher prices. For example:

Suppose the United States levies a 10% tax on vibranium from the nation of Wakanda (sometimes a fictional example is simpler to follow than a real-world one). Since Wakanda is the only nation in the world that sells vibranium, American buyers cannot go elsewhere for the product; and the product is really valuable to them, so they are not very price-sensitive (at least, not at 10%). So the Wakandan seller marks up its sale price by 8% to cover the tax, passing on most of the cost to the initial buyer—say, Stark industries. Because the cost of vibranium has gone up, they have to buy less of it—or forego other purchases they had planned on making (in either case, they bring fewer products to market). And since their production costs have gone up, they in turn raise the prices on the vibranium shields they produce for their consumers—maybe by 6%. Thus the cost of the tariff ends up divided between the Wakandan seller, Stark industries, and the American buyers of vibranium shields (who in this case paid the most). Meanwhile, fewer shields overall have been sold—or if just as many have been sold, then that means the buyers have less money to spend on other things; so there is still an additional opportunity cost, as fewer products overall are traded in the economy—but nobody can know how many, because nobody knows what each of those buyers of vibranium shields might have spent their money on otherwise.

Or, if you must have a more real-world example: in February of 2018 a tariff on imported washing machines went into effect (20% on the first 1.2 million imports, and 50% on all thereafter); that cost translated into an increase in the consumer cost of washing machines by 16.4% by April—in fact the largest price increase ever recorded for this product. Overall sales of washing machines declined accordingly.

Less overall economic product means less wealth—fewer real goods and services—traded and enjoyed by the citizens of the nation. So when asking, "who pays for the tariff?" the answer must include not only the buyers and sellers of the taxed good—they pay the nominal cost—but also all those who lose the opportunity to make a trade favorable to them—the deadweight loss in mutually beneficial trade. And this reduce in trade affects in turn all participants in the national economy, who also suffer the opportunity cost of foregone wealth production. The nation, in aggregate, is left poorer than it would have been if the trade had not been impeded. (Importantly, although the nation is poorer in aggregate, it is important to note that some sector of the nation may be left wealthier: specifically, those people and businesses who trade in a good that competes with the Wakandan vibranium—such as a nascent adamantium industry, for example.)

Ethical Considerations

A small tariff on all imports might be justified to pay for the navy which protects shipping to a country safer; but tariffs are generally not supported on these grounds. In actual practice, tariffs are supported instead upon the grounds of Protectionism and "Fairness" (a word of dubious content, if allowed to be examined). Significantly, both of these grounds depend upon a national identity, and the assumption that citizens of a country are obliged to give some amount of preference to their fellow citizens over against foreigners (and their own selves). We will consider both of these in turn. But first, let us consider how tariffs stand against our preliminary ethical principles.

The first one, representation, is tricky: for tariffs are applied to goods imported from foreign governments, and we cannot apply the principle of representation across national borders. But since we identified that much of the actual tax incidence is passed from the sellers to the buyers, we can consider the principle of representation there: and on this ground, tariffs seem to do alright, insofar as consumers do have the opportunity to vote for or against the politicians who support the tariffs. When we consider participation and appropriateness, however, tariff policy holds up less well, because the essence of a tariff is to award a benefit to one portion of the population (the firms protected from competition) while applying the cost to another portion of the population (the firms and end consumers who must pay higher prices). Though on the positive side, we must acknowledge that the costs of a typical tariff is likely to afflict a majority of voters rather than a minority of them; so on this dimension the tax is more ethical than one which focuses the harms on a minority which could not effectively respond through the vote.

Regarding honesty, tariffs seem to be promoted not so much out of deceit as out of economic misunderstanding. However, there is one feature that is possibly deceitful: that is the executive power to impose a tax in the name of "national security." For typically—and Constitutionally—it is the American Congress which has the power to tax, not the American president; however, Congress has passed several laws (e.g. Trading with the Enemy Act of 1917, Trade Expansion Act of 1962, Trade Act of 1974, and the International Emergency Economic Powers Act of 1977) which give the president the power to tax imports when there is a war, a threat to national security, or certain other emergencies. Consequently, President Johnson in the 1960s and President Trump more recently both cited "national security" concerns to levy tariffs—even while each advocated their policies with rhetorical appeals to "fairness," and "protecting" Americans jobs. Insofar as a president cites "national security" to justify other goals, the policy is deceitful.

Meanwhile some other instances of apparent deceit may actually reflect economic ignorance or imprecise language rather than dishonesty. For example, when the US House of Representatives circulated a "fact sheet" regarding tariffs which read *"Under our current broken tax code, U.S. companies pay a tax when exporting products, but not when they import products. To avoid paying that tax on exports, U.S. companies move jobs, research, and headquarters overseas,"* one might cite them for being dishonest, because the United States cannot and does not impose taxes on exports. Or one might simply understand them to be using the phrase "tax on exports" to actually be referring to the import taxes that other countries impose on American products (effectively, other countries' taxes on American exports).

Regarding openness, tariffs are not explicitly hidden: anyone can review the 3,700+ page Tariff Schedule, right? Well, technically; but in practical terms, this is hidden knowledge, for voters typically do not have the free time to read this and deliberate upon it. As far as the average voter is concerned, the cost of the tax is quite hidden: for as the tax is not directly applied to them, but upon "imports," and they never see what amount of that tax gets passed on to them, it is effectively invisible to them. Newspapers may print articles cataloging the increase of prices—but newspapers also print stories arguing the opposite side also, so they may not be regarded as reliable information. Thus when the consumer pays an additional $60 for their washing machine, they may have no idea whatsoever that they are paying for the tariff. (And remember, it is not only the washing machines imported from China which cost more, but also the American-made washing machines, since they are no longer forced to compete against a lower Chinese price.)

As for appropriateness, tariffs are fundamentally problematic: their very function is to benefit one group of people at the expense of another—raising the taxes on Peter in order to pay Paul (or to keep Paul's job secure from competition). Insofar as Peter (that is, all the voting Peters in the nation) approve of this transfer and willingly sacrifices for it, it may be regarded as ethical. How far is that?

Regarding the minimizing of harms, tariff policy has significant faults. As noted above, tariffs raise prices for consumers, which in turn reduce their ability to buy other items they desire, lowering demand for other products. For every job "saved" by a tariff, uncounted others are lost by the increased price of inputs and the decreased demand. The damage is distributed unevenly, but ripples out; and the damage gets magnified when other countries respond by passing their own tit-for-tat tariffs. The increased tariffs not only reduce overall trade (that is, reduce the number of mutually-beneficial exchanges) in the short run, but signal to investors that they will receive less profits in the taxed industries, reducing capital investment (and consequently, all the economic growth that results from capital investment). Now if all these harms were honestly discussed and weighed against any anticipated/perceived benefits, that would be one thing; but insofar as political debate ignores these costs, it is flatly unethical.

Regarding the justice/punishment criteria, some tariffs are unequivocally unethical, as some are passed with the specific purpose of punishing another government. In fact they doubly fail this measure, for not only are some tariffs intentionally punitive, but they also punish the wrong people. For example, when West Germany imposed a tariff on US frozen chicken, the Unites States responded with a tariff on light trucks—the US punishing West Germany (and still punishing unified Germany today) for injuring the US economy. Except that it is not the United States and West Germany who were trading chickens and trucks: it was individuals in both of those countries who were trading with each other. In reality, the West German government interfered with the freewill trades between American chicken farmers and German consumers, injuring them both; and the American government responded not by retaliating against the West German government, but by inflicting injury upon West German truck dealers and American consumers. They did not punish the individuals for the "crime" of imposing tariffs; *they punished entirely different individuals who happened to live in the same country*. We often miss this important distinction when we talk about nation trade, imagining different countries to be single entities; but ethically, just as we ought to refuse to punish all people of a particular race for the actions of some, we should also refuse to punish people of a particular nationality for the actions of others in that nation. As a punishment, tariffs are flatly unjust.

Finally, regarding peace, tariff policy has problems here also: for after a tariff raises costs for importers of the taxed product, the most powerful of those importers then turn to lobbying the government for exceptions for themselves—exceptions which they must compete for, against others in their industry who want the same. For example, after President Trump increased taxes on imports of Chinese steel and aluminum, several companies immediately applied to the executive branch for exemptions. Some received exemptions; most did not. But all who applied knew that they were competing with other businesses for those exemptions; and whoever had the strongest lobbying arm had the greatest chance of obtaining the special exceptions distributed by the government. Thus the tariff, in addition to the economic effects enumerated above, has the additional effect of increasing the power of the government to dispense favors to that please them; and all businesses, in order to remain competitive in the economic market, must also divert resources to competing in the political market, lest their economic competitors win any advantage over them in political favors. And these are just the businesses that get most injured; for on the other side, those business which are protected by the tariffs become increasingly dependent upon the government policy, and to maintain it they must devote lobbying dollars as well—lest their politicians change their mind to satisfy consumers who would like lower prices. Protected businesses, which could make money by better serving their consumers, are instead incentivized to view them as political enemies, since they have the power to change the tariff policy.

Lobbying and Corruption

Corruption was not mentioned among the ethical principles listed above, since it more properly applies to the people who operate the government than it does to a specific tax policy—for an ethical tax may still be administered in a corrupt fashion (for example, by collecting it from some but not others), while an unethical tax might be administered with perfectly regular application, showing no favoritism. However, it is true that some kinds of taxes are particularly exploited and/or exploitable through lobbying efforts (which is counted by many as a kind of corruption—although other people might just call this democracy at work).

In 2016, a private equity company named One Rock Capital Partners, LLC, acquired the North Pacific Paper Company (Norpac), which produces newsprint for newspapers. At this time, many newspapers imported their newsprint from companies in Canada. So in 2018, as the Trump administration was levying new tariffs (ostensibly for national security purposes) One Rock lobbied the Commerce Department to tax imports of Canadian newsprint, *on the grounds that American imports of Canadian newsprint was harming their investment.* The Commerce department obliged the American firm by levying a 30% tariff on Canadian newsprint, which allowed Norpac to raise the price of their newsprint, and consequently turn a hefty profit.

The increased cost of newsprint is paid by newspapers around the country, which will reduce their profits. Thus the effective lobbying by one firm has transferred money from one set of firms to one particular firm which can operate the levers of government power.

Meanwhile, the sheer amount of money that businesses must spend on lobbying represent an additional economic harm, as money spent on lobbying does *not* create economic growth (wealth), but rather diverts money away from both production and investment, which would promote economic growth (wealth). Surely this is a harm we ought to minimize.

Summary Report Card – Tariffs

Representation/Participation   **Pass**
Voters can theoretically respond to tariffs by changing their representatives.

Honesty   **Problematic**
Tariffs can be passed under the guise of "national security" when in fact they are being passed for multiple other reasons.

Openness   **Problematic**
Consumers have no idea how much they pay for these taxes.

Simplicity   **Problematic**
The tariff schedule in the United States is more than 3,700 pages long.

Appropriateness   **Doubtful**
One population (generally, consumers of a particular product—both individuals and firms) is harmed in order to benefit a separate population (generally a set of domestic producers of a particular product).

Consideration   **Doubtful**
Since much of the cost of the tariff is passed to the consumer through higher prices (not only for the imported goods, but for the domestic goods which are no longer forced by their foreign competition to sell at a lower price), many tariffs functionally transfer wealth from poorer people (end consumers) to richer people (owners of protected businesses).

Minimizing Harms   **Fail**
Politicians don't count the harms, but only the [perceived] benefits.
Meanwhile, trade wars significantly reduce the overall production of wealth.

Justice   **Flatly Unethical**
Tariffs are passed to punish people—except they punish the wrong people!

Peace   **Fail**
Tariff policy pits firms against each other in political battle for government favor. A firm must devote money to lobbying the government to protect itself from other firms which are lobbying the government; and the most effective lobbyists get to invoke the power of government inflict harms on other firms.

So far, tariffs are not looking so good—but surely they are "fair," or are necessary to protect jobs or industry, right? At least, those are the common ethical justifications advanced for them; so let us now consider these arguments.

The argument from "fairness" contends that because country X imposes tariffs against country Y, then it is only fair for country Y to impose tariffs on country X. However, given the negative economic effects of a tariff borne by the country that imposes a tariff, this is a little like saying that because country X punches itself in the face, then country Y should punch itself in the face as well. A little like, but not entirely: for we did acknowledge that tariffs do inflict costs/harms upon other countries as well, so a country is in fact doing more than punching itself in the face—the West German tariffs on American chicken, for example, significantly reduced the market for American chicken, thus injuring—that is, reducing the sales and profits of—the American chicken farmers.

Except we already saw that this concept of fairness only makes sense if a country is composed of a single entity, rather than many (or many millions) of individuals trading in the market. Responding with a "fair" tariff—whether against West Germany in 1964 or against China in 2018—isn't simply responding to that country, but to a subset of trading individuals within that country, who may have nothing to do whatsoever with the "unfair" exchange.

An additional problem with enacting a "fair" tariff is that a government represents a third party to an economic exchange, attempting to determine what is "fair" between other parties already engaged in freewill transactions. If I freely choose to buy a Chinese product at a given price, then both the seller and the buyer/myself have already determined that the price is fair—if I did not think it fair, then I would not make the purchase. How does the government—which itself is not an individual person, but a number of diverse agents all with different values and different amounts of information about the market, yet lacking the specific information that affected my individual purchase—determine a more "fair" price that what we have already agreed upon?

Ah, but the "unfairness" is not so much between the buyer and seller as it is between competing sellers: the foreign seller is "unfairly" selling their product at a lower price than the domestic seller, and this is "unfair" because the domestic seller misses out on the sale. But what is the complaining seller properly appealing to? Does the domestic seller have any particular right to my business? What obligates me to purchase from the domestic seller when I can choose to purchase from a foreign seller who offers my the same quality for a lower price (or, in other contexts, better quality for the same price, or even better quality for a higher price)? What makes my freewill choice "unfair" to the domestic seller? And if it is "unfair" for a foreign seller to offer a lower price, does that mean it is also "unfair" for a second domestic seller to also offer a lower price—does the complaining seller need to be protected from his neighboring countrymen as well?

Of course most people argue that there is some significant difference between competition among businesses in the same country and competition among business in different countries (although interestingly, businesses frequently do in fact apply for protections against local competition as well—but that is a separate issue from tariff policy). One of the more commonly cited reasons is that foreign countries have an unfair advantage in the price of labor: frequently (at least, in cases like China) they can pay their workers less, which gives them the ability to sell for less; the tariff is needed to balance this unfair advantage. But there is a great economic problem with appealing to the national government to balance comparative advantages between nations: it reduces overall wealth production—whether one is measuring both economies together, or even just measuring the economy of the nation "protecting" itself. This type of fairness necessarily results in people (as a whole) being poorer (although the subset of the people who receive the direct benefit of being protected from competition are initially better off—and somehow promoting the good of a subset of the population against the good of the whole of the population is "fair.").

But jobs will be lost if tariffs are not erected, the protectionist may point out. And this is true—just as it is true that jobs are lost in one firm or industry any time another firm offers the same or better products and service at a lower price. *Some* jobs are lost, while on the whole, *more* jobs are created, because there is more *wealth* created and exchanged. This wealth creation and exchange is done through the freewill transactions of buyers and sellers—by what method do we determine a more fair standard for deciding which jobs need to be preserved and which jobs need to be prevented? Who decides, and by what established principles do they decide, that it is fair to protect 25,000 jobs in the steel industry at the cost of 400,000 jobs in other industries (different economists will dispute over the exact proportion here, but the general agreement is that more jobs are lost than are saved). This ethical problem is intractable: there *is no established, universally agreed-upon principle* anyone can appeal to which can help a government (either the chief executive, the legislative body, or the individual bureaucrats who operate the machine) decide which jobs are more important than others. There is, however, the politician's principle: favor those jobs which will net the most votes.

But what about domestic security and autarky? And what if a nation has a nascent industry that may become competitive, but initially needs some protection to get it started? The nascent industry issue makes a lot of sense to many people, particularly if they perceive that the nation needs the new industry in order to become more independent and less vulnerable to trade fluctuations in the rest of the world.

And indeed, it would make sense, if the nation were owned by a single individual who was administering their own property in the way they best saw fit; but in reality, when the national government does not own the businesses of their citizens, such "administration" is unavoidably the government choosing to favor some part of its population over another part—and the part that it favors is invariably the part that can provide the most political support (in money, influence, and votes). Furthermore, such "temporary" tariffs tend to be rather permanent—forever protecting, and forever hampering, the formerly-nascent industry in the global competitive market.

The domestic security issue can be more complicated, and may have more ethical ground—and indeed, the various trade acts referenced earlier, which allocated taxing power to the president, were all concerned with this issue. For theoretically, an enemy nation could disrupt or even destroy an industry through selling a product at such a low cost that American businesses could not compete. Right? Except this is probably an economic myth—or at least, there is no historical record of it having ever been successfully accomplished. For any nation that tried to undercut a particular industry through selling at low prices would just be increasing that country's wealth, as the buying nation acquired more goods for less money. Yes, particular industries would be injured—temporarily—and there would be some [potentially large] economic disruption; but on the whole the targeted nation would still benefit. Consider if China attempted an "act of economic warfare" by "dumping" steel at such low prices that the American steel industry collapsed (I use China as an example again because the recent tariff levied on Chinese steel was levied specifically under the legal pretense of protecting national security). The result would be that Chinese firms (which are being directed by the Chinese government in this hypothetical scenario) would earn less profit, potentially even losing money; and the longer they tried to maintain this the worse would it would be for the *Chinese* economy. Meanwhile American industries which used steel (automobile manufacturers, equipment manufacturers, construction firms, etc.) would all be making greater profits—they might welcome such an "attack" as that.

But what about the trade deficit? Aren't Americans getting an unfair deal when we import more from China than China imports from America? Isn't that unfair and should be rectified? Most assuredly not: for if it is true that Americans import more from China than China imports from America, that would imply that America is *gaining more wealth from China than it is trading them in return*. But in fact this is not true: the "trade deficit" is a myth, an artefact of government accounting. For the "trade deficit" results from counting only the flow of goods, and ignoring the flow of capital investment; when both are counted together, the supposed deficit disappears. As it has to: for every $1 of money exchanged for a $1 of goods has an equal value. I do not claim to have a "trade deficit" with my local grocery store, though I buy goods from them and sell no goods in return; we make equal, freewill exchange, and count it that way. In the same way, when Americans (not America, as an entity, but Americans, as millions of individual trading entities) buy goods from Chinese (not China), and the Chinese buy stocks, bonds, treasury bills, and other investment products from Americans, it is always an equal exchange—unless we stubbornly insist upon counting one kind of commerce and not the other.

With such myths as the trade deficit and the specter of economic attack through price dumping dispelled, do we have any other ethical grounds for supporting tariffs?—Actually, let us not move on just yet; for it is quite likely that my brief arguments have been insufficient to change anyone's mind on the issues of domestic security and trade deficits. Let us instead suppose for a moment that I am mistaken about their economic effects: if so, could we then count tariff policy as ethical for these protectionist purposes? I still think not: for in both cases, the ethical construction rests upon perceiving entire nations as individuals, or at least as individual firms, directed by government leaders. But is this an appropriate model? It is simple, certainly, and may be of some practical use in some situations; but it does not at all match the economic reality of millions of individuals making freewill exchanges in pursuit of their own subjective goals. Protectionist policy elevates the perceived needs of the nation over the real needs of individuals—except in practice, "the nation" always refers to some subset of the nation, to some particular individuals and/or firms. Thus protectionist tariff policy *necessarily* intrudes upon the freedom of some individuals in order to confer benefits upon other individuals, in the name of a national identity which rhetorically disregards the importance of individual economic valuation and exchange. This is ethically problematic, even if trade deficits represented real harms instead of misunderstood accounting labels, and even if it were somehow feasible for another nation to sustain some sort of price-dumping "attack" upon another nation.

So, with protectionist arguments being ethically problematic, are we left with any other grounds at all to justify tariff policies (to justify interfering with the freewill exchange of goods across national borders)? Perhaps there is one, but it rests upon another set of ethical assumptions:

When a nation imposes regulations upon those who do business within its borders (such as safety codes, licensure and quality control, labor controls, and many more legal restrictions), it increases the cost of doing business within that nation. But as such regulations cannot be applied to business in other nations, it does not raise the cost for those firms. Consequently, the foreign businesses without these costs have an advantage, an "unfair" advantage, over the domestic firms—and this advantage seems to come at the cost of their own workers' safety, their own workers' income, and their own products' quality. Since the regulating nation has imposed a cost upon its own businesses, is it not consequently obligated to recompense those businesses with a protective tariff?

Perhaps it is. That is, if you believe that the initial regulatory action was ethically justified, then you may consistently believe that the consequent tariff is ethically justified, for the tariff makes it more possible for the regulated businesses to do what they are being required to do. Furthermore, it might incentivize foreign firms to adopt similar regulations, if you could promise them the tariff would be reduced if they did so. Importantly, this ethical rule would not justify all tariffs, but only the amount of tariffs that would balance the additional costs of complying with the government's various regulations.

An Almost Analogous Case in California

What might be the merits and demerits of a tariff designed to uphold a domestic regulation? We can actually see an example of this play out within the United States, between California and other states in the union. While this example does move us from discussing foreign trade to discussing domestic trade, it highlights the economic contest at work in both cases; I leave it to you to decide if the ethical question has changed. Anyway: in 2008 the state of California passed a law requiring that egg-laying chickens be kept in larger cages (giving farmers until 2015 to make the change). The egg farmers rightly pointed out that this would increase their cost of doing business, and so risk putting them out of business, as they would not be able to compete with the lower prices on eggs imported from Iowa, Missouri, and other states. So in order to protect their own farmers, California banned the import of eggs from any farm that did not meet the California standard: if farmers from other states wanted to continue to sell to Californians, they would have to change their business practices and increase their own costs to do so. In consequence, the price of eggs has gone up—not just in California, but nationally, as egg farmers in other states do change their production in order to access the large California market. But since the farmers in the other states rather resent California imposing its law on their productions, 12 states have jointly sued California. California now argues that its law regarding egg imports is for health concerns (dishonesty!), and doesn't really injure the other states' economies; meanwhile Americans pay an additional $350 million for the same amount of eggs, with almost $100 million of that increase coming from the poorest fifth of the population (taxing the poor?).

Now imagine that instead of California attempting to impose its law on other states through a ban on imports, this were a country attempting to impose its regulations on another country—or just trying to protect its own businesses from the costly effects of these regulations—through a tariff. If you support the original regulation, this may seem easy—but what if you did not support the regulation: would your ethical calculus be the same, or different?

But suppose Americans agreed that a particular cost peculiar to American businesses (such as safety regulations, "decent" wages, etc.) warranted a protective tariff (note that this argument can only justify a tariff against a nation that does not have these costs, such as China; when trading with other nations that do have such costs, or have even greater costs—such as many European nations—no tariff could be justified with this argument): the next thing to consider then would be the resulting trade-offs, and if the net result would bring greater harm or greater good. For some of the costs of such a protective tariff would still include the following:

1. Since Americans would pay more money for the same amount of product, they would have less money for the consumption of other products; and consequently, the overall wealth production of the nation would be reduced, resulting in slower job growth and slower growth in average earnings.

2. Since the protective tariff benefits American producers unequally, and establishes the possibility of other protective tariffs in the future, American firms must divert productive wealth to pay for lobbying the federal government, further reducing the overall production of wealth and further slowing the growth in average earnings.

3. If the foreign country impacted by the tariff responds with its own retaliatory tariff, then there is the additional cost to American producers who are rendered unable to sell in markets where they had many customers. This sudden and drastic reduction in customers frequently results in firms being forced to lay off workers, or sell off capital that they had invested in as they grew to serve the larger market. This destroys prior investments of wealth.

    When retaliatory tariffs (and possibly a full-blown a trade war) result in harms to domestic firms (or entire industries), the government politicians—who depend upon votes for re-election—often respond with further "protective" measures: for example, after China levied retaliatory tariffs against the United States for President Trump's aluminum and steel tariffs, the Trump administration announced that it would seek some $12 in subsidies for American farmers hurt by the Chinese tariffs. This $12 billion is part of the cost of the aluminum/steel tariff, paid through borrowing money from investors (including Chinese investors!)—which diverts $12 billion from being invested in the economy (in real estate, new businesses, expansion of existing businesses, capital improvements, and every other places investors place their money to make a profit from anticipated economic growth).

Counting all of these costs, even an ethically warranted protective tariff may easily cause more overall harm than good.

But what if we can Win a Trade War?

Although all countries involved in a trade war suffer harms, it is true that harms are not distributed equally; and it follows that it is possible for a more powerful country to do less damage to itself in a trade war than a less powerful country is doing to itself. In such a situation, the economically less powerful country may eventually capitulate to the demands of country with the more robust economy in order to end their trade war; and we can call this "winning" a trade war. So, if winning such a trade war is possible—or even probable—would that justify waging it? For economically, it would be trading a short-term loss for a long-term gain.

This calculus might make sense if each nation were an individual entity (as we tend to think of them in the abstract), allowing one to determine the value of such a trade war with some cost-benefit analysis. But the moment we recall that it is not a national being involved in trade, but millions of individuals involved in trade, we cannot escape that such a war still means that some individuals are harmed in order to bring benefits to other individuals. And even supposing that all the individuals within a nation were in agreement (which they certainly are *not*), one would still be advocating causing harm for the purpose of forcing people in one nation to conform to the dictates of another—which is pretty clearly unethical to the party being subjugated, at least.

Mental/Emotional Roadblock: Fairness

Frequently, a person who agrees that tariffs are harmful (and who even agrees that they are ethically problematic), and who consequently agrees that two countries would be better off if both eliminated their tariffs, nevertheless *is still resistant to the proposal that their own country should reduce/eliminate their tariffs,* unless other countries agree to do the same at the same time. The mental (and emotional) obstacle here is that it seems "unfair" if one country eliminates their tariffs while another does not: for why should the US charge no tariff if France/China/wherever continues to charge x%? Isn't that unfair to Americans? Aren't they being ripped off?

No. Unequivocally, no, they are not being ripped off. Recall that an American tariff means that *American buyers* must pay a higher price for their goods; so eliminating that tariff is making them better off, not worse. But, the questioner may still object, American *businesses* (and consequently, American workers), are made worse off, because they still have foreign tariffs imposed upon their products sold overseas. But again, no, unequivocally no: for those businesses have not had their foreign sales injured if the other country refuses to change their tariff, and the foreign country is *not* going to respond to a lower tariff by increasing theirs (that would be the absolute opposite of how nations have always responded historically); so no harm is being done to American businesses (in aggregate) by the elimination of tariffs (although specific, *uncompetitive* businesses which have been protected from competition by tariffs will be forced to adapt, or close down as foreign businesses do a better job of meeting customers' demands). But! the emotional objection continues, it is still unfair that one country can sell to us without a tariff so long as they don't let us sell to them without a tariff! Well, there is a type of unfairness here, but it is an unfairness that hurts the unfair party: for if the Chinese/French/etc. insist upon keeping their tariffs, they are being unfair (causing harm) mostly to Chinese/French citizens.

The truth is the country that unilaterally reduces/eliminates tariffs, even when other countries do not, *benefits* from their action. This might be counter-intuitive—actually, it only seems counter-intuitive if one has on some level bought into the notion that tariffs are a good thing—but intuition aside, it is a question of fact that can actually be resolved by looking at historical data throughout the world. For example, jurisdictions like Hong Kong, Singapore, and Macau impose virtually no tariffs or trade restrictions, regardless of what other countries do, and these are some of the richest places in the world (although to be sure, they have other policies helping them, such as low taxes, small government, and minimal red tape). Meanwhile New Zealand reduced their tariffs—they went from an average of 20% tariffs in 1992 to under 10% in 1996 to eliminating nearly all their tariffs by 1999, bringing their average down to about 2% today—without concern for whether or not other nations reciprocated, and consequently entered a period of great economic growth (although again, one must note that this was supported by other pro-market policies as well). Similarly, Great Britain began the 19th century willing to reduce tariffs only when other nations did, but about halfway through determined to decrease their own unilaterally, beginning with the repeal of the Corn Laws in 1846—and that country too experienced great economic growth (again, helped by other pro-growth policies and innovations).

But as with any question of data, a person is not likely to be convinced by data reported by the person they are debating—you must really investigate the data yourself. The intellectually lazy person will not pursue the data, but instead revert to whatever they believe "intuitively" to be the case ("intuitively" is placed in quotation marks, because what we call our intuition is often misinformed). The intellectually responsible individual will investigate the data, and discover that, all other things being equal, unilateral reduction of tariffs coincides with economic growth. Because we do not need to wait for other people to stop punching themselves in the face to benefit from ceasing to punch ourselves in the face.

4

Excise Taxes (Sin Taxes)

Excise taxes (or, if you want to split hairs regarding definitions, excise *duties*) are taxes levied directly upon goods at the time of their production—and consequently passed along to consumers in the form of higher prices upon those goods. Such taxes are typically levied upon items which are considered "bad" for individuals and for society as a whole, in which case they are also termed "sin taxes." Throughout the world, sin taxes are most commonly levied on alcohol, tobacco, and gasoline; the United States does the same—although some jurisdictions also levy sin taxes on other items, such as soft drinks or other sugary items.

Description and Purpose

In theory, excise taxes are a way to get people to pay for externalities—the negative effects upon other people resulting from use a product which are not accounted for in the product's price. For example, the consumer of cigarettes pollutes the air with secondhand smoke, causing ill health effects for other people without compensating them; the consumer of alcohol decreases community and traffic safety and increases the risk of nondrinkers without compensating them; and the consumer of gasoline pollutes the air with carbon monoxide without compensating all the other breathers of air and subjects of the global environment. Since society (or more accurately, the body of individuals within a society who have inclination and power to act upon the laws) regards these external effects as bad, and they want to reduce these negative impacts (or at least obtain some way of funding their responses to them)— and because these type of effects are [perceived as] difficult to address through tort law—they levy a tax upon these products to transfer some of the costs of the externalities from society back to the consumers of the products themselves. (Or as some non-economical people might phrase it, to "punish" those who cause harm through using/overusing these products. This "punishing" aspect is important to some voters and policy makers, while totally irrelevant to others.)

In practice, excise taxes are frequently used simply to generate revenue. For it is very difficult (if not impossible) to determine a "correct" amount of tax to cover the harms of the externalities (for how do you determine the dollar amount of damage cause by secondhand smoke—in a way that the majority of experts and voters will agree with your assessment?), and when "punishment" comes into play, different legislatures, voters, and other judges will assess wildly different amounts, according to their own subjective measures of the value of punishment. Meanwhile, since no specific amount can be easily justified, but the basic concept can be, it is a simple matter to just advocate any arbitrary amount based upon the basic concept instead of upon any economic analysis—and consequently, to increase that amount whenever additional revenue is desired. Thus excise taxes vary significantly between different state and local governments (the tax on a box of cigarettes in 2018 ranges from $0.17 in Missouri to $4.35 in New York; and the state tax on a gallon of gasoline ranges from

14.65 cents in Alaska to 58.7 cents in Pennsylvania, on top of the 18.4 cents levied at the federal level); and the variance does more to describe the revenue demands of the governments of each state rather than the cost of the externalities borne by the residents of each state. Similarly, one of the main arguments advanced in favor of legalizing marijuana is that the state can gain an additional revenue source from taxing it—clearly indicating that the tax is more for the purpose of generating revenue than for discouraging use of the product.

Highest & lowest gasoline taxes by state		
Rank	State	Tax per gallon
1	Pennsylvania	58.7 cents
2	California	55.22 cents
3	Washington	49.4 cents
4	Hawaii	47.88 cents
5	New York	45.76 cents
46	Arizona	19 cents
47	New Mexico	18.88 cents
48	Mississippi	18.79 cents
49	Missouri	17.35 cents
50	Alaska	14.65 cents
(data as of July 2018, sales taxes not included)		

Highest & lowest cigarette taxes by state		
Rank	State	Tax per pack
1	New York	$4.35
1	Connecticut	$4.35
3	Rhode Island	$4.25
4	Massachusetts	$3.51
5	Hawaii	$3.20
46	North Carolina	$0.45
47	North Dakota	$0.44
48	Georgia	$0.37
49	Virginia	$0.30
50	Missouri	$0.17
(data as of July 2018)		

Theory and practice align better with the other major function of excise taxes, which is to change consumer behavior. Since the tax increases the cost of the "bad" item, consumers tend to buy less of it, as they do not have infinite money and would have to forego other purchases in order to pay the increased costs. Thus, a government which wishes to reduce the amount that people smoke may increase the tax on cigarettes, or a government which wishes to reduce childhood obesity might pass or increase a tax on sugary drinks. Sometimes, this purpose is primary, with revenue generation being a secondary purpose; in other cases, revenue generation may be the primary purpose, with the change in consumer behavior being considered an added bonus. When advocating excise tax increases, either or both purposes may be advertised (however, the advertising does not reveal the legislators' purpose so much as it reveals which purpose will most appeal to the voters who watch the advertisements; consequently, a legislature which is seeking additional revenue may prefer to advertise the benefits to the public health that accrue from reduced smoking, drinking, or air pollution, instead of advertising how much money they expect to make from the proposed tax).

In the United States, excise taxes are regulated by the Internal Revenue Service (IRS) and the Alcohol and Tobacco Tax and Trade Bureau (TBB). Gasoline/fuel generates the most excise taxes, followed by alcohol, tobacco, and firearms. (In the interest of confining this text to the ethics of taxation, and avoiding adding in a debate on gun control, I will not be using any examples of firearm taxation below.) These have been commonly taxed throughout history and throughout the world both for the purposes of discouraging their purchase and generating government revenue; and most people understand why these particular kinds of items fall into the same category: each represents a product that can cause harms (or, in simpler but less accurate terms, are "bad"); and generally we accept this as justification for a tax.

But "causing harms" is a very loose, very subjective category. Consequently, many other goods and services are taxed on the same justification. Some of the excise taxes might still make a lot of sense (although, particularly regarding the items that cause environmental harms, there is much debate about the dollar value of those harms), while others may not make so much sense to as many people.

In addition to firearms, the United States also applies an 11% excise tax to bows and arrows. In addition to gasoline, several other excise taxes are levied to reduce environmental harms, including coal (tax varies with the type of coal, and may be assessed at a per-ton rate or at 4.4%), tires, cars that get less than 22.5 miles per gallon, heavy trucks/trailers/semitrailers, electric outboard motors, and air travel. And in addition to tobacco, the federal government also taxes e-cigarettes (which contain nicotine but not tobacco—more on that below), and many states tax marijuana.

Meanwhile the Unites States also taxes several items of dubious harm. Insurance purchased from a foreign insurer is taxed at 1-4%. Sport fishing equipment, including fishing poles, is taxed at 10% (capped at $10), to compensate for the harms caused by... sport fishing? Indoor tanning salon services are subject to a 10% excise tax. Local telephone service is subject to a 3% excise tax. And certain vaccines (vaccines!) are taxed at 75 cents/dose (in this last case, the government is clearly not trying to dissuade purchases—for they may even mandate the purchases—but is collecting more stable revenue).

At the local level, many jurisdictions tax sugary foods/drinks, attempting to change (improve?) people's diets and health. (These tend to be very unpopular among the voters, who rather resent such paternalistic taxes.)

And there is growing support for creating new excise taxes for meat products to discourage the consumption of meat, as raising and eating meat is perceived by such supporters to be a source of unsustainable environmental harm.

Economic Effects

As noted above, the immediate effect of a tax upon a specific good is that it raises the cost of that good, which in turn results in less of it being sold. How much less sold depends upon the *price elasticity of demand* for that good. If demand is highly elastic—that is, small changes in price result in large changes in demand—then a tax increase will significantly reduce the sales of that item (and consequently, result in a smaller amount of revenue being generated by the tax); but if the demand is highly *in*elastic—that is, consumer behavior does not change much with a small change in price—then a much higher amount of tax can be levied before sales begin to significantly decline. The price elasticity of demand is affected by several factors, such as the perceived necessity of the item, the percentage of income being devoted to the purchase, and the availability of substitute goods. Thus a product like insulin has a very inelastic demand—even if the price were doubled, people would still buy it, because their lives depend upon it (and for which reason, it is generally accepted to be highly *un*ethical to tax)—while a product like chicken has a much more elastic demand—since people could easily buy other meats for dinner, or even less meat altogether. Now the demand for "bad" items like alcohol and tobacco is affected by their addictive qualities: when prices go up, addicted people will tend to divert more income from other purchases to maintain their consumption—but even addicted people run into limits (they do not have infinite money), and eventually reach the point where they must change their behavior. Meanwhile an increase in price for gasoline will also affect different consumers differently: if one depends upon their own automobile for transportation to work, they will continue to buy the gasoline they need to get to work when they price goes up, even as someone else with available alternatives is able to switch to carpooling, or public transportation, or to a different place to live that is closer to work.

If the tax increase is great enough to result in a significant change in consumer behavior, then the cost of the associated externalities—the negative effects of consuming these products not ordinarily accounted for in the products' prices—are presumably reduced. For example, a reduction in cigarette smoking is expected to result in a [future] decrease in health care costs (both for the person smoking less, and for those who would have developed health problems as a result of second-hand smoke, and for the market generally due to a reduced demand for medical services)—although it is difficult to accurately estimate these cost savings, as many of them don't materialize until many years later, and many other variables are in play throughout that time. Similarly, a reduction in alcohol consumption has similar medical cost savings, in addition to a reduction in damages to property and loss of life that results from drunken behavior, including driving. On the other hand, the economic savings resulting from less driving is harder to calculate, as we have no economically-accurate predictive models of the relationship between driving and the environment (we have multiple theoretical models, with great variance among them).

Cigarette Taxes in California

Although cigarettes are considered addictive, data from recent tax increases indicates that cigarette smokers will change their behavior if the tax increase is large enough. For example, the state of California used to levy an \$0.87 tax on each pack of cigarettes sold, but then increased their tax rate to \$2.87 per pack. Consequently, cigarette consumption fell from an average of 34 packs per person per year to only 26 packs per person per year. (Notice the Laffer Curve here: the tax rate was more than tripled, but the revenue only went up by about 2.5 times. It appears that California has not yet reached the revenue-maximizing point for this particular tax: their legislature could probably increase the tax even further before they started getting less revenue from the increase.)

Meanwhile the change in consumer behavior—including purchasing less of the "bad" items being taxed at a higher rate, and the diversion of funds from other purchases in order to maintain consumption of the "bad" items being taxed at a higher rate—has several additional economic effects:

1. Other industries, besides the industries being taxed, experience a drop in sales. This is because in order to pay the higher prices resulting from the tax increase, consumers of cigarettes/alcohol/gasoline/sugar/etc. must divert their spending from other purchases. Frequently, this means less spending on "nonessential" items, such as lattes and Legos and other little luxuries.

2. Specifics business experience an increase in revenue—specifically, those firms which become the recipients of the new tax revenue. For example, the government may spend the money on an advertising campaign to discourage smoking, or to pay a construction company to build/repair a road or bridge. This is the flip side of the first consequence; taken together, what is happening is that the government (the legislature, and the bureaucracies and agencies funded by the legislature) attain a greater measure of power in directing economic activity, at the expense of the consumers' power to direct economic activity. In many cases, this also entails *moving* economic activity from throughout the region to specific locations which receive the government funds; typically, an excise tax (along with many other kinds of taxes) transfers funds from the less populated regions to the more populated regions (where government services are deemed more important—or at least where more voters are), particularly the capital city of that region.

3. Overall economic activity is reduced. When money is spent on a good or service, the supplier of that good or service then spends that money on the purchase of other goods and services that they desire. When the money is spent on a tax, the government in turn also uses it to purchase goods and services—but at a slower rate of circulation (how much slower depends upon the efficiency of the government collecting and distributing the taxes, relative to the level of activity in the economy being taxed).

4. A black market may develop. The higher the tax, the greater the incentive for tax evasion. Excise tax evasion is a significant concern for many countries and local jurisdictions, and is one of the reasons that tax revenues begin to fall after pushing the tax rate past a certain point (for a comparison of international tax rates and policies regarding tobacco tax rates and revenues, you may be interested in Arthur Laffer's *Handbook of Tobacco Taxation: Theory and Practice*). On the black market, the "bad" product continues to be sold, but without reporting the sale to the government and without the tax. These may be large scale operations, or even individual transactions: for example, in New York City, many people buy and sell cigarettes "singles" in order to avoid paying the tax assessed per pack (in addition to the $4.35 tax levied by the state, New York city adds another $1.50, bringing the tax on a pack of 20 cigarettes to $5.85). This illegal activity then introduces additional costs paid by the government to enforce its tax laws (increased policing, booking, and trying of crimes—and the social cost of applying violent force to prevent petty economic transactions between individuals).

5. When the tax is local, some economic activity moves to neighboring regions. Thus, the 1.5 cents per ounce tax on sodas in Philadelphia and the 1.75 cents per ounce tax on sodas in Seattle both resulted in many consumers who live on the outskirts of those cities changing where they buy their groceries, since driving a few more miles to a store in the next city could save them money.

These effects occur whether the product being taxed is tobacco, alcohol, gasoline, sugar (sometimes assessed not on the sugar directly, but on a class of "junk" foods, or on sugary sodas), or anything else; although the significance of each effect will vary according to how high the tax rate is set, and how much economic product is being taxed.

> **Brick Tax**
>
> From 1784 to 1850, Great Britain had a Brick Tax on each brick produced. People adjusted by increasing the size of bricks (until the government doubled the tax on large bricks) and by choosing to use more timber instead. By changing the price, excise taxes change economic behavior.

Legislating in Ignorance of the Laffer Curve

Just how big of a problem is economic ignorance? And what happens is lawmakers pass a tax without considering Laffer Curve effects? Let us consider the example of New Jersey:

The state of New Jersey used to have the next to lowest gasoline tax in the nation, at 14.5 cents/gallon. But in search of new revenue, the state lawmakers raised the rate to 37.1 cents/gallon as of Nov 1, 2016. The new tax was expected to raise some $2 billion dollars for the state—but in case it didn't, the bill included a clause that *automatically raises the rate if it doesn't produce the target revenue.* Since you have read this far in the book, and have learned about the Laffer Curve, you can guess what happened: people responded to the higher price of gasoline by changing their behavior, driving less; and since people purchased less gasoline, the tax raised somewhat less revenue than the legislators anticipated. Consequently, on Oct 1, 2018, the rate was automatically increased to 41.4 cents/gallon (now the 9th highest in the nation).

What will happen next? Will the higher rate be enough to raise the $2 billion target revenue? It depends upon how much people change their behavior. In this case, New Jersey is somewhat protected by its neighbors: New York assesses several gasoline taxes totaling around 45 cents/gallon, and Pennsylvania has the highest gas tax in the nation, at 58.7 cents/gallon; so New Jersey Drivers who live near the border cannot simply purchase gasoline across state lines. Meanwhile they still have to drive enough to get to work, so maybe they won't be able to reduce their driving enough, and the state will hit its $2 billion annual target this year around. Or, they will reduce their driving enough, and the state lawmakers will try again with a higher rate—even as they wonder why all other economic activity associated with driving (including vacationing and other recreational trips) is declining.

Another way New Jersey drivers can reduce gasoline purchases is by switching to more fuel-efficient cars; so maybe new car sales will increase in New Jersey, even as used car sales and auto service on used cars declines. Interestingly, both state and federal governments have pushed for more fuel-efficient cars, and those legislative actions have in part caused the decline in revenue collection from gasoline taxes. Unfortunately (at least for New Jersey drivers), lawmakers are trying to recover the lost revenues through higher rates, rather than considering other tax policy options.

Tax Incidence

Though levied directly upon goods at the time of their production, excise taxes mostly get transferred to the consumer at the point of sale: frequently, these amounts are even posted at the place of sales (for example, at many gas stations, one can find a placard detailing the amount of taxes included in the price). When excise taxes are increased on gasoline, tobacco, alcohol—products which consumers desire to continue buying even when the price goes up—sellers typically raise their prices to match, or nearly so (in theory, one seller could raise their prices by a smaller amount, reducing their own profit margin in an attempt to undercut the prices of their competitors; but in practice, the bulk of the tax gets passed to the final price of the product). Individual customers bear a greater or lesser tax burden according to how much they are willing to change their own behavior.

> **Gasoline Taxes in California**
>
> As of July 2019, the price of a gallon of gasoline in California includes the following taxes:
>
> Base state excise tax: 30 cents
> Variable state excise tax: 17.3 cents
> Federal excise tax: 18.4 cents
> Underground storage fee: 2 cents
> Plus state sales taxes: (2.25%)
> Plus local sales taxes: (varies)

For example, a person who is able to reduce their consumption of cigarettes and/or alcohol pays less tax than the person who cannot overcome their addictive habit(s). The significance of this fact depends upon one's view of human agency: if one believes that people are entirely in control of all of their decisions, then this simply means that people pay the prices they are willing to pay for the products they like; but if one believes that cigarettes and alcohol are medically additive—that there is some loss of decision-making ability that accompanies the use of these products—then this means that the tax falls particularly upon the people who are the most sick or most injured by the products being taxed. Now if the tax is an effective medicine for their illness—that is, if it is effective at changing their behavior (and it does change some behavior), then this may be regarded as medically appropriate; but if the tax is *ineffective medicine, then it just makes the lives of sick individuals that much poorer.

While not medically addictive, gasoline consumption is similar to alcohol and tobacco consumption, in that some individuals are more capable of changing their behavior than others. For some people, an increase in the gasoline tax is adjusted to by reducing recreational driving, or by increased carpooling, or by increased use of public transportation. But for other people, who have fewer alternatives available to them—such as those who commute to earn their income, and must drive their own car on account of no carpool or public transportation options being workable—the increase in gasoline tax can only be adjusted to by forsaking other purchases, since they need to purchase the gasoline to get to work and earn their money. Thus the people with the least amount of freedom are most impacted by the burden of the tax.

Similarly, when any excise tax is passed by a city government (such as Seattle's tax on soda, or New York City's tax on cigarettes), those residents who live and work in the center of the city bear a greater burden than those who live near the borders, or who otherwise regularly leave the city. The more mobile residents simply change where they make their purchases, buying soda pop, cigarettes, or gasoline in the next city over, while the less mobile (that is, those who tend to have fewer economic options, those who are the most disadvantaged) bear the full burden of the tax. Additionally, besides reasons of fewer alternatives being available, it is also true that (on average) poorer people tend to spend more cigarettes and soda than do richer people (regarding alcohol, poorer and richer people tend to buy rather different kinds of alcohol, with beer being more common among lower-income people). Consequently, tax increases on beer, cigarettes, and soda pop are tax increases that disproportionately impact the poor. Finally, gasoline taxes have an additional impact upon many other prices, by increasing the costs of transportation. Thus grocery prices go up (and/or grocery firms' profit margins go down), once again having a disproportionate impact upon lower-income households, who spend a greater percentage of their income on food than do wealthier households.

Sales Taxes on Specific Kinds of Services

One of the things which distinguish an excise tax from a sales tax is that an excise tax is applied to a good at the time of production (and usually, but not always, at a fixed rate), whereas a sales tax is applied to a good at the point of sale (generally as a percentage of the sale price). While this is a meaningful distinction for manufactured goods, which can be produced at one time and sold at another, it is less meaningful for services (such as a taxi ride), which are produced and sold simultaneously. Taxes on services may be classified as sales taxes; however, if a tax is levied on a specific kind of service, and particularly if it is applied for the purpose of changing (or punishing) consumer behavior, then it is functionally equivalent to an excise/sin tax. Such is the case with taxes levied on ride-hailing services (such as Uber, Lyft, and Via). Like other excise taxes, these taxes discourage particular consumer behaviors and economic activity, have greater impacts upon those people who have less economic freedom (fewer alternatives available), and generate revenue with noticeable Laffer Curve effects. Accordingly, targeted sales taxes on ride-hailing services will be considered alongside more traditional excise taxes when discussing ethical considerations below.

Ethical Considerations

The standard ethical case for excise taxes is that they compensate society for harms resulting from the sale and use of particular products. Cigarettes, for example, produce secondhand smoke which must be breathed by other people who are not compensated, and they increase the burden on the health care system, much of which is publicly funded; thus a tax on their use can recover some portion of those costs (or at least the costs borne by the government—it is rather difficult to assess the monetary costs of secondhand smoke, and even if it were easy, it is the government which collects the taxes, not the harmed individuals). Alcohol is taxed for the same reason: here, it not only increases the burden upon the health system, but also increases the risks to other people's safety, and the cost of policing (thus, alcohol was taxed long before governments started paying for health care). Gasoline produces air pollution, which again harms other people (though again, it is the government rather than the harmed individuals which collect the tax), and incurs costs upon whatever group is responsible for cleaning pollution; additionally, too much air pollution and traffic condition can deter in-migration and increase out-migration, reducing a city's own potential economic growth and tax base. Finally, sugary drinks contribute to obesity, which also burdens a publicly-funded health care system.

Other Methods of Compensating those Harmed

Many of the justifications above are made meaningful by the fact that the government pays for a great deal of health care (more than 50% in the United States). But even if it did not, one could still point to "externalities"—that is, unpaid-for harms resulting from the sale/use of certain products. If there were no tax, how might these be addressed?

One way there are addressed is through insurance premiums: smokers pay higher health insurance premiums, and those with who get tickets for drunk driving pay higher car insurance premiums. A second way is through social costs: restaurants and apartment complexes may refuse to accommodate smoking, and individuals may discourage smoking through their own freewill social organization.

Another alternative to taxation is could be legal action, treating the harms produced by certain products under tort law. However, this is very difficult to quantify and prove in some cases (such as with secondhand smoke, or pollution produced by myriads of individuals who drive); and in the case of pollution, American law has been written specifically to protect businesses from such tort suits.

However, for many legislators and voters, excise taxes represent more than simply recovering the economic costs of externalities: they are also actively pursued as a means of making other people behave "better." The voter or governor who does not like smoking or drinking, and who desires for other people to do less (or stop it altogether), passes the tax to discourage the bad behavior. When this motive is at work, Laffer Curve effects on tax revenue become irrelevant: if a tax rate is pushed high enough to discourage the bad behavior so much that tax revenues fall, that is all the more desirable within this paradigm. However, this paternalistic ethic is not so commonly shared as the other ethical principles discussed in this book: for while some regard paternalism as a legitimate function of the ruling elite, many others regard it as a fundamental tyranny of some people over others. The ethical position that it is appropriate to use government power (that is, taxes and police force) to enforce "good" decisions regarding personal health is much contested.

Similarly, those who would make the case that taxes on sugary drinks "protect" children from obesity are also making a hotly contested ethical case: for they are arguing that some adults have the right to inflict costs on other adults in order to direct their parenting behavior. While one might make the case that this is necessary and appropriate, since children do not have the means to protect themselves—and people generally agree that it is entirely appropriate to protect children from child abuse—parental laxity regarding children's diets is *not* commonly accepted as actionable child abuse. Consequently, we refrain from bringing legal action against parents for allowing their children to drink [too much] soda pop; and yet somehow many people think it is perfectly acceptable to fine the behavior through taxation.

But how does excise taxation stand up to our more agreed-upon standards? Beginning with representation—do voters have a say in the tax—it seems to hold up fairly well. Excise taxes are frequently passed though popular votes (such as on propositions submitted to the voters); and when passed less directly through elected representatives, voters may change their representatives. However, we do run into a problem whenever the subjects of the excise tax are only a minority of the population—as smokers increasingly are. For when the taxed population is a small enough minority, they no longer have sufficient voting power to prevent the majority from continuing to vote ever-increasing taxes, taxes far beyond the ethical justification of paying for harms, levied instead for the sake of general revenue. When this is the case, the tax is flatly unethical, a means of diverting some of the overall burden of taxation from a majority population to a minority one. And when such action is taken under the pretense of promoting better social outcomes, it violates the ethical principle of honesty as well.

Now it is important to note before proceeding that such ethical problems are not inevitable (although, they are perhaps likely, given the incentives at work in government). Rather, they vary with the particular good being taxed, and the amount of tax, and the level of government assessing the tax. Taking these different factors into account, we may conclude some excise taxes are more ethical than others; according to the level of representation/participation in each tax. Excise taxes levied by city governments, for example, are much easier to respond to than state or federal taxes: for many people may be able to vote with their feet, by moving to another jurisdiction, even if they do not have enough power at the ballot; so one may say that local ethical taxes *tend to be* more ethical than national excise taxes, at least in terms of representation and participation.

Although there is an important caveat to make about local taxation: sometimes, voting with one's feet is *not* so viable an option, depending upon the circumstances of the tax. Consider for example the Washington DC tax on ride-hailing services (considered as an excise tax here, although it is technically a sales tax levied on a specific kind of service): a provider cannot avoid the tax without disengaging from their source of revenue, and users of such services may find all of their alternatives to be much costlier. But so long as the population of Uber/Lyft/Via users remains smaller than the population of nonusers, the city can continue to increase the tax (recently increased from 1% to 6%) without a voting challenge.

Turning to the ethical considerations of openness and simplicity, excise taxes fare much better than many other kinds of taxes. Excise taxes tend to be very open, often posted near the point of sale, and explicitly advertised as part of the campaign to discourage the taxed economic activity. They are also very simple: a fixed amount per unit (or occasionally, a fixed percent), easily understood by all involved. (A slight exception to this would be California's variable excise tax on gasoline, which is levied on top of a base excise tax; but this amount is expected to be set at a fixed rate in July 2019.)

Unfortunately, excise taxes don't stand up so well on the measures of appropriateness and consideration. For as we noted, excise taxes most heavily impact those people with the fewest viable alternatives and least economic freedom—i.e. the poor. Now when these tax revenues are then used to serve this same population—for example, by using gasoline taxes to maintain roads, alcohol taxes to maintain safety, and cigarette taxes to promote health—we can call these taxes appropriate (insofar as they serve the population taxed—for now, we leave aside the more debated question of individual freedom vs. paternalistic care). However, in many cases, the excise taxes are used to serve entirely different populations, such as whenever the revenue is put into the general fund to be spent on everything else in the budget. And in particularly egregious cases, excise tax revenues are even earmarked to be spent on entirely different populations, as in the case of the DC ride-hailing tax, which is used to fund their metro system.

____

The DC Ride-Hailing Tax

Washington D.C. has a metro system which depends upon public subsidies to operate, in addition to the fares it collects from riders. Theoretically, public subsidies help keep the fares low, making it more accessible to poorer riders. However, no public transportation system can meet every individual's needs, and many people prefer the much more flexible alternatives provided by taxis and ride-hailing services like Uber, Lyft, and Via—particularly when parts of the metro system are experiencing problems.

Now the city must collect taxes to keep the metro functioning, so they have decided to assess an excise tax on ride-hailing services (currently 6% of the fare).—a service which directly competes with the metro. In most situations, people would immediately recognize the evil of taxing the customers of business A in order to keep business B aloft; but the city argues exactly the opposite here: they note metro fares have declined precisely because ride-hailing services are so popular, so ride-hailing services have "harmed" the metro, and thus should compensate the metro for that harm. The result is that people who choose to take their business elsewhere are still forced to pay for a service that they explicitly abandoned. Using the city's ethical logic, we might next levy a tax on private colleges for competing with state colleges, or upon new medical technologies which give people an alternative to checking into a state hospital—or even, if voters are not particularly attentive, upon entrepreneur Bob for competing with politically-connected businessman Jeff.
____

Recently, many states have begun legalizing marijuana—and then immediately taxing it. So far, no state has passed such excise taxes in order to raise revenue specifically for addressing marijuana harms, or serving the marijuana-using population; on the contrary, in every case legislatures have simply seized upon the legalization as a new source of general tax revenue, to fund other projects and make up for prior budget deficits. Throughout these cases, very few (if any) legislators have paused to wonder if it is appropriate to make marijuana users pay more for the same government services as nonusers. Indeed, there is something perverse about immediately creating a new financial penalty in response to the popular movement to decriminalize marijuana (for the states are legalizing them through propositions put to the voters); yet so normal is the assessment of new taxes that few stop to question it.

Regarding the criteria of minimizing harms, it is difficult to evaluate excise taxes, since the taxes are passed for the explicit purpose of mitigating other harms (such as air pollution, lung cancer, and obesity), so any further harms created by the taxes will always be weighed against that—and differently for each voter, according to their separate values. For some, harming evil tobacco companies is precisely the point, so they have no interest in minimizing economic damage to that industry (including potential job losses). If Americans agreed that tobacco use is objectively evil (or alternatively, if they agreed that it was a perfectly acceptable activity) then we might make some judgment here; but since Americans very much disagree on this point, any cost-benefit analysis of harms here will equally contentious. Meanwhile, this contention poses further problems for us on the criteria of justice and peace:

For as we acknowledged in chapter two, punishment is properly a function of criminal courts, administered after determining criminal guilt, and observing due process to minimize the possibility of punishing the innocent. Unfortunately, many people seek political means of punishing those they do not like, enacting legal penalties through the bureaucracy or through the vote when they cannot determine guilt through the courts. Such is frequently the case with excise taxes, when unable to satisfactorily demonstrate liability or guilt through the courts, people can instead muster a popular vote to administer a financial penalty anyway. And unfortunately, when a group of voters determines that they need to punish "evil" tobacco companies, or "big oil," or irresponsible parents who let their kids drink too much soda and become obese, there amount of punishment demanded (what in court would be termed "damages") is always More. So long as some individuals engage in behaviors that others do not like, there will always be a motivation to increase the level of punishment ("deterrence").

Consequently, excise taxes do *not* promote peace and unity among the citizens of the nation, but rather the opposite. Those people who want to smoke (either cigarettes or marijuana), or drink (either alcohol or soda pop), or use alternatives to public transportation (either their own gas-guzzling vehicles or through hailing an Uber) are in continuous political battle with those who prefer they not do these things. The taxers continue to propose new taxes, and the targets of the tax must practice defensive voting to avoid them—and as tobacco and beer companies spend millions of dollars on lobbying and advertising to defend against the new taxes, the taxers cite this as proof of their evil power and why we need to get money out of politics (lest you think this is an exaggeration, look up pro-tax television ads whenever a proposition for increasing an excise is put to the voters, or review the pro and con arguments on your voter information guide: the pro-tax side invariably laments, often in ALL CAPS, how much money their opponents are spending to fight their very reasonable tax proposal).

This conflict has the additional economic effect of diverting great amounts of money from more productive use to lobbying government and lobbying voters through political advertisements and extended campaigns—which might be rather beneficial to the media companies and lobbyists and legislators themselves, but it represents an opportunity cost of all the other economic transactions and wealth creation that might have otherwise come to pass. (The same harm was noted regarding tariffs; although in the case of excise taxes, more money is spent lobbying voters directly during election years when propositions are on the ballot.)

Summary Report Card – Excise Taxes

Representation — **Varies with level of government**
The more local the tax, the better: for when an excise tax affects a local area only (e.g. a city), tax payers can vote with their feet, taking their business elsewhere. But voters have very little impact on national excise taxes.

Participation — **Highly Problematic**
For many excise taxes, a larger population (such as nonsmokers) has power to continue to increase taxes for a smaller population (such as smokers).

Honesty — **Varies**
Excise taxes are frequently pursued as a revenue source, but advocated for reasons of public health.

Openness and Simplicity — **Good**
Rates tend to be simple, and are frequently posted.

Appropriateness — **Varies**
Ethical whenever the funds from the excise tax are used for related services (e.g. using gasoline taxes to improve roads); unethical when the funds are used indiscriminately (put into the general fund), or used to fund directly-opposing services (e.g. using taxes on ridesharing services to fund public transportation).

Consideration — **Doubtful**
Excise taxes on tobacco and sugary drinks are paid mostly by the poor.
Excise taxes on gasoline disproportionately affect the poor.

Minimizing Harms — **Debatable**
Excise taxes are passed explicitly to reduce particular societal harms, and any new harms created by the taxes are measured against those: results will differ according to voters' various value systems.

Justice — **Flatly Unethical**
Excise taxes are frequently used by some voters to punish others for behavior they do not like.

Peace — **Fail**
Consumers and businesses harmed by excise taxes are pitted against their neighbors politically.

Emotional Objections to the Ethical Principles of Justice and Peace

In chapter two, I tried to identify ethical principles which were more commonly agreed upon, rather than trying to foist a particular set of ethics on the reader; and I believe that among Americans, there is a common support for certain legal principles as being counted innocent until proven guilty, the importance of due process, the right to a fair trial, and the necessity of demonstrating liability before assessing damages in court—hence my conclusion that it is unethical to use taxes to administer punishment, as that violates all four of those commonly held legal principles. Yet when excise taxes are discussed, many people entirely change their mind about these principles, and argue that it is absolutely appropriate/ethical to use taxes to punish people for buying and [particularly] selling such "bad" products as tobacco and alcohol (and, to a lesser extent, gasoline and soda pop). Moreover, so many people feel so strongly about the ethical virtue of taxing tobacco, etc. that one may quite object to my branding it "flatly unethical" here, arguing that I am attempting to foist some uncommon and even individual judgment upon them after all. How can I possibly claim to be pursuing a common ethical examination of tax policies if in fact I am just shilling for big tobacco and arguing that people should just be allowed to whatever they want?

But I am not shilling for either the tobacco or beer companies (they pay me nothing, and lo, I pay them nothing, as I neither smoke nor drink alcohol—though I do buy gasoline and soda pop); and I am attempting to find some common ground. Only here, the common ground is on our legal ideals; and it seems contradictory to abandon those legal ideals when it comes time to discuss tax policy. And that is the very reason why we need to have this discussion; for as noted in the first chapter, much of our problem with discussing ethics and tax policies is that we *don't* bother to think about them ethically, and that we *don't* bother to be consistent with our other beliefs—and this failure needs to be redressed. We need to be honest with ourselves about punishment, and careful about invoking it where we have very dubious authority.

Perhaps we can again find common ground in this: no one wants the fickle electorate to declare punishments for their own pet behaviors. Before you concede to such fines, you would demand a just hearing, and a reasonable assessment of damages, as opposed to an arbitrary fine according to a vague and undefined "badness" of your activity, subject to increase whenever the legislature found itself in need of greater revenue. Whatever limits on taxation you would demand to protect yourself, you should abide by those same limitations when raising taxes on others.

A Case of Contention: Minimizing the Harms of E-Cigarettes

The excise taxes on e-cigarettes (vaping) is an interesting example of both the confusion and contention involved in tax policy. To begin with, the taxes and regulations are dubious legally: for e-cigarettes are subject to laws and regulations which govern tobacco products, despite the fact they have no tobacco (they do have nicotine), but beginning with the Obama administration the Food and Drug Administration (FDA) passed a rule *deeming* e-cigarettes to be tobacco products, and therefore subject to tobacco regulation. This is an example of a government agency expanding its own legal mandate—and while some would argue that this expansion of definition makes sense (since nicotine is found in tobacco), others would disagree (since it is not the nicotine which causes cancer or the other ill health effects associated with secondhand smoke); and one might want some limitation on a bureaucracy's ability to redefine laws in ways that expand their power. Meanwhile, this redefinition calls into question the purpose(s) of the tax: for if the tax is being levied because tobacco use has harmful externalities, we cannot use the same justification to tax vaping products which remove those externalities. Or were we taxing it because it's addictive instead? Or, perhaps, to generate revenue? For the popularity of vaping would threaten the tax revenue collected from smoking, as smokers switched from cigarettes to e-cigs.

Proponents of taxing e-cigs argue that while e-cigs do not cause cancer, they encourage children to take up smoking, and therefore must be in turn discouraged through taxation. (Note here the fundamentally paternalist ethic here; as noted before, this ethic, being in opposition to freedom, is *not* universally accepted, but instead considered absolutely reasonable common sense by some, and particularly dangerous by others.) But those in opposition to taxing e-cigs point out that the more than 90-99% of e-cig users are *former* smokers, not new smokers; and these former smokers experience better respiratory health and longer life spans. So if one wants to *reduce [overall] harms*, one should be in support of vaping and oppose the taxes that would discourage the single most successful quit-smoking tool. On that ethic, it comes to a question of preventing harms among the few teens who might be tempted by e-cigs to smoke regular cigarettes, or reducing harms among those many adults who already smoke and might be tempted to quit. (Assuming, of course, that it is one's duty to provide paternalistic direction at all.)

Or, perhaps the question is really about generating revenue—in which case, tax away, and ultimately, who cares about the further justification?

5

Luxury Taxes

Luxury taxes are frequently categorized as excise taxes, for like other excise taxes, they are applied to the sales of specific goods and services; but as they are very different in purpose and involve some additional economic factors, they warrant separate consideration here. This discussion may even be more useful, as luxury taxes [in the United States] are not as entrenched as excise taxes; voters and legislators may be more open to examining the economic and ethical issues associated with a theoretical future tax than they are to challenging people's [and their own] investments in current tax/revenue policies.

For while various luxury taxes have been implemented throughout the world and throughout history, they are currently not a significant feature of United States federal tax policy. The last major national luxury tax in the United States was passed in 1991, but then repealed only two years later. However, there is always the possibility of passing new luxury taxes in the future; and besides taxes at the national level, individual states may also pursue luxury taxes to fund their own budgets.

Description and Purpose

A luxury tax is a tax levied on goods or services considered "nonessential" to daily living, generally purchased by wealthier people. The goal is to raise tax revenue from those people most capable of paying additional taxes, and specifically avoid burdening poorer people with taxes that would increase the costs of meeting their basic needs. Historically, they are frequently levied when the state finds itself in urgent need of additional funding, such as when financing a war; but they may be levied at any time the state (or local jurisdiction) is in search of greater revenues.

Since luxury taxes attempt to focus the burden of taxation upon the wealthy, one might expect them to be quite popular among the less wealthy. However, the category of "nonessential" items is highly subjective, and subject to change over time (the specific definition of "wealthy" is also subjective and changes with time, although the abstract concept is more consistent); so there is always the possibility that what is deemed a "nonessential" or "luxury" good today will become common or even indispensable tomorrow. For example, when the United States first began to tax telephone services, this only affected 1% of the population; but now telephone service is considered so essential that the government now buys cell phones for people who cannot afford it. Similarly, Norway at the beginning of the 20th century levied luxury taxes on oil-powered cars, sugar products, and chocolates; today, none of these are regarded as luxury goods—but they remain subject to luxury taxes. Accepting any luxury tax on one day admits the possibility of a legislator defining some new item as a luxury subject to tax on a future day.

Common targets of luxury taxes are expensive cars (exactly how expensive varies between tax jurisdictions), expensive houses, yachts, private airplanes, jewelry, travel accommodations, and entertainments (sometimes referred to separately as "amusement taxes"). Some of these products, such as yachts and private airplanes, are exclusively purchased by those considered wealthy; while others, like room rental in hotels and payment for concert tickets or amusement park entrance, are purchased by many people not considered to be wealthy (just wealthy enough to have some amount of disposable income on such "frivolities"). As a population grows wealthier and has more disposable income, cultural attitudes change regarding what is or is not "frivolous" (entertainments, for example, while still recognized as less essential than food and shelter, are increasingly considered important purchases impacting mental health and personal well-being). Legislators interested in keeping the tax burden on the wealthy would have to occasionally update their luxury taxes; in practice, however, some governments do (India, for example, recently revised their luxury tax policy) while many others do not—for a revenue-hungry government will always be reluctant to let go of a revenue source (as John Donne put it in a poem once, "as princes do in times of action get new taxes, and remit them not in peace"). And as a population gets wealthier and develops more disposable income (that is, income which can be spent on "nonessential" items), this increases the size of the tax base for "luxuries."

Luxury Taxes in India

In India, the old luxury taxes have been updated under their Goods and Services Tax (GST), which defines different tax rates (0%, 5%, 12%, 18% and 28%) for different categories of goods and services. Essential items are taxed at 0%, with less essential items given a higher tax rate according to how legislators decide to classify them, with the [theoretically] least needful items assigned to the highest tax rate. Goods taxed at 28% include molasses, aerated water, and sunscreen; paint, wallpaper and ceramic tiles; water heaters, dishwashers, washing machines and vacuum cleaners; ATM and vending machines; and automobiles, motorcycles, and aircraft for personal use. Services taxed at 28% include authorized private-run lotteries, race club betting, and cinema.

In the United States, luxury taxes have not been a significant feature of national tax policy since the 1990s (which will be discussed below); but they are a feature in the tax policies of many states and local jurisdictions. For example, New York and New Jersey both have luxury taxes on homes which sell for $1 million dollars or more; Maryland has a tax on amusements (such as concerts and amusement parks); and Atlantic City in Georgia has a luxury tax on room rental in hotels, inns, rooming, or boarding houses, cover or entertainment charges, beach chairs and cabanas, admission tickets, and the sale of alcoholic beverages served for consumption on the premises of the sale (e.g. drinks at a concert).

Discrepancy between Theory and Practice – Luxury Taxes and Veblen Goods

There are some economic phenomena which can be observed in very particular circumstances, but which do not generalize to larger contexts. Unfortunately, sometimes people make this very mistake, imagining a general principle or pattern to exist when one in fact does not, and unfortunately, sometimes tax [or other governmental] policy is created based upon such faulty generalizations. Such is the case with the so-called "Veblen Good."

Veblen Goods (named for economist Thorstein Veblen, author of *The Theory of the Leisure Class* in 1899) are goods (and services) which [appear to] violate the Law of Demand (which states that, all other things being held equal, the quantity demanded does down as the price goes up). For some [very specific] goods [in very specific contexts], demand actually goes up when the price is increased [at a particular point]: for example, demand for a particular wine at a posh restaurant may go up if the wine's price is increased from being the cheapest on the menu to being a middle-priced wine, as wealthy socially-conscious and status-seeking diners seek to avoid the negative social judgment that comes with buying the cheapest wine; similarly, the demand for a particular designer handbag may go up when its price is raised to the point of it becoming a sign of social prestige, if the number of new wealthy status-seeking buyers outnumber the number of less wealthy or less status-seeking would-be buyers who no longer demand the more expensive product. (Unfortunately, most descriptions of Veblen Goods omit many of these qualifying phrases, presenting a simpler and more readable—but less accurate—formulation.)

Demand may go up when the price increases because wealthy buyers might purposely be spending more in a display of conspicuous consumption (they are in fact paying for social status in addition to paying for the product); or because buyers are using the price as an indication of product quality (assuming the more expensive item to be of higher quality, and therefore desiring it more than the less-expensive alternative); or because the buyers see the price increase as a signal of future price increases, and seek to "stock up" before the price goes even higher. However, in every case, the increase in demand cannot be extrapolated to all prices. If it could, then sellers would simply continue to raise the price, competing with each other to have the highest price; but in fact this never happens: for at some point the increase in price becomes no longer worth the perceived benefit of social status, and demand once again falls with further increases in price. Thus every description and graph of Veblen Goods depicting an ever-increasing demand is patently fallacious. In the world of real human interactions, we cannot generalize a specific increase in demand at a particular price range to imagine a similar increase in demand at all price levels.

Unfortunately, human beings tend to overgeneralize, and the concept of Veblen Goods continues to be taught in a simplified, less-accurate form, omitting the qualifications and restrictions that would make the concept more accurate. Abstract examples can always be supplied, but finding empirical examples is more difficult; and when they are found, it is always for a specific context, at a particular price range.

Consequently, and even more unfortunately, legislators tend to fail to recognize these limiting factors, and instead imagine an entire class of Veblen Goods as ideal targets for taxation. The theory—frequently cited in descriptions of luxury taxes—is that a tax placed on a Veblen Good actually increases the demand for that good, and therefore generates more revenue with no adverse economic effects. But instead of placing a luxury tax within the specific window of effectiveness for the specific goods with Veblen effects, and in the specific contexts that produce those effects (which are subject to change), luxury taxes get applied to entire classes of products imagined to be Veblen goods, like fine wines, luxury cars and yachts.

The actual application of such luxury taxes has shown—and will continue to show—that this theory (taxation of certain goods actually increases the demand for those goods) is patent nonsense. Now if everyone relied upon empirical data, the historical record of luxury taxes and their effects should settle the question; but the theory is so simple, and so attractive, and so useful a support of luxury taxes, that it has not gone away, even after much empirical evidence.

Economic Effects

Before discussing the economic effects of luxury taxes in general, I would like to describe the documented effects of a particular set of luxury taxes, which I believe is a representative illustration of the effects we can generally anticipate.

The United States Federal Government most recently experimented with significant luxury taxes when it passed the Omnibus Budget Reconciliation Act of 1990. The act raised individual income tax rates, and created a 10% luxury tax on several items: jewelry and furs valued over $10,000, private airplanes valued over $250,000, boats/yachts valued over $100,000, and cars valued over $30,000. The taxes were anticipated to collect $9 billion dollars in the next 5 years—based upon the assumption that the wealthy status-seeking buyers of furs, private airplanes, yachts, and expensive cars would continue buying the same (or more, if these were Veblen goods) amount of these products at the higher prices. However, that is absolutely NOT what happened. Higher prices as a result of new taxes in no way increased the status of these goods for the purposes of conspicuous consumption, and wealthy buyers instead responded to the increased prices by changing their buying behavior, seeking out less expensive alternatives—such as by buying their yachts outside of the United States.

The year after the tax went into effect, sales of American yachts dropped more than 50%—a result quite consistent with the Law of Demand, yet somehow not anticipated by the United States Congress which passed the law. Now the Unites States government still managed to collect some $16.6 million dollars in revenue from taxes on the yachts that were sold; but since the American yacht industry lost more than 7,000 jobs in the first year due to reduced demand for their services, the government had to pay even more than that in Unemployment Insurance benefits—meaning the government passed a new tax, and then *lost* money on the deal. So disastrous were the results, the yacht tax was quickly repealed in 1993 (most of the other luxury taxes were likewise repealed, although the tax on cars remained in effect until 2002).

Although the yacht tax was short-lived, its impact was enormous. In just a few years, some 25,000 laborers lost their jobs building yachts, while another 75,000 jobs were lost at companies that supplied the yacht manufacturers with materials and supplies. About one-third of American yacht manufacturers stopped producing yachts, with many going bankrupt; other firms survived with drastic reductions (Viking Yachts, for example, trimmed its workforce from 1,400 employees to less than 70; Ocean Yachts from 350 to only 50).

Not every luxury tax will be as disastrous as the above example. Even in this example, the 10% tax rate was not so damaging to the other industries: jewelry manufacturing lost only 330 jobs, and the aircraft industry about 1,500—significant losses, but not so industry-destroying. Had the legislators selected a smaller tax rate, job losses in these industries might have been much lower, and the tax might have actually accomplished the stated goal of earning revenue. But how much smaller—5%, or 2%, or half a percent—we cannot know for certain, without running a full-world simulation of every consumer at every tax rate. All we can be certain of is that the revenue peak for this Laffer Curve lies at some point less than 10%.

Economics v. Politics

After the 1990 luxury tax fiasco, you might think that politicians would be more careful in proposing significant luxury tax policies. And one might say that they are, insofar as no major luxury tax has been enacted in America since then—but that hasn't stopped some politicians from *campaigning* on such issues; for even if one knows that a certain policy is economically disastrous, it might still be good policy in terms of garnering votes, so long as the voters are ignorant. Consequently, luxury tax proposals will continue to be brought up in political debates, *even when the politician is not serious about passing them* (though of course, we cannot read anyone's mind, and it is always possible that the politician is economically illiterate), so long as the politician perceives a political advantage in advocating such policy.

While the luxury tax enacted in the Omnibus Budget Reconciliation Act of 1990 is only one example of the negative effects of a luxury tax, it is quite representative of all such taxes in this way: luxury goods are purchased by people with disposable income, which means these consumers have alternative ways to spend their money, and therefore respond to the change in prices created by the tax. Despite the fantasies of tax-hungry politicians, there *are no Veblen luxury goods to tax* (although some particular goods might be subject to a Veblen effect at a particular price difference in a particular context)—if there were, governments would certainly tax them, to reap the rewards of both the tax revenue and the increased economic production. Instead, taxes on luxury items have the same effect that taxes always do: they provide a reason for consumers to change their behavior.

Such a change in behavior has also been observed in response to the mansion tax in New York (beginning in 1989) and New Jersey (which passed the tax in 2004). This tax affects homes costing one million dollars or more: so a property which sells for $1,000,000 ends up costing $10,001 more than a property selling for $999,999. Naturally, it becomes foolish to try to sell a house for $1,000,000, when one can avoid the tax simply by dropping the price by a dollar. But it also becomes more difficult to sell any house for a range of prices above that, because they all cost at least $10,000 more. Consequently, the Real Estate Board of New York reported that properties selling from $1 to $1.075 million spent more time on the market than more expensive and less expensive homes, and many of these ended up sellers ended up ditching their realtors and selling themselves for less than the $1 million.

You may not care particularly about the hardships imposed upon people who can afford million dollar houses, but you can still recognize the principle at work: taxes motivate changes in behavior, and discourage economic exchange. If the tax is on luxury houses, that affects where people choose to live. If it is on luxury cars and yachts, it affects how people choose to travel—and also affects the livelihoods of all those who build these items. If it is on "luxury" chocolates and other "non-essential" items, it affects how many of those items are sold—and the livelihoods of all the chocolatiers and producers and retailers of other "non-essential" items (and woe to them whose government determines that their livelihood is "non-essential" for society). Perhaps your particular brand of coffee is nonessential, and luxurious enough to be taxed (Seattle actually tried to tax espresso in 2003, but voters rejected the proposal). Perhaps your gaming computer is nonessential. Perhaps your business suits are—if they are above a certain point. You can be sure that if any of these taxes were enacted, buyers of these items would change their behavior, and the producers and sellers of these items would lose—or go out of—business. Entire industries would be affected, less wealth would be produced overall (money would be spent elsewhere, but there would be costs associated with repurposing machinery, buildings, and labor).

Tax Incidence

As with excise taxes and other sales taxes, the direct burden of a luxury tax is divided between the buyer and the seller, as some (or even all) of the tax is passed along to the buyer in the form of higher prices. How much is passed to the buyer depends upon how sensitive consumers are to the price increase: if they are very sensitive (quick to change their buying habits), the seller bears most of the tax burden (they raise prices less than the amount of tax, allowing their profit margin to be reduced in order to pay the tax); whereas is they are less sensitive (slower to change their buying habits), a greater portion of the tax is paid by charging a higher price. However, even when consumers are very sensitive, the seller cannot eliminate their profit margin entirely, so in competitive markets (where profit margins are tighter), they are forced to pass the tax along in the form of a higher price—and when this higher price results in too great a reduction in demand, it no longer becomes profitable to sell the taxed item, and businesses close.

Buyer or seller, it at first appears that in either case the tax is being paid for by the "rich"—that is, by those people who are wealthy enough to afford "luxury" goods. But the producers of luxury products are not always "rich;" and the strain on profit margins means that they, too, bear the burden of the tax, in the form of less work (either being laid off or having their hours cut), and/or lower wages (a lower profit margin reduces the amount of money available to a business, such that raises for the workers may no longer keep up with inflation).

A Luxury Tax by any other Name

Excise taxes, luxury taxes, and sales taxes (which are discussed in the next chapter) are all different types of consumption taxes (taxes assessed at the point of sale); and they are similar enough that their economic effects and moral considerations might be considered together. What distinguishes them is the target of the taxes: sales taxes are generally applied to all (or the majority) of goods (frequently, goods considered to be necessities are excluded from a sales tax), excise taxes applied to specific goods perceived to cause harms, and luxury taxes to goods and services considered to be non-necessary and usually purchased by the rich. However, all of these categories overlap, and depending upon who is making the determination, a tax might be called by one name or by another. What is a good is considered to be both a luxury item and a harmful one? What if a good is considered to be an unneeded luxury but is simultaneously bought mostly be the poor? And at what point does one demarcate where "rich" and "poor" begin and end? Additionally, the same goods and services may be categorized differently at different times: chocolate, for example, was once considered (and taxed as) a luxury good, but now chocolate is an inexpensive pleasure consumed in great quantity by people at all levels of income, including the bottom quintile. Likewise playing cards were once taxed as a luxury (or perhaps as a sin, as they were associated with gambling, but deemed a non-necessary item whether a luxury or a sin).

Sometimes, the proper name of a tax is hotly contested. For example, a 1936 Louisiana luxury tax designated many items as luxuries that common people regularly purchased, including rolls (made from the same dough as untaxed bread), pork and beans (the 10-cent can was not taxed, but the 13-cent can was), and suits above $3 (about $55 in 2018 dollars). Naturally, the tax met with much opposition (although it was still passed) from people arguing that it was in fact a sales tax burdening the common people, rather than a 'luxury' tax on the rich. More recently, a Maryland luxury tax proposed in 2012 would have counted boats and vehicles over $35,000 to be luxuries (a little over $38,000 in 2018 dollars, which is not much higher than the median new car price of $34,000). Such definitional disputes highlight the tension elected governments face when trying to develop a new revenue source that is both effective at generating revenue and yet still confined to a small enough part of the population that they don't get voted out of office for passing the tax.

Luxury taxes also can overlap with property taxes or use taxes, as in the case of boats. The use tax on boats and automobiles will be addressed in the next chapter, on general sales taxes, as it will be particularly relevant to the discussion of tax differences between jurisdictions.

And finally, luxury taxes have in the past also overlapped with employment taxes. Such was the case of the British tax on particular manservants first levied in 1777. Here, the legislators took explicit effort to be careful to distinguish what they deemed to be a luxury manservant and a non-luxury manservant, so that the tax would remain a tax on luxuries as opposed to becoming a tax on employment. Thus the employment of coachmen, footmen, grooms, butlers and the like was taxed; whereas the employment of farm laborers, factory workers, shopkeeper assistants, servants of tavern keepers and the like were not taxed (unless such servants also performed personal or domestic services for their employers). However, the class of taxable servants was subsequently broadened, so by 1812 it included shopmen, porters, warehousemen, factory managers, and stewards as well. (This provoked more strenuous tax evasion efforts, and the taxes were reduced in 1823, but the tax was not repealed until much later, in 1889.) Now the taxation of servants may seem not at all relevant to us today; but it is very useful to note that the British legislators considered the effects of their tax upon employment, and tried to frame it in such a way that the employers of servants did not become incentivized to lay off large numbers of working class servants. For as noted before, "luxury" taxes often affect the working class in more significant ways than they do the rich people they are meant to soak.

Ethical Considerations

The basic ethical case for luxury taxes is that they are applied to the population that can most easily afford them—thus they seem to quite satisfy one of our common ethical criteria, consideration for the poor. However, while this is satisfactory in theory, in actual practice the poor who are employed in producing the taxed goods or in providing the taxed services end up being burdened with a more significant cost. For in practice, taxes alter prices, and the change in prices affects consumer behavior—even the consumer behavior of the wealthy—and the subsequent change in market demand impacts economic production and employment. Still, in theory, if the luxury tax is kept low enough, the change in consumer behavior could be small enough that useful tax revenue could be generated without bringing about disastrous effects: perhaps the American yachting industry could have endured a 1% tax where it could not endure 10%.

This presents an interesting challenge for legislators: for they will have many political and personal incentives to advocate for a higher luxury tax rate, even when a lower tax rate would be much more net beneficial. To begin with, their primary goal is to get re-elected [generally by satisfying the demands of their constituency], and their constituencies might not consider a small tax rate to be high enough—for economic knowledge is not particularly common, and many voters are wont to assume that higher tax rates always result in higher revenues. Particularly if the constituency's rallying cry is that the rich much "pay their fair share," a proposal for a low tax rate may actually be rejected as offensive. But it is morally imperative to consider the likely consequences of a policy, rather than consider only the desired consequences. A small enough luxury tax rate will satisfy both the ethical criteria of consideration and minimization of harms; but a too-large rate will not only fail these criteria, but reach another level of wickedness: for when a rate is set high enough that the tax not only harms people more than it helps them, but even costs the government more than it collects, then it has not only failed all ethical criteria but also functional criteria as well.

But supposing the rate is kept small, how do luxury taxes fair on our other ethical criteria? They can be advocated without deceit, so they appear to meet the criteria for honesty; and when passed, they can be made simply and easily enough understood (although they are not always made so)—there is at least nothing intrinsic to this type of tax that runs afoul of openness or simplicity. And just as with sin taxes, when passed on a local level they satisfy our need for representation: for those taxed can, if defeated at the ballot box, still vote with their feet by moving to other localities (and the rich are more capable of moving)—although, also like sin taxes, this makes a national luxury tax more problematic. A luxury tax passed by a state would therefore be preferable to one passed by the federal government, and a luxury tax passed by a county or city even better still.

But we do find some ethical challenges when we look more carefully at democratic participation: for the luxury tax, by design, is directly applied to a minority of voters—yet all voters may have a say in designing it. In addition to being vulnerable to the tyranny of the majority, this makes it even more likely that a luxury tax will end up being a poorly-designed tax: for people who are not directly affected by it are less likely to fully consider the costs of the tax. For what does X care what Y has to pay in taxes, or what changes will be likely in Y's spending? Applying a tax to any minority population is a sure structural recipe for poorly-designed policy, so long as majority voters do not perceive a cost to themselves.

Fortunately—from the perspective of this particular minority population—the rich have better access to the levers of government power, so they are not without defense against untrammeled and uninformed majoritarianism. But unfortunately—from both the minority rich and the majority non-rich perspective—this only highlights the imbalance in political power/access between the two groups in contest, and so exacerbates the resentment of class divisions. Those without political access resent those with access—even when that access is used defensively. Consequently, a luxury tax is not at all a recipe for peace in a democratic society.

Regarding the appropriateness of the luxury tax, we must answer that it unequivocally does not serve the needs of the population being taxed—but this answer, while entirely consistent with our original formulation of appropriateness, is distressing to many, who find it absolutely "appropriate" that we should tax the rich to serve the needs of the poor. If we defer to the common usage of the term "appropriate," we must mark this ethical issue as debatable: for there is no common agreement on this issue. But it does highlight an interesting inconsistency in our society's ethical practice: for almost everyone recognizes that it is unethical to tax women in order to serve men, or to tax Asians in order to serve blacks, or to tax Californians to serve New Yorkers—but simultaneously many believe that it is quite ethical to tax the buyers of furs to serve those who don't buy furs, and the buyers of yachts to serve those who have nothing to do with yachts, and the buyers of above-average vehicles to serve those who buy below-average vehicles.

Finally, we have an additional ethical conundrum, in determining how "luxuries"—and "unnecessary" items—are to be defined. Affirming the principal of the luxury tax necessarily affirms the power of some group of individuals to determine the "correct" buying habits of the whole of the people, and to back up that determination with financial penalties. But who gets that power? Me, we all hope, or people like me. Only tomorrow, people who are not like me may have the reins of power, and that spoils our enthusiasm for government. And so long as we cannot be at peace with other people having the power for such decision-making, then luxury taxes quite fail the ethical criteria for peace.

Summary Report Card – Luxury Taxes

Representation   **Varies with level of government**

The more local the tax, the better: for when a luxury tax affects a local area only (e.g. a city), tax payers can vote with their feet, taking their business elsewhere. But voters have very little impact on national luxury taxes.

Participation   **Problematic**

A majority population (the non-rich) are tempted to pass taxes which apply only to a minority population (the rich); but the rich have greater means to lobby government against these attempts.

Honesty   **Good?**

Luxury taxes tend to be openly advocated as a way of taxing the rich. (It is difficult to tell if politicians are being dishonest about their other effects, or if the politicians are just ignorant of other effects.)

Openness and Simplicity   **Fair to Good**

Historically, luxury taxes have sometimes been simple, and other times more complex. In either case, the people affected are generally aware of the rates.

Appropriateness   **Debated**

Luxury tax revenues are raised explicitly to transfer wealth from one group to another. While most people accept this as unethical between groups of economic equals, many people make an exception when it comes to transferring wealth from a wealthy population to a poor population.

Consideration   **In Practice Disastrous**

Although aimed at the rich, luxury taxes more significantly impact the producers of the luxury products, who are often working class.

Minimizing Harms   **Disastrous**

Luxury taxes often have negative economic effects that far outweigh the value of the revenue generated.

Peace   **Fail**

Luxury taxes tend to be advocated from a rich vs. poor standpoint, contributing to the class warfare mentality and incentivizing richer people to invest more in lobbying government to protect themselves from excessive taxation—which in turn further exacerbates the resentment of the poor toward the greater political power of the rich.

Furthermore, the principal of the luxury tax concedes power to others to decide for us what goods and services are "necessary" and which are not; and this places us ever in contention with other parties in politics.

Why talk about an abandoned tax?

The United States has not attempted another national luxury tax since that disastrous attempt in the 1990's; and prior to that, luxury taxes have never been a significant source of revenue for the federal government. Furthermore, luxury taxes are not a significant source of revenue for any other country, either; and are absent from many countries also. So why invest a chapter discussing it, when there are so many other kinds of taxes which are much more common? Particularly if government legislators have learned their lesson and forsworn such taxes.

Except it is not clear that legislators have learned their lessons. For historical examples aside, there is still faulty theory out there (like the idea that luxury taxes can easily and productively be levied on Veblen goods) that continues to be taught in some colleges and universities which produce government legislators—and politicians (along with all other people) certainly have a tendency to seize upon whatever part of a theory that seems to justify what they already want to do (for example, a politician in favor of increasing spending for their pet projects will cite Keynesian theory supporting deficit spending to recover from a recession, and then ignore the same Keynesian theory which advocates reducing that extra spending during times of economic growth). Additionally, even if legislators have learned, it is certainly clear than many voters have not (history is easily forgotten, and other people's history even more so, thus the vast majority of those who have no connection to the yachting industry have absolutely no awareness of what happened to it only a few decades ago); so the legislator who is an elected politician always has an incentive to at least talk about and even propose a luxury tax, to please those voters who want more revenue extracted from other people to pay for the government they want.

Yet despite such a constituency, luxury taxes are not currently popular among governments throughout the world; but perhaps the biggest reason for that is this: luxury taxes are not a broad-based tax, but by definition are applied to a smaller sector of the economy—and a revenue-hungry government will tend to select taxes which can apply to more people and generate significantly more revenue. For that reason alone, governments in need of revenue will tend toward income and sales taxes, which generate hundreds or thousands of times more revenue, being collected from hundreds or thousands as many taxpayers. Luxury taxes represent an economically high-risk, low-reward source of revenue; they are high risk not only in terms of detrimental economic effects, but in terms of encouraging out-migration to other jurisdictions with less onerous tax rates. Luxury taxes at the State level in the United States (and to some extent, at the national level among European countries) are simply discouraged by the reality of tax competition between jurisdictions that allow for easy migration.

6

Sales Taxes

Tariffs, excise taxes, and luxury taxes are taxes that targeted a restricted range of goods and services; in contrast, general sales taxes are applied more widely, to all or to most goods bought and sold, raising revenue from overall economic activity rather than trying to affect people's purchases of particular products. Currently, the United States has no federal sales tax; but most states do (45/50, as of January 2019), and many localities have additional sales taxes on top of these.

Highest Sales Tax Rates by State		Lowest Sales Tax Rates	
California	7.25%	Colorado	2.9%
Mississippi	7%	Alaska	0%
Indiana	7%	Delaware	0%
New Jersey	7%	Montana	0%
Rhode Island	7%	New Hampshire	0%
Tennessee	7%	Oregon	0%

Description and Purpose

Sales tax is another example of a consumption tax, which refers to any tax levied at the point it is purchased by the consumer. The tax is generally a percentage of the sale, and is commonly restricted to goods, but may also be applied to services. The tax is collected by the retailer, who then must forward the revenues to the government—or governments, as state, county, and city governments all have the option to levy such a tax. For example, California has the highest sales tax rate in the Unites States at 7.25%, but 32 of its 58 counties charge additional amounts, and many cities charge as well.

Sample of Sales Tax Rates within California (State + Local) as of Oct 2018			
Sacramento County	7.75%	San Francisco County	8.5%
City of Sacramento	8.25%	San Bernardino County	7.75%
Los Angeles County	9.5%	City of San Bernardino	8%
City of Downey	10%	Riverside County	7.75%
City of Long Beach	10.25%	City of Riverside	8.75%
City of Santa Monica	10.25%	City of Palm Springs	9.25%
San Diego County	7.75%	Orange County	7.75%
City of Chula Vista	8.75%	City of Westminster	8.75%
Fresno County	7.975%	Santa Clara County	9%
City of Kingsburg	8.975%	Monterey County	7.75%
Kern County	7.25%	City of Monterey	8.75%
City of Ridgecrest	8.25%	City of Salinas	9.25%
Alameda County	9.25%	Ventura County	7.25%
City of Newark	9.75%	City of Ventura	7.75%

Sales taxes are one of the simplest forms of taxes, insofar as their only purpose is to generate revenue. From the perspective of taxpayers and most voters, revenue generation is the fundamental purpose of taxation; but as we have seen with tariffs and excise taxes, legislators often try to use taxes for other purposes—like "protecting" domestic businesses or discouraging "bad" behaviors. When tax policy is used as a tool to manipulate economic or social outcomes, it introduces additional levels of debate, complicating discussion of the issue:

Tax Purpose	Primary Questions to Debate
Revenue Generation	Does it generate enough revenue for the government services we desire, without causing harms which might outweigh those benefits?
Change Economic Activity	Is the economic outcome desired by the government what the voters/taxpayers actually want (and if so, why aren't the voters/taxpayers bringing about that economic result through their own freewill transactions)?
Change Social Behavior	Is the change in social behavior desired by the government what the voters/taxpayers actually want (and if so, why do they need to be incentivized to adopt this behavior through taxation)?

Sales tax policy is almost entirely confined to this first purpose. (Later, when we discuss income tax, we will examine how the complicated income tax code aims at all three of these purposes—which is one of the reasons the code is so complicated.) In trying to generate revenue, legislators try to estimate the revenue to be gained by an increase in the sales tax rate (which is generally a single rate), and then weigh out some of the harms:

1. How much will the sales tax in our area (state, county, or city) reduce people's buying power? Since every item will be marginally more expensive, consumers will have to buy fewer items; and this means they will enjoy less real wealth, and there will be fewer market transactions overall, which means fewer jobs. Does the value of the government programs funded by this tax outweigh the value of this lost wealth?

2. How much economic activity *and* revenue will be lost to people transferring their activity to lower-tax jurisdictions (i.e. the next city/county/state over)?

3. And how much can we get away with before the taxpayers recognize these harms? (Because it is the harms that the voters *feel*, rather than the actual costs, that impact the results of the next election.)

The states, counties, and cities within the United States apply their sales taxes to the final sale of a product to the consumer; transactions between producers and wholesalers are not taxed. In this way, each product is only taxed once, when purchased by the person who actually uses—consumes—the product, instead of being taxed multiple times, as it passed from producer to distributer to wholesaler to retailer to finally the consumer. Additionally, not every product purchased by the consumer is taxed: typically, items like unprepared food and sometimes other "essential" items are left untaxed. This is done to reduce the cost to the poor. Exactly what is exempt from sales tax may vary from state to state; for while such exclusions are common, they are not intrinsic to the sales tax itself, which may just as simply be applied to everything. Similarly, while many states have begun taxing services as well as goods, precisely *which* services are taxed vary greatly between states, with some taxing a wide variety, and others only specific kinds of services.

The Value-Added Tax (VAT)

Outside of the United States, many countries apply their sales tax not only at the point of final sale (consumption), but at all points along the production process where the product is improved—where "value" is added to the product. Typically, only the addition in value is taxed; for example, a widget produced and valued at 10 euro is taxed on its 10 euro value, but when that widget is afterwards transformed into a doodad worth 12 euro, it is taxed at that point on the 2 euro addition to the value of the product. Depending upon how many production steps the product goes through before finally being sold to the customer, it may be taxed several times in total (and at each transaction, there would be different impacts upon how much of the tax gets absorbed by the seller and how much gets passed on to the buyer, as compared to an untaxed transaction).

There is one great advantage—from the point of view of the tax collector—that the VAT has over a sales tax assessed at consumption only: it's more hidden from the voter. For with a sales tax applied at consumption, the consumer can look at their receipt and see exactly how much sales tax they paid (7.75% where I live, or 8.75% where my brother lives; in both cities the law allows the sales tax to be listed separately from the price, and we recognize that the consumer pays this tax). But with a VAT, the total value of the tax is not so listed, as it will vary depending upon how many times value has been "added," and the different demand elasticity at each of those points. The total tax may not be indicated to the consumer at the final point of sale—meaning the voter is less likely to "feel" the tax, and therefore less likely to act through the ballot box. Thus sales taxes rarely exceed 10%—voters consider them too onerous—but VAT taxes can be (and are) raised much higher, with less fear of tax evasion or ballot box retaliation.

Economic Effects

Since sales tax increases the unit price of goods, the most direct impact of sales tax is to reduce the number of things that consumers can buy. Consequently, the overall number of market exchanges is reduced, and consumers enjoy less overall wealth. Theoretically, consumers' foregone purchases are replaced with government purchases using the collected tax dollars, so overall economic activity should remain roughly the same, only with different outcomes: consumers retain less *personal* wealth, but that foregone individual wealth is merely exchanged for more shared forms of wealth, including public schools, an adequate police force, maintenance of roads and parks (as well as less shared forms of wealth, including government salaries, kickbacks to partisans, contracts awarded to private interests, etc.—but these elements apply to all forms of taxes, not just sales taxes). The more local the government, the more equal the exchange between foregone consumer activity and increased government activity; but as the collecting government extends over a larger area, the greater the potential for tax revenues to be collected in one location and spent in another. Thus the citizens of Palm Springs, CA, can be confident that the 1.5% they pay in sales tax to their city will be spent on city improvements; but the 0.5% they pay to their county might end up being spent in the city of Riverside, and the 7.25% they pay to their state might end up being spent in Sacramento and elsewhere throughout the state.

When the sales tax is applied to all goods (and services, if the state has chosen to tax services as well), there is relatively little economic distortion: since all (or nearly all) prices go up, consumers may continue to buy a relatively similar mix of goods and services, since there is not much change in their values *relative to each other*. But when the sales tax is confined to a particular class of goods and/or services, the natural consequence is for consumers to demand less of the more expensive goods and services. For example, a state that chooses to tax only amusement and recreation services (Arizona, Utah, Alabama and Kentucky all fall into this category) might find that their citizens spend less on concerts and amusement parks than do citizens in neighboring states, switching their recreation dollars to other entertainments. Similarly, when a state taxes services to real property, such as lawn service and landscaping, its citizens might, in aggregate, start preferring smaller yards that don't require so much service. But the more general the taxation, the less change in behavior can be expected; consequently, sales taxes tend to do less to alter/distort market activity than do tariffs and excise taxes.

Sales taxes have more significant effects upon consumer behavior at the borders of the taxed region. For when it is easy for people to cross the border to make purchases elsewhere, they will often do it. This will tend to be most common where the difference in tax is the greatest; for example Californians who live near enough to the Oregon border may cross over to save themselves 7.25% on their purchases. (Actually, somewhat less than that: for the increased demand for goods on the Oregon border results in a price increase there, although generally still not as high as the California price, so long as the Oregon stores still want to attract the Californians' business.) As such travel is easier between counties, and even easier between cities, counties and cities must keep their additional tax rates lower—people may not find any value in driving a few more miles to save only 1% on their purchases. Big, attractive cities and isolated towns are typically able to manage some tax without affecting their commerce overmuch, while smaller towns immediately neighboring other jurisdictions tend to find their residents more ready to shop elsewhere. And in addition to merely shopping elsewhere, those with the economic means also have the option of moving to a new jurisdiction entirely; so there is tax competition between different jurisdictions that applies a downward pressure on tax rates.

Use Tax

State governments with high (relative to their neighbors) sales tax rates run the risk of driving some amount of business—and tax revenue—out of their state. This is particularly the case with large purchases, such as cars and boats, where a small percentage difference in tax is nevertheless a high enough amount in absolute dollars that the buyer finds it to be worth their time and effort to cross state lines to avoid the tax. Consequently, many state governments in the United States have implemented a strategy for disincentivizing such behavior: the use tax.

Use tax is a sales tax applied to purchases of goods made *outside* a tax jurisdiction, but then brought into the jurisdiction. For example, if a Massachusetts taxpayer travels across state lines to New Hampshire to buy goods there (there is no sales tax in New Hampshire), their home government of Massachusetts will then charge 6.25% use tax on those goods when they return home. Similarly, any goods purchased from a seller in another state via the internet is also subject to the use tax, so the Massachusetts resident becomes unable to avoid their state's usual 6.25% sales tax rate.

Of course, consumers do not always report their purchases, and so still attempt to avoid the tax. But for some kinds of purchases, the use tax is unavoidable: for example, if I were to buy a car in Oregon (no sales tax), I would be discovered by my home state of CA when registering the vehicle, and therefore be subject to the use tax. In this way the state of CA continues to tax their residents wherever they choose to shop—and tax also people who migrate into the state with their vehicles purchased elsewhere.

Government officials in search of revenue hate tax competition, since it limits their ability to raise revenues. This is one reason that pro-tax groups, such as the Organization for Economic Cooperation and Development (OECD), argue in favor of tax harmonization between jurisdictions. From a market perspective, this is akin to collusion between firms (in this case, providers of government services) fixing prices—an arrangement generally considered unethical and in most places made explicitly illegal whenever it occurs in the marketplace. Fortunately for taxpayers, not many nations or local jurisdictions hold to such agreements (just as firms in the marketplace frequently violate agreements to collude), as individual actors recognize the gains to be had for themselves if they charge a lower price/tax. For government jurisdictions, the gain is increased in-migration (and/or decreased out-migration) of business.

But such downward pressure upon sales tax rates is not equal in all places: for some geographic areas are simply more attractive than others to many people, well worth a few percentage points of sales tax. And just as a superior product on the market can command a higher price, so a superior geographic region can command a higher price among people able to choose where they would like to live. Thus a state like California, renowned for its sunny weather, for Hollywood, and for its many other attractions, can command a higher price (including tax rates) than next door Arizona; and a city like New York, with all of its cultural attractions, can command a higher price (including its tax rates) than nearby Newark (in this case, New York State actually has a lower sales tax rate than the state of New Jersey—4% versus 6.625%—but New York City has additional local taxes which put their residents' rate at 8.875%, while Newark adds nothing to its residents' tax burden).

Taxes are the price of government, but mobile people may not even be shopping for the local government they like so much as they are shopping for other features (weather, culture, career opportunity, etc.). The price of the local government becomes an incidental consideration; and for the most mobile (often, the most wealthy), sales tax rates alone may not be important enough to affect their decision; consequently, the most attractive regions can raise their sales tax rates further before experiencing any negative effects upon migration—although, when all other taxes are taken into effect, wealthy people may choose to move explicitly for tax reasons. Thus states like Florida, with a 6% sales tax, 1.1% property tax, and no income tax, continues to attract upper-income migrants from states like Illinois and New York (Florida surpassed New York's population in 2014, and continues to increase). As an attractive geographic area itself, Florida could probably command a higher tax rate and still experience some in-migration; but like a competitive market firm, its government has (so far) pursued a policy of lower tax rates specifically to attract business from other states. Such policy is consequently much resented by the governors of New York, which would prefer a more harmonized—they would say "fairer"—sales tax system.

Tax Incidence

Since sales tax (and use tax) is applied to a wide variety of goods (and sometimes services) instead of a narrowly defined set of goods and services, the tax burden is distributed among the entire population instead of focused upon a particular group. But as a consumption tax, applied at the point of sale to the consumer, such taxes are felt more by poorer people more than by richer people, since poorer people spend a greater portion of their wealth (savings and investments are not subject to sales taxes, so people wealthy enough to save and invest pay a smaller proportion of their income in sales taxes—although they have to pay other kinds of taxes on their savings and investments, so their overall tax burden is higher). Consequently, it is often described as a *regressive* tax (a regressive tax rate gets lower as income increases, whereas a *progressive* tax rate gets higher as income increases). This is another factor limiting the sales tax: any politician who promotes increasing the rate knows that they will be raising taxes on the "poor," and upon the majority of voters (and their political opponents will make sure that the voters know this too).

To reduce the impact of the sales tax upon the poor, governments typically exempt grocery and other "necessary" (in quotes because different lawmakers define what is necessary rather differently) purchases. The class of exempted foodstuffs may be restricted to "basic" items (again, as defined by the lawmakers), or might apply to all food items. So in one state, donuts might be subject to sales tax (it is a snack item instead of a grocery item), while in another state they are exempt (as a grocery item), while in another state it depends upon where the donut is sold (a box purchased from the grocery store is exempt, but a dozen bought from the donut shop is taxed as a prepared food item). Some states exempt certain articles of clothing from sales tax; some states exempt medical prescriptions. Others still tax these items, but at a lower rate. Meanwhile some "necessary" items, like toilet paper, remain taxed (only two states, New Jersey and Pennsylvania, exempt this item from their sales tax).

Tampon Tax

Not exempted from most sales taxes are tampons and other feminine hygiene products. Since such products are generally considered essential for daily living, many people argue that these products should also be exempted from sales tax, and refer to their non-exempt status as a "tampon tax" unfairly levied upon women for being women. When discussing this topic, it is important to remember that there isn't any such actual tax, but only a want of a sales tax exemption.

Finally, state and local sales taxes are *never* applied to purchases made by the United States federal government.

Ethical Considerations

The ethical justification for sales taxes is fairly straightforward: they are forthrightly a means of collecting revenue for government, obtained from the general population benefiting from that government in a way that shows minimal favoritism to any subset of the population. These taxes do not try to further justify themselves with debatable propositions about also being a tool to change people's behaviors; and this makes them much simpler to evaluate than tariffs, excise, or luxury taxes.

As local taxes (in the United States), sales taxes are highly responsive to voter representation: for even when neglected at the ballot box, voters can still vote with their feet by moving to a new jurisdiction. State taxes are of course harder to vote against in this way than are city or county taxes, but still much easier than the national sales taxes (generally VATs) assessed elsewhere in the world. The highly visible nature of sales taxes in the United States, being generally printed on receipts, increases the populations' awareness of the tax; and being applied to the entire voter base makes them even more subject to the will (or at least ire) of the people. While these downward pressures upon the sales tax are unpleasant to governments in want of revenue, these same limitations make sales tax a much more ethical means of taxation than most alternatives. However, it must be noted that while voting by out-migration *may* provoke legislators to reconsider their high rates, it also may result in the opposite effect, as legislators who are ignorant of the Laffer Curve (or who otherwise fail to recognize the tax rates as a reason for out-migration) might respond by *increasing* their rates in a misguided attempt to make up for missing revenue.

In contrast to most other kinds of taxes (and especially income taxes), sales taxes are readily understandable to voters. They are simple, visible, and common to their fellow voters. Increases in their rates are readily perceived/felt, and voters have power to respond accordingly—power increased not only by their ability to live and shop elsewhere, but also by the odds of finding common ground with other voters.

The more local the sales tax is, the more appropriate it is, in that revenues collected locally are spent locally, thus benefitting the population taxed; and since tourism is voluntary, this criteria is still satisfied, insofar as the tourists' tax dollars improve their chosen destinations. However, in larger states the sales tax can become less appropriate: for if a state favors particular areas with its spending (such as larger cities with more voters, and particularly the state capital), then the sales tax becomes an instrument of transferring wealth from one geographic region to another. When this happens, the tax policy also fails the representation criteria, as rural populations cannot muster the votes to overcome the interests of the urban populations (and in this case, voting with their feet by moving only further diminishes the voting power of those who remain).

Meanwhile the exemption of groceries (and in some cases other "essential" items) relieves the poor of some of this burden. Now some people still argue that such exemptions are not considerate enough, since the poor devote a larger share of their income on consumption than do the rich (who are able to save/invest more of their income). Consumption taxes are often referred to as "regressive" taxes, meaning that the greater a person's income, the smaller the percentage they pay in taxes: richer people are able to devote some amount of their income to savings/investment—which are often subject to other taxes—so the smaller proportion of their income spent on immediate consumption means they pay a smaller percentage of their income in sales taxes (of course they still pay a larger *absolute* value in consumption tax).

Fair Tax

There is a proposal for a national sales tax in the United States, known as the *Fair Tax*. The proposed tax would replace the established income and payroll taxes with a national sales tax rate levied on all consumption (services as well as goods) of about 30% of the sales price (as compared with traditional tax-exclusive sales tax rates; it is often represented as a 23% tax-inclusive rate, as a more direct comparison to the income and payroll taxes it proposes to replace).

While such a tax would eliminate all the economic harms of the income tax (discussed in the next chapter), many people object to it based upon the ethical principle of consideration for the poor, since the poor would find their effective tax rate increased. In response to this argument, the Fair Tax proposal introduces the *prebate*, a tax rebate received in advance (or "pre-received"), which would be an amount of money given to every taxpayer on a monthly basis in anticipation of the amount of tax they would have to spend on their basic needs. If set at the mathematically appropriate level, poor Americans would experience no sales tax burden, as the money coming in each month would match or exceed the sales tax going out.

As a technical device, this could conceivably resolve the consideration question— yet many voters on the political left simply disregard the new concept (or at least find it inadequate), and many on the political right regard the prebate as a kind of government benefit (such as universal basic income), so the concept has not gained much popularity since its first proposal in 1999.

The proposal is still out there, though, and I would recommend anyone interested in discussing taxation and ethics to check it out from the source directly, instead of second-hand. You can review the arguments in favor of this proposal at fairtax.org.

Interestingly, this tension in America is not experienced the same way in Europe: for while American politicians who raise their sales tax rates are considered to be taxing the poor, European politicians who raise their VAT rates are *not* held to the same account by their voters—that is, Europeans voters allow their politicians to set much higher consumption tax rates to be borne by the poor. Whether this is because the European VATs are less visible to voters (and so less felt by them), or because European voters agree that public benefits for all should be paid for by all, one can debate. Or perhaps the European system of collecting much of their revenue from consumption taxes simply reflects the realities of the Laffer Curve: they have already found limits in taxing the incomes of the wealthier people who have more freedom and ability to evade the taxes by moving to other jurisdictions, so they tax those less free/able to move out of necessity. Whatever the reason(s), it is important to note that the European social welfare programs are financed by general consumption taxes which collect substantial revenues from the middle class and from the poor, instead of financing them primarily though income taxes levied upon the rich. But in America, the political and popular demand is for social welfare spending to be financed by taxing the rich, generally though higher income taxes.

In light of this debate, we should recognize that the ethical principle of *consideration* is somewhat debated. I have proposed, "It is less ethical to tax the poor to fund necessary government than it is to tax the rich to fund necessary government. It is even worse to tax the poor to serve the needs of the rich." Others might prefer a principle along the lines of "It is unethical to tax the poor." Meanwhile people on the opposite side of the political spectrum might find no ethical difficulty in taxing the poor to provide services for the poor(er). The value I have proposed can be common ground for people on both sides of the political spectrum (it is logically consistent with both); but this common ground can easily be rejected by people who demand a value that accords *only* with their own, excluding the values of their opponents. Unfortunately, rejection of common ground changes political engagement from a process of negotiating a solution acceptable to all sides into a combat where each side attempts to force the other to surrender—it turns from seeking solutions to seeking only power. We shall make better political progress if we can remain in the common ground, that we should not tax the poor to serve the needs of the rich, than if we insist upon a more contested ground about whether the poor should be exempted from taxes entirely.

Meanwhile, the apparently ethical opposition to a national sales tax replacing the income tax is somewhat belied by the fact that the political wing most opposed to the idea is at the same time the political wing most supportive of passing a VAT *in addition to* current income taxes. Such a stance is logically consistent if the primary goal is simply to increase tax revenues, but it is not at all consistent with any stated ethical purpose of protecting the poor from taxation.

Our next consideration, minimizing harms, is not subject to the same kinds of value disputes (although people often dispute upon the economic facts, as well as the relative valuation of harms). But since sales taxes are applied to goods generally, instead of being targeted at specific groups of goods, they minimize harms by minimizing price distortions in the market. Also, since [in America] sales tax rates tend to be lower, there is less harm resulting from excessive taxation. However, harms are incurred at the borders of different tax jurisdictions, by the residents of the higher-tax jurisdiction, as the difference in tax rates incentivizes people to move their business from one location to another. Thus any city, county, or state which continues to raise its sales tax rates significantly above that of its neighbors harms its own taxpayers by driving economic activity to other cities, counties, and states (which does benefits those other locations). However, this harm is not particular to sales taxes: it occurs with every kind of tax, when there is a noticeable difference in rates along borders that people can freely cross.

Finally, in considering the ethical principle of peace, it is interesting to note there is more potential conflict than there is actual conflict at the moment. For peace is most jeopardized when a tax policy confers either benefits or burdens upon a specific group, forcing groups to compete/lobby to get the best deal among their neighbors. Since sales taxes are applied generally, there is not so much competition. However, as long as sales taxes are applied to goods but not services, there is a potential conflict between the providers of goods and the providers of services, as providers of goods may complain that they bear an unfair burden when compared to the sellers of services, who enjoy all the same benefits of government without paying so much of the cost. However, at the current time this is not a much-contested political issue, nor has it been so in the past decades. Now if it should ever come to pass that a national sales tax is implemented, and if that tax exempts services or particular goods (such as foods, medicine, etc.), then we would expect greater conflict, increasing with the size of the tax, as the larger the tax gets, the more significant it is to place the tax burden upon one business but not another.

On the whole, sales taxes appear much better—from an ethical perspective—form of taxation than the other taxes we have examined so far; and as we shall see in the next chapter, a much better ethical option than our current income tax system. But if they are so much more ethical, why do Americans persist in using income taxes rather than sales taxes to fund the bulk of their government? There are a few reasons. First is custom/inertia: people tend to do what they have previously done. Second is uncertainty: legislators are not sure how high a sales tax rate would need to be to replace the current income tax to generate the same amount of revenue; they fear setting a rate so high that they lose their next election, but also fear setting a rate not high enough, resulting in major deficits. But third, and perhaps most significantly, is that a change from income tax to a national sales tax would transfer some amount of the current tax burden from the wealthier to the middle class and to the poor—even with some kind of "prebate" implemented to reduce that shift. And many people find that to be flatly unacceptable, no matter how well sales tax might score on all other ethical measures.

Summary Report Card – General Sales Taxes

Representation   **Good**

City taxes being better than county, which are better than state: tax payers can vote with their feet, taking their business elsewhere. However, Use taxes are problematic, as they apply taxes to economic transactions made *outside* a jurisdiction's borders.

Participation   **Excellent**

The tax is levied upon the whole of the population.

Honesty and Openness   **Excellent**

Sales tax is passed to raise revenues, without subterfuge, and the amount of the tax is highly visible to those being taxed, being identified at every purchase. (But the VAT is problematic on the openness criteria, being generally hidden.)

Simplicity   **Excellent**

Generally, sales taxes are applied at a single understandable rate.

Appropriateness   **Fair to Excellent**

Varies with the size of the jurisdiction: excellent when a local population is taxed to provide local benefits, less so when centralizing benefits around a state capital.

Consideration   **Contested**

Grocery exemptions to sales tax reduce the burden upon the poor—but a sales tax that could replace income taxes would increase the poor's overall tax burden.

Minimizing Harms   **Good**

Lower rates and even application reduce harms. Yet particular harms result when a local jurisdiction's tax rate drives business to neighboring jurisdictions; but the very threat of this tempers the tax rate. (European VATS, being set at much higher rates than American sales taxes, are more harmful.)

Justice   **Pass**

Sales taxes are generally not used to administer justice (but are still often used to transfer wealth from some people to others).

Peace   **Good to Excellent**

Although there is a potential battle between providers of goods and providers of services, that battle has not become manifest; and consumers show great unity.

Also important to note is that some of the ethical advantages of sales taxes discussed in this chapter are tied to the fact that these taxes are—in the United States—more local. Being more local taxes, general sales taxes are more responsive to citizen opinion (either through the votes at the ballot box, or—often more significantly—through their dollar votes, according to where taxpayers choose to shop and live); at a national level, the same tax would not score so well (at least in the United States; for there is some difference between the United States here and Europe, in that travel between nations in Europe is much more common than between nations in the North American continent). Similarly, the downward pressure provided by tax competition at the local level is also diminished when a sales tax is applied nationally; for the United States Federal Government does not need to be much concerned about the possibility of American citizens crossing the border into Mexico in order to purchase goods there. Finally, the problem of rural tax collections being reallocated to city (and particularly the capital city) spending increases with the size of the tax jurisdiction; and what is already a problem at the national level with income tax—with a significant concentration of wealth around the nation's capital—would not be changed for the better by switching from an income to a sales tax.

Sales Tax on "Fair Market Value"

State taxes can be ethically dubious in cases as well:

Since sales tax is based upon the price of products, revenue-hungry governments may object to buyers and sellers agreeing to lower prices, since it reduces the state's share of the transaction. Thus the state of Michigan stipulates that their 6% sales tax rate applies to the greater of either the purchase price, or the "fair market value" as determined by the state. So, if person A sells a used car to person B for the price of $7,000, but the state auditor challenges the sale price and determines that the vehicle was "really" worth $10,000, then the state can tax the sale as if it had sold at the higher price. In other words, the state of Michigan asserts the authority to tell private parties in a mutually beneficial and agreed-upon sale what the price *should* be, and if those parties are "undervaluing" the transaction. Whatever written contract exists between buyer and seller is unimportant: the *state* gets to decide the taxable value of the item. This can make quite a difference to the state in terms of annual revenue from large-item sales such as automobiles, boats, and airplanes—and it can make quite a difference to the buyer in any individual transaction, who may be forced to pay several hundred (or in the case of a boat or airplane, several thousand) more in tax to complete the purchase.

The revenue-seeking state is incentivized to value items at a higher amount; what prevents them from artificially inflating values in order to extract more revenue?

7

Personal Income Taxes

Finally we come to the type of tax that most Americans think of when they consider "paying taxes," or voting on tax policy: the income tax. But the income tax is complicated—extraordinarily complicated, with more than 2,600 pages of statues (with another 6,000 pages of IRS regulations and revenue rulings, plus more than 60,000 additional pages of case law commenting on all of this)—so any description will only barely scratch the surface. To navigate such complexity, many Americans hire tax professionals—but with such extraordinary complexity, IRS audits discover that even paid professionals make many mistakes—and so does the IRS! For example, General Accounting Office audits of IRS phone advice have found a 13% error rate in its 2006 audit—an improvement over the prior year's 24% error rate. Yet the official IRS position is that the advice they give over their telephone help line is "advisory only" and the IRS is *not bound to recognize it* when examining tax returns! In other words, if a taxpayer follows their explicit directions, that taxpayer can still be found to be in error when preparing their return!

Meanwhile, this stupendously complex code is ever-changing. Congress made more than 5,000 changes to the tax code just between 2001 and 2013. So how is a voter supposed to begin to make sense of all this?

Description and Purpose

The United States first passed an income tax in 1861 to help pay for the Civil War. Income taxes were repealed in 1872, and not enacted again until 1894—at which point they were challenged in the Supreme Court, and ruled unconstitutional on the grounds they were direct taxes and therefore had to be apportioned according to state populations. Thus Congress proposed the 16th Amendment, ratified in 1913, to give the federal government the power to levy income taxes without such a restriction.

The 1913 income tax was only 1% on income over $3,000 (about $76,000 in 2019 dollars) and another 6% on incomes above $500,000 ($12.7 million in 2019 dollars), so it originally only impacted the very rich. But as of 2019, the income tax is collected from more than half of all American households. (A much higher number of households *file* taxes, but receive credits that equal or exceed their tax liability, resulting in those households receiving money from the income tax, rather than having to pay anything. In common parlance, Americans call these "refunds," but in such cases, the term "negative income tax" would be more accurate.) From its inception, the income tax had multiple tax brackets/rates, which progressively increased as taxpayers' income increased. The rates for the different brackets have varied over time, with a high of 94% in 1944 to the current rate of 37% on income over $600,000.

In the United States, each bracket rate only applies to the income amounts within that bracket, *not* to the whole of the income. Thus, a single person who increases their taxable income from $35,000 to $40,000 pays the top marginal rate of 22% only on the income above $38,791, while paying a smaller rate on the income below that. As of 2018, the brackets for a person filing their taxes singly are as follows:

Taxable income	Marginal Rate	Tax Owed
$0 - $9,525	10%	10% of taxable income
$9,526 - $38,790	12%	$953 + 12% of income over $9,525
$38,791 - $82,500	22%	$4,464 + 22% of income over $38,790
$82,501 - $157,500	24%	$14,080 + 24% of income over $82,500
$157,501 - $200,000	32%	$32,080 + 32% of income over $157,500
$200,001 - $500,000	35%	$45,680 + 35% of income over $200,000
Over $500,000	37%	$150,679 + 37% of income over $500,000

The progressive tax structure allows the government to lay the tax burden primarily upon the wealthiest people (a structure that satisfies our ethical principle of *consideration* for the poor, but which runs afoul of our ethical principle of *representation*, since it results in one portion of the population being able to dictate terms to another). As of 2018, the top 20% of households paid 87% of all income taxes collected; more than half of the total income tax collected by the federal government came from just 3% of American households. This income tax revenue makes up approximately half of all federal revenues (another 35% is collected from payroll taxes, 9% from corporate income taxes, and the remainder from all other sources).

The tax brackets indicated above only apply to those who file singly; those who are married filing jointly have different brackets (reflecting income for a household of two adults). Those who are married filing separately have the same tax brackets as those who file as Single, excepting the final bracket (which starts at $300,000 instead of $500,000), while those who file as Head of Household (single people with dependents) have different brackets entirely. Not only has the different rates for each bracket varied over the decades, but the number of brackets has varied also, being as few as 2 (as recently as 1988–1990) and as many as 24 (for Head of Household in the latter part of the 70's).

But while these tax brackets start at $0, that doesn't mean every dollar is taxed, for some amount of income is excluded from taxation before the brackets are applied: the standard deduction (currently $12,000 for unmarried individuals and $24,000 for married couples). (In the past, this deduction was smaller, but then an additional amount of money was exempted for each person in the home; this personal exemption was eliminated when the standard deduction was nearly doubled.) So for a single person earning $20,000 gross income, they would only pay 10% tax on $8,000.

In addition to the income excluded from taxation by the standard deduction, taxpayers with children also benefit from the Child Tax Credit and (for lower income households) the Earned Income Tax Credit (EITC), which are money the government "credits"—that is, gives—to the taxpayer. The EITC (which varies according to income level) is entirely refundable, and $1,400 of the $2,000 Child Tax Credit is refundable—"refundable" here meaning the tax filer gets to keep it even if they owe no taxes. Thus a married couple with two children and a gross income of $30,000 will not have to pay taxes on their $6,000 of taxable income: instead, the amounts credited to them will result in them receiving almost $7,000 "refund" in negative income tax.

But the exclusions don't stop there: additionally money spent on particular purchases are not counted as taxable income, so the married couple with two children and gross earnings of $42,000 who has spent $12,000 on their health insurance will discover that only $30,000 of their gross income is countable gross income, so they also will receive almost $7,000 in negative income tax (which will be called a "refund").

Negative Income Tax vs. Refundable Tax Credits

In the American political discourse, refundable tax credits are almost never referred to as "negative income tax;" instead they are termed "refunds," conflating these payments with actual refunds to people who have overpaid their taxes throughout the year and are getting their own tax dollars back. But as transfer payments (money moved from one portion of the population to another portion of the population) administered through the tax code, they are in fact a negative income tax (as the tax filer receives, rather than pays, taxes), and are properly counted among other means-tested transfer payments, such as cash aid welfare, food stamps, Supplemental Security Income (SSI), and other such payments. But by administering this payment program through the tax code, politicians can separate this spending from the related political discourse—and in people's minds (recipients of the negative income tax do not identify themselves as receiving a government handout paid for by other taxpayers). Perversely, increases of these payments get termed "tax cuts" instead of spending increases. (That is, they are termed so in political discourse; the actual budget correctly identifies them as payments.) Meanwhile the term "negative income tax" gets reserved for a hypothetical payment that would be explicitly identified as such in the tax return, as proposed by Milton Friedman and supported by President Richard Nixon. But in truth, the negative income tax is not hypothetical, but was enacted in another form through the Earned Income Tax Credit in 1975. (Interestingly, Friedman had proposed it as an alternative to the welfare system; but instead the American politicians decided to go with both.)

In addition to the deduction for health insurance premiums, the current tax code also allows taxpayers to deduct from their countable gross income payments to health savings accounts, student loan interest payments, IRA contributions, and a few other defined expenses. Meanwhile higher-income families may opt to forego their standard deduction in favor of "itemizing" deductions, if the total of itemized deductions exceeds their standard deductions. Similar to how the writers of the current tax code have decided that money spent on health insurance premiums or student loan interest should not be taxed, itemized deductions cover other purchases deemed important enough to warrant not being taxed, including money spent on mortgage interest on a home, charitable contributions, certain qualifying medical and dental expenses, and some amount of money paid in taxes to state and local governments. The purpose of allowing such deductions is to encourage particular economic behaviors: the government *wants* its citizens to buy homes, go to college, save for retirement, stay in good health, and give to charity, so it reduces the tax burden for people engaging in those behaviors.

The State and Local Tax (SALT) Deduction

One of the most significant of the itemized deductions is the deduction for money paid for state and local sales taxes. As a result of this deduction, wealthy taxpayers (poor taxpayers and middle-income taxpayers who don't own their own homes typically take the standard deduction, which for them is larger than the itemized deduction) in higher-tax states experience some relief, as their overall tax burden goes down for the year. However, this relief enables state and local governments to raise their tax rates, confident that their taxpayers will not feel as much of the pinch. The taxpayers, being less price-sensitive to the change in tax rate, are less likely to change their behavior (in this case, which state they choose to reside in). However, the Tax Cuts and Jobs Act of 2017 capped this deduction at $10,000 (capping the deduction meant collecting more income from wealthy persons, offsetting the anticipated revenue loss from the tax cuts part of the bill). With this cap, the wealthiest tax payers feel the impact of their local/state taxes more acutely (and if the SALT were ever repealed entirely, they would feel it more acutely still); consequently, more wealthy taxpayers have changed their behavior in response—by moving to lower-tax states. While not everybody is motivated to move, enough wealthy taxpayers have moved that the governor of New York has complained that Florida is "stealing" their wealthiest tax payers, and the governor of New Jersey even considered (briefly) suing the federal government over the change. New York, New Jersey, Connecticut, Illinois, Rhode Island and California are losing tax revue as a result of such movement; while Texas, Florida and Nevada have experienced increased in-migration of these wealthy taxpayers.

The existence of so many deductions in the American income tax code means the income tax is not only a means of raising revenue, but also a means of encouraging (or discouraging) particular economic behaviors. To the legislator interested in planning/directing the economy, the tax code presents a host of levers and switches to manipulate that economy. However, the national economy, being the product of the independent decisions of more than three hundred million Americans, plus millions of non-Americans contributing to the economy, is even more complex than the 60,000 pages of tax code; so would-be planners often (if not always) discover different results than what they anticipate.

The Mortgage Interest Deduction

One of the most popular—even sacrosanct—deductions is the deduction for mortgage interest on a home. As a result of this deduction, more people are motivated to buy homes, knowing that they will be able to write of the interest and thus save money on their tax bills. Consequently, demand for homes goes up—and so does the price of homes, immediately eliminating some of that savings. Worse still, the taxpayer who finds the standard deduction to be more valuable than the itemized deduction (much more common since the standard deduction was increased in 2017) will end up with no tax savings at all—a fact many homebuyers do not discover until they do their taxes the next year. But the price of homes remains higher so long as the deduction is advertised and not examined mathematically by the home-buying public.

Meanwhile all these various tax brackets and rates and deductions and exclusions and credits (refundable and non-refundable) are subject to constant debate and negotiation; and it is this process of negotiation that results in the great complexity and expansion of tax law. For every deduction—and every definition—will affect some people more than others, and those most affected will be highly motivated to apply political pressure to make [perhaps small] changes to protect themselves, while the less affected have no incentive to fight that (the cost being distributed among so many, and being zero to many more). The very definitions of what economic transactions count as income, and as what "type" of income, get debated—and make up a significant portion of the tax code. Thus a thousand independent parties can be motivated to advance a thousand different changes; and the complexity of the economy itself (more than 300 million individuals making independent decisions) revealing thousands of more questions unanticipated by the original legislators and needing clarification from the courts. Amidst all this complexity, politicians discover that the complexity becomes not so much a bug in the system as a useful feature: for they become the recipients of all the lobbying money spent on adjusting the tax code.

Just as the tax rates indicated above do not apply to all income, they do not apply to all *types* of income; for the United States tax code distinguishes between different income sources, and has different rules for different types. (Some of these types, such as income for corporations and income from capital gains, will be addressed in separate chapters, as they introduce unique economic effects and ethical considerations.) A significant portion of the tax code is devoted simply to defining income in all of its forms, and delineating the various methodologies for classifying and counting the different types of income for taxable purposes. Some types of income require separate tax worksheets to compute what amount is taxable, some refer the taxpayer to tables and schedules, some get taxed in some conditions but not others, and some types of income are excluded from taxation. Child support, for example, is not taxed; but for 70 years, alimony received has been taxed. Social Security payments are not taxed—unless the taxpayer has enough income from other sources, in which case they are taxed. Gambling winnings are taxed—unless they are exceeded by the prior year's gambling losses. Some kinds of court awards, disability payments, and gifts are taxed; other kinds are not.

Many of these decisions were made independently of each other; others were created as a package. But for each rule, either elected politicians and legislators (with the help of their staffs) or unelected bureaucrats debated and decided when it would be fair, appropriate, or just plain possible to tax these different sources, and the tax code is the product of these myriad separate disputes over time. With so many decisions and rulings, and with taxpayers generally occupied with their own employment, it is useless for most individuals to keep track of it all—so they depend upon tax professionals to keep track of it. And when taxpayers do look at the rules, they often find that the tax code answers some of their questions very differently than they would have answered them themselves:

- Should barter (that is, trade of goods and services without money, such as an exchange of ten chickens for one pig) be taxed? The federal income tax code says yes: the people engaged in the barter must work out the money equivalent of the exchange and each of them count that as income. If a man builds his neighbor a new wooden deck in exchange for his neighbor doing some landscaping for him, then one neighbor would count the value of their new deck as taxable income, while the other neighbor would count the value of the landscaping as taxable income.
- Should a discharge of debts be counted as income? The IRS says yes: if you are forgiven a debt of $10,000, you must count that as $10,000 worth of income, and pay income tax on it.
- What if someone else pays for something on your behalf (car repairs, for example, or utility bill to keep your electricity from being shut off)? The IRS counts that as income, too.

- Does that include when an employer pays for travel expenses? The IRS says yes it does, if the trip was considered an award to the employee (but it wouldn't count as income if the economic gain were subordinate to business purposes).
- What if you loan your friend money; is either the loan or the repayment taxed? The IRS says the loan itself is not taxed, but the interest income is—even if you did not charge interest. For the IRS will *impute* interest income to you, and then tax you on the amount they suppose you "should" have charged and collected.

Just as with the selection of brackets/rates and deductions and exclusions, all of the various rules and regulations for the different kinds of income are also subject to continual negotiation and revision—the rules regarding alimony, for example, were changed by the Tax Cuts and Jobs Act of 2017 (previously, alimony paid was deducted from the payer's taxable income, and considered taxable income for the recipient; but for divorces filed after January 1 of 2019, the recipient no longer has to pay taxes on this, while the payer no longer gets to deduct it). Some changes (like the change in alimony) affect many individuals, but no coalition, and so are not met with much resistance (in terms of lobbying); other changes affect larger interests or coalitions of people that can afford lobbying, and are therefore met with more resistance—and with more money spent on lobbyists who in turn spend that money on the legislators themselves in attempts to secure results which are more favorable—or at least less damaging—to them. (In fact, much tax lobbying is defensive in nature, insofar as deciding not to lobby makes one vulnerable to tax increases which have been lobbied for by others. We will be considering this in more detail later, when we discuss taxes on business income.)

Meanwhile some provisions of the tax code are indicated from inception as temporary, with "sunset" dates for when they will end—except that such "temporary" provisions may be extended, if legislators determine that such extensions are warranted (read: if they have political incentive to do so). In these cases, those who benefit from the "temporary" measures lobby their legislators to extend these temporary provisions; and the legislators can either make them permanent or continue the tax extenders for another set time period—at which point the legislators get to benefit from an additional round of lobbying. For every possible change in the tax code is an invitation for lobbyists to spend money on legislators to secure more favorable results. Unfortunately, this means that there is a structural incentive for politicians to create "temporary" provisions and then maintain them through "extenders." It would be more beneficial for the nation if businesses were able to count upon a stable law, and make future investments accordingly; but it is more beneficial to the recipient of lobbying monies to collect those monies repeatedly.

Thus the income tax accomplishes four major purposes:

1. Like all taxes, it raises revenue for the government (in fact, about half of all federal tax revenues come from personal income tax);

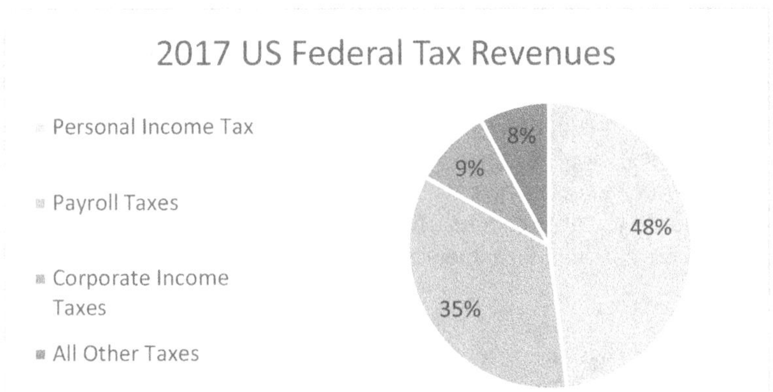

2. Like tariffs (and to a lesser extent, excise taxes), it provides the government with various means of manipulating the economy (if "manipulating" has too negative a connotation for you, read, "incentivizing or dis-incentivizing specific economic behaviors");

3. The income tax transfers wealth from rich to poor through the refundable tax credits, which amount to a negative income tax; and

4. Like tariffs, it provides politicians with an additional source of personal income through lobbying (much of which is defensive in nature, for if a firm may be particularly hurt by a proposed change to the tax regulations, it may be forced to spend its profits on lobbying against that change just to survive).

Historical Significance of the Personal Income Tax

Since the personal income tax is such a significant source of government revenue today, discussing the ethics of this tax presents a greater challenge than discussing the ethics of tariffs and excise taxes: for while people may consider the possibility that an insignificant (in terms of revenue generated) tax might have ethical problems, the same people may refuse to even consider this possibility for a tax that sustains their current government. To even suggest that there are ethical problems with the personal income tax threatens many people's worldviews, and also their hopes, and—in some cases—their personal well-being. Yet this was not always the case; and it is worth considering how this change in perception of the needfulness of the income tax came to pass.

Prior to the introduction of the personal income tax, government revenues were much smaller—both in absolute terms, and as a share of a country's economic product—and government was also much smaller. Consequently, government was much more limited in the number of projects it could undertake—and this was true not only for the United States, which had a written constitution which legally limited the powers of government, but also for other countries which had no such formal legal and philosophical limitation: they simply could not afford to do everything that government today now does. Government relied upon others taxes—particularly tariffs, excise taxes, and land taxes—to provide law, wage wars, and enrich the king (and the governors, officials, and bureaucrats subordinate to the king). Such taxes were largely borne by the merchant and landed classes—which made sense, as these were the primary sources of taxable wealth in any nation.

But after the industrial revolution, wealth began being produced on a much greater scale, by many more people. This opened up the possibility of a much much larger income for the government; and simultaneously, the rise of representative government opened up new possibilities for the *function* of government: for a government (and tax system) which exists to serve the will of the people (or at least, of those people who are represented in the government) will find many more needs than the government (and tax system) which exists to serve the will of the king. However, historical patterns do not change immediately, and the rise of participatory government did not immediately create government on the scale which is normal to us today. Instead, governments at first continued to rely upon the limited sources of income from traditional taxes. But as expenses and deficits increased, governments (now representative governments) began to consider the new income potential.

In both the United States and Great Britain, the immediate occasion for introducing the income tax was war. Historically, governments have been limited in their ability to wage war by the amount of money they can muster to pay for soldiers, ships, and other armaments; and wars have ever been a reason for increasing all kinds of tax rates (which increases are sometimes remitted in peace, but often not). Thus Great Britain introduced an income tax during the Napoleonic Wars in 1799, then abolished it a year after the Battle of Waterloo in 1816. In the United States, the personal income tax was introduced in 1861 to pay for the Civil War (actually, it had first been proposed during the War of 1812, but that war had ended without it being passed), and was abolished in 1872.

However, as the governments of both the United States and Britain grew, and found deficits even in peacetime years, they reintroduced personal income taxes to pay for peacetime endeavors. Great Britain brought it back in 1842. The United States brought it back 1894—but the Supreme Court declared it unconstitutional in 1895 (since the United States Constitution required direct taxes to be apportioned among the states according to their populations), and it was not until the 16th Amendment was ratified in 1913 that personal income tax become a legal and permanent feature of United States. In both countries, personal income tax was originally applied only to the very wealthy; but it did not remain that way.

In 1913, the US Congress passed a now-legal income tax applying to the wealthiest Americans; it had a progressive rate structure and a top rate of 7%. In 1916, with tariff revenues having been reduced by WWI, the income tax was increased; its top rate was 15%. In 1917, the rates were raised again: now the top rate was 67%, and the personal exemption was cut, expanding the tax base to include more people. In 1918, the top rate was again raised, now to 77%, which provided political cover for raising the lowest rates. It had only taken 5 years for a small tax applied to only the wealthiest to become a substantial tax applied to a much broader base. And when the war ended, tax rates were reduced a little; but with half of the nation's revenue coming from personal income taxes as of 1925, there was no going back to small budgets and limited government. For decades, the Progressive movement in America had been agitating for greater government, and growing in popularity and power; its goals had been thwarted largely by a lack of revenue, and with that obstacle removed by the personal income tax, the purposes of government were redefined.

This redefinition of government, and that visions absolute need for a larger revenue source, brought with it a redefinition of the government's right to taxation. In the early years of the United States, citizens and the states understood that the federal government's power to tax was limited (the individual states retained greater powers of taxation), and was for the purpose of providing specified services. But in modern times, it has been understood that the government may tax whatever it will, and that it has a right to a share of people's productive activity, to provide whatever services the people and their representatives demand by vote. And it *must* have this right, if the people are to obtain the services they desire.

The Significance of Withholding

When the federal income tax was first passed, taxpayers paid the amount they owed once a year, as a [large] annual sum. Writing a check out to the government made the cost of this tax very clear to those few who had to pay it—few, because originally, the income tax applied to only the very wealthy. Well, the wealthy could afford it—except not really, because the United States Federal Government needed even more money to finance WWI, and then to finance new government programs during the Great Depression, and then to finance WWII. What it wanted was a broader tax base; but it was difficult to get all the middle class to consent to paying such significant amounts—to budgeting all year long so that they would be able to pay such significant amounts.

In WWI, most of the expenditures had to be financed through debt, rather than current taxes, and one of the consequences of this was massive inflation leading to a doubling of market prices. So as WWII loomed, the government was concerned about how to avoid this problem. One of the young economists working at the Treasury Department at this time was Milton Friedman, who, in the interest of preventing the inflation problem and helping the government to win the war, helped develop the program of tax withholding, whereby employers would automatically collect income taxes from employees throughout the year. This would enable the government to have a continuous revenue stream to finance the war, instead of having to budget from the amount received once annually; and it would allow the government to raise tax rates, since forcing taxpayers to pay in installments would make the burden easier to bear (for the same reason that consumers tend to buy new cars in installments, rather than paying the full price in cash outright).

In 1942, Congress took advantage of withholding to drastically increase the size of the tax base, taxing all income above a $624 exemption—and the income tax became a mass tax instead of a class tax. The measure—which Friedman later wished could be abolished—allowed the government to raise tax rates on the less wealthy even after the war was over, since the annual price of the increase was spread out over the course of every paycheck—and entirely disguised at tax time, when extra withholdings are refunded (without interest, of course) to taxpayers who were forced to overpay throughout the year. The expansion in size and scope of government following WWII was only possible because of withholding, which made it both practically and *psychologically* feasible to collect income tax revenues from so many who had never before been subject to income taxation.

Economic Effects

The single most significant effect of the personal income tax is that it has allowed for a great expansion in the size of government. Whether the size of that government is a net good or a net evil is much debated: many Americans believe that their current government is far too big, while many others would like to see it even bigger. As of 2018, the United States Federal Government's spending accounted for about 35% of the nation's economy; while in Europe, some governments account for more than 50% of their nations' economies. This increased size allows the government to take on more functions—particularly welfare programs, including social security (total spending on Social Security is about one quarter of the entire federal budget, and spending on Medicare and Medicaid takes up another quarter)—and gives it a greater capacity to wage war. Note: this is not to say that the funds are *needed* or even desired for waging war—these are much-debated statements—but it merits listing here because the size of military budgets in peacetime is and can be so much greater than before. Military spending in 2015 accounted for a little more than half of discretionary spending, or about 16% of the total US federal budget.

It is difficult to describe the effects of a government directing so large a share of the economy, because the values of these varied effects are much debated. Additionally, the effect cannot be counted the same between different nations, for governments vary considerably in quality; we could only properly compare the size of one government to the same government at a different size—but those comparisons only exist in theoretical models, because we cannot clone entire countries in a lab and test them with different policies. Nevertheless, some economic impacts can be anticipated through consideration of basic economic principles.

The first principle to consider is the matter of economic calculation, or how different goods and services are valued in order to allocate them productively. Market economies use prices to allocate resources; prices in the market are set by the myriad of individual exchanges between buyers and sellers according to every individual's subjective needs and valuations, with the aggregate of all those expressed needs becoming represented by the price (which may vary between regions). Collectively, this system directs producers to produce those goods and services which are most valued, whether that be steel or corn or computers or hot dogs. Businesses have to choose between trade-offs in the production of goods and services, always considering their own cost; and this forces them to make efficient use of scarce resources, or they get out-competed by other businesses. Consumers also choose between trade-offs as they attempt to satisfy their unlimited wants with limited means, which forces them to make more efficient use of their resources.

In contrast to business and private spending, government spending is very different: first, in that it does not benefit from the same level of information through the price system (first, because it tries to fix prices at "fair" levels through legislation, depriving itself of market information; and second, because the prices of many of its social services are also decided by lobbying power or legislative fiat, instead of through the use of market information); second, in that those in charge of spending the money are not spending their own money (as a rule, people are much more careful with their own money than they are with others' money); and third, in that it is not so constrained by costs, since it has given itself permission to run at a deficit. Consequently, government spending is, on average, less efficient than private spending in terms of allocating scarce economic resources. How much less efficient varies greatly between governments, according to their myriad policies. For example, the French government appears to be a little less efficient than the German government, in the sense that the French government consumes a greater share of its economy than does the German, without providing noticeably superior services; and both are more efficient than the Spanish, Italian, or Greek governments by the same metric.

This is a general principal, and you do not need to believe that it applies to every single dollar of government spending universally. For it may be the case that in some situations, government might be able to spend money more efficiently than private spending: for example, it might well be more efficient to pay for a single military, a single police force, and a single court system, rather than have multiple competitive providers on a market. (Although, for any given expenditure within those categories—say for example the purchase of a fighter jet—the particular government agency may quite fail to get a competitive price, so long as the individual members of the military or the bureaucracy do not have personal incentive to get the most competitive price.) But as government multiplies, and as the features that incentivize frugal use of scarce resources decrease (features like personal incentive, price information, and reliable feedback.)

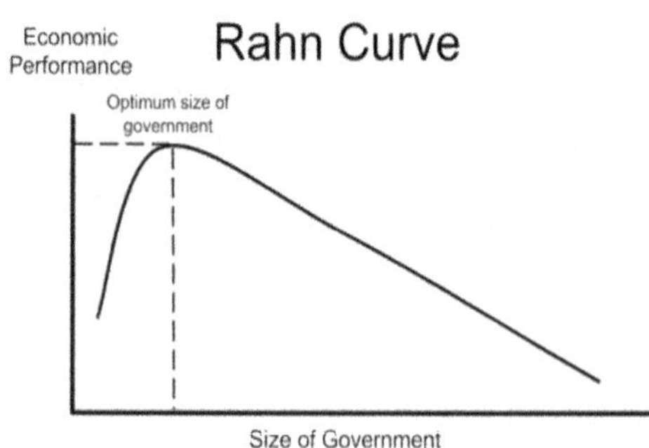

This trade-off was described by economist Richard Rahn as a curve: initial government spending improves a state's economic performance, but after a certain point, each additional dollar of government spending reduces the economy's overall performance, with each additional dollar being spent less efficiently than the one before.

Note than the differences in efficiency between government and private spending matters for all tax policies, the point applies more particularly to the personal income tax, since that is the greatest revenue source for the United States federal government, and has enabled the greatest increase in the size of government. (If you are reading this in Europe, however, you may also apply these observations to your nation's VAT.)

Again, we must acknowledge that Americans do not agree on how efficient their government is when compared to private spending; and while Richard Rahn estimates the peak of his curve to be somewhere between 15% and 25% of the economy, other economists may argue that the peak is significantly higher. We will not be able to solve this debate in any one book, so we will move on to consider other economic effects which are not so debated.

Another result of increasing the size of the tax base is that it enables a government to borrow more money. Governments have always borrowed money to cover deficits; and lenders offer the money always on the expectation of being repaid. Such expectation is based upon lenders' estimate of borrowers' ability and likelihood to repay; and a nation's tax base represents its ability to make those payments. Today, most government borrowing is done in the form of issuing bonds; such bonds are purchased in the open market by banks and other investors for the purpose of making a profit on the interest promised by the government. The government makes up its deficit by borrowing money from the pool of capital being invested for profit; or in other words, it *diverts* money from being invested in other income-producing projects that are anticipated to be more risky or to yield a lower return than the interest rate promised by the government.

Consequently, the greater the amount of government borrowing, the more money is diverted from investment activity which promotes the growth of new businesses and industries. (And again, this fact is common to all government borrowing, but is mentioned here because the personal income tax, through the expansion of the tax base, enables the government to overspend its budget even more, since lenders can look to the size of the tax base as a sign that they will be repaid.) How much economic growth is lost to this process? Again, no one can ascertain for certain; we just know that all existing companies and start-ups must compete with the government for a limited pool of investment funds, and we can never measure just what businesses might have been created but weren't on account of this. (This inability to measure what might have happened impacts every economic prediction in all matters, not just tax policy; and it is one of the most significant reasons one can find economists expecting entirely different results from any given government policy, including the setting of tax rates.)

The next [again, debated] result of the personal income tax applies to nature of the tax specifically, rather than to its scale, and has particular consequences resulting from the progressive structure of the tax. Taxing productive behavior (that is, income-producing behavior) reduces the incentive for productive behavior, thus reducing the amount of production overall—the economy grows more slowly, resulting in less overall wealth than there would be at a marginally lower tax rate. Interestingly, this simple economic principle—that raising the price of something reduces the demand)—is completely accepted in virtually every other instance, yet it is debated here. For example, we saw that excise tax policy is explicitly based upon the truth that raising the price of an item through taxation will reduce the demand (if you want less of something, tax it); yet many people do not expect the same fundamental principle to apply to personal income.

To understand why this is the case, let us recall from chapter 2 our discussion of the Laffer Curve, and how different tax types have different curves (just as different products sold by a business have different price curves). For example, an excise tax or capital gains tax might have a curve resembling the one depicted below on the left; which the personal income tax might have a curve more closely resembling the one depicted below on the right, which peaks at a much higher point. Moreover, the curve below on the right appears fairly straight at the beginning, indicating that initially, increases in the tax rate do not do much to alter [income-producing] behavior. But why would this be the case?

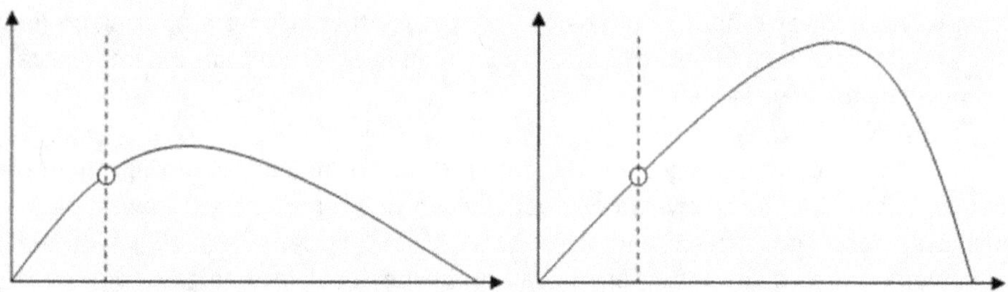

Here, it comes down to the *marginal utility* of each dollar. For the person with little income, each individual dollar represents a larger share of their total income than it does for the wealthy person—each scarce dollar is more important to them to satisfy their needs. Consequently, an increase in their tax rate—for example, from 10% to 20%—might not do much to change their income-producing behavior; indeed, they might even seek to work more if they absolutely need that money to pay the rent. But the wealthier person, who is already able to pay their rent and satisfy their other needs, has a lower *marginal value* for each additional dollar they earn; and consequently, they value their leisure time at a higher rate. The increase in the tax rate reduces the value of their work hours as compared to their leisure hours.

The trade-off between work hours (that is, productive, or income-producing hours) and leisure hours is experienced at all income levels, and we do see lower-income individuals also respond to changes in the price—which is why workers need to be paid overtime for extra hours. Now a worker who is paid time-and-a-half is more incentivized to work extra than a worker who gets the same rate of pay for the additional work; and a worker who is paid double time is more incentivized still; yet even poor people will sometimes turn down double time pay on some occasions (for example, they may prefer spending Christmas with their families to making double time at the store). Thus we have experiential evidence (that conforms to fundamental economic theory) that people change their productive behavior according to the price.

Consequently, if we were to tax overtime earnings, we should expect the aggregate of all workers to work fewer overtime hours, with some workers preferring their leisure time to the now-lower-value of extra work. And if you encounter someone who insists that increases in income tax rates do not reduce work hours, just challenge them with a few questions: would you pick up an additional shift at work if that shift paid 10% less than what you are used to making? 15% less? 20% less? And if all of your working hours paid less, how many hours would you be willing to work before you decided to change your budget? 45? 50? 55?

For while the declining marginal value of work is more readily apparent with overtime hours, it applies to all earnings. As an hour of income-producing activity becomes less valuable, people—in aggregate—will exchange some of those hours for more leisure time. And if the new tax rates result in their regular earnings becoming insufficient to meet the needs of their chosen lifestyle (including rent, clothes, food, entertainments, and everything else), many will choose to live more frugal lifestyles rather than choosing to work additional hours (for example, by moving in with parents or roommates to reduce living expenses). Consequently, personal income tax rates *do* produce a Laffer Curve; although a change in the lowest tax bracket may do less to change taxpayer behavior than a change in the highest bracket may.

Wealthier businessmen might forego additional income not only because they prefer leisure hours, but for other reasons also. For example, in 1960, George Romney (father of 2012 presidential candidate Mitt Romney) declined a $100,000 bonus (about $850,000 in 2019 dollars) offered to him by his company. He cited social reasons—he didn't think any businessman "needed" such income—but it must've occurred to him also that this $100,000 bonus was only going to net him $9,000, since the tax rate on the highest income bracket at that time was 91%. Romney the businessman knew that it would cost his company $100,000 to pay him only $9,000—*not* a particularly efficient use of scarce funds. So he declined the bonus (he ended up declining some $268,000 in pay over a five-year period); and the federal government missed out on $91,000 in personal income tax revenue from the foregone bonus.

We have evidence of changes in behavior because the top tax rates have been changed so often. We saw a particularly significant change when President Kennedy cut the top tax rate from 90% to 71%: total federal revenues actually increased (since the 91% marginal tax rate was to the right of the peak of the Laffer Curve), deficits shrank, and the nation's economy experience a surge of new growth. We saw it again when Reagan brought the top marginal rate down from 70% to 28%: between 1980 and 1988, total tax revenue from those making more than $200,000 quintupled. (Note: these two examples are so often cited in arguments that tax cuts pay for themselves, that I would reiterate here that only *sometimes* cuts in tax rates generate more revenue—specifically, when the initial rate is beyond the peak of the Laffer Curve—but in other instances, when the initial tax rate is at or below the peak, the tax cut will only result in reduced revenue.)

Meanwhile Canada has recently provided an example of the opposite process. In 2015, they raised their top tax rate (affecting income above $140,000) from 29% to 33%, anticipating an additional $3 billion in revenue on the assumption that people would *not* change their behavior. But the wealthiest 1% of Canadians did in fact change their income-producing behavior, resulting in a *loss* of revenue for the Canadian government of $4.6 billion dollars, as more than 30,000 Canadians dropped out of that tax bracket and others simply reduced their taxable income within that bracket. (Important to note here is that some amount of this revenue loss was the result of wealthy people choosing to realize some of their income prior to when the new rates took effect, so the 2016 drop was larger than subsequent years. But the net result years later was still less revenue than anticipated, a reduction in the Canadian tax base, a smaller private sector, and reduced competitiveness with its neighbor to the south.)

Changes in personal income tax rates inevitably impact income-producing behavior, with higher rates resulting in fewer hours spent in income-producing work. While the change in behavior is most noticeable at high tax rates, and at the borders of tax brackets (where people are more acutely aware of the change in the value of each additional hour of work), even among lower tax rates people will make different decisions about how much time they spend working versus how much time they spend in leisure. Collectively, this means that higher tax rates slow overall economic growth, while lower tax rates encourage it.

Unfortunately, we will not observe this as an instant effect in a nation's economy the year after a change in tax rates, as many economic policies and factors in addition to tax rates will impact economic growth; but we can review a comparison of different nations, and observe that similarly-sized nations with lower tax rates tend to experience faster economic growth than their counterparts with higher rates—but even here, the correlation is not satisfactory to critics, because they can likewise assert that a myriad of other economic policies and factors were at play. But while the data on economic growth can be ascribed to so many factors besides tax rates, we can anticipate certain expected results simply by applying the fundamental economic principle that people will change their behavior according to their circumstances, in order to better accomplish their goals (such as obtaining what they believe is a better quality of life through the use of their scarce money resources). And from this principle we can expect the following:

1. Wealthy people will preserve some amount of their income from taxation by taking advantage of tax shelters, using available deductions, and moving income to other places or sources; and these actions tend to reduce the formation of capital (such as investment money) available to the economy.

2. Since capital formation is a major driver of real wages, a reduction in capital formation will tend toward lower average wages.

3. People (not every individual person, but people in aggregate) will work fewer hours, resulting in less overall wealth production / less economic growth; and

4. Some amount of people will emigrate to lower-tax jurisdictions (this will be most common among those who already spend much of their lives in other jurisdictions).

We may also anticipate other effects based upon historical precedent (these are *not* certain based upon fundamental economic principles, but are nevertheless nearly certain based upon prior experience):

1. Increases in tax rates for the wealthiest people will be followed by increases in tax rates for less-wealthy people.

2. Overall complexity of the tax code will increase, as politicians seek to disguise tax impacts or at least shift them to less significant voting blocs, and as those most impacted by the highest rates find more incentive to lobby for specific breaks carved out of the tax code to fit their personal income arrangements.

Beyond the change in tax rates, there are many other aspects of the tax code which have significant impacts upon the economy. As we discussed earlier, the various deductions allowed for income do much to incentivize particular economic behaviors, such as buying a home, or creating a medical savings account. Such "savings" become more important to taxpayers as their tax rates increases. But the savings here translate into higher prices in housing (as demand for housing increases, price increases), so the deduction in the tax code translates into a price distortion in the market—and a tax savings enjoyed by the wealthy becomes a price paid by the less wealthy (those who choose to buy a home, but who do not benefit from the special deduction).

Finally, there is one other economic impact that actually can be quantified [relatively] easily: that is the cost of tax compliance. Currently, the tax preparation industry earns some $10 billion dollars annually; and Americans will spend more than two and a half billion hours just on filing their personal taxes. Now the value of those two and a half billion hours cannot be computed (presumably, those hours represent lost leisure time, rather than lost income-producing time; and besides, each person's hours are valued differently); but the $10 billion dollars spent on hiring tax professionals and the like is an identifiable sum that, under a simpler system, could be spent on real wealth—computers or clothes or toys or education or anything else taxpayers would freely choose to purchase with their own dollars.

International Taxation and the Exit Tax

While most countries in the world only tax their citizens on money earned within their borders, the United States asserts the power to tax their citizens living abroad on all the income they make outside of US jurisdiction. This includes people born American citizens abroad due to having citizen parents, but who live their entire lives abroad without ever setting foot in the United States. (Additionally, the United States also taxes noncitizens who have had a "significant presence" in the US within the prior three years.) While the US does allow a tax credit for taxes paid to foreign governments, this does not always work out dollar-for-dollar as advertised, and Americans abroad consequently experience increased taxation.

This tax burden is onerous enough that more than four thousand wealthy Americans renounced their citizenship in 2015, followed by another five thousand in 2016 and another five thousand in 2017. Most of these renunciations were made for tax purposes. But the United States government, unhappy to lose such tax revenue, makes sure to charge an Exit Tax on persons renouncing their US citizenship if they have a net worth of $2 million or more: the IRS determines the value of the expatriate's assets as if they were sold on the day they renounce citizenship, and then taxes that. (They also will continue to levy income tax on these individuals for the next 10 years if they spend more than 30 days in a year within the United States.)

The United States also goes after less wealthy individuals renouncing their citizenship as well, by charging a $2,350 fee for renouncing or relinquishing citizenship (or more than 20 times what other high-income countries tend to charge, while many other countries charge nothing at all).

State Income Tax

The United States Federal Government is not the only governing entity within its borders which collects income tax; forty-three states also levy this tax as well. (Some states fund their governments through sales taxes, some through property taxes, and some through income taxes; some states use a combination of these options—California, for example, collects all three types.) While eight of these states charge a flat tax rate (all taxable income is taxed at the same percentage rate), the remaining thirty-five have progressive income tax systems similar to the federal government, some with fewer brackets, some with more.

As with high sales tax rates, each state's income tax rates are limited by the competition of other states: for wealthier and more mobile people may relocate to another state with a lower rate. In 2016, a net amount of

State	Top Marginal Rate as of 2019
California	13.3% on income over $1,000,000
Hawaii	11% on income over $48,000
New Jersey	10.75% on income over $500,000
Oregon	9.9% on income over $125,000
Minnesota	9.85% on income over $156,911
New York	8.82% on income over $1,077,550

about 280,000 household (almost 600,000 people) migrated from the 25 higher-tax states to the 25 lower-tax states. New Yorkers move to New Hampshire, or more often Florida, neither of which have an income tax (in fact, while New York receives more international immigrants than any other state, it loses a greater amount of population to out-migration to other states). Californians move most frequently to Texas, Nevada, or Washington, all of which are without an income tax. Such movement has increased as a result of the recent cap to the State and Local Tax (SALT) deduction, which places a greater pressure on states to limit their own taxes (and spending, presumably)—although the most immediate effect of the change to SALT was to increase federal tax revenues. Tax migration can have a significant on states' budgets, particularly when it results in revenues coming in under the projected figures.

As with federal income tax, state income tax also has impacts upon productivity. But the most immediate impact might be simply the size of each state's government, with higher rates generally supporting more expansive governments with more spending programs. Interestingly enough, however, there does not seem to be much relationship between tax rates and government debt: for the high-tax states of New York and California have still managed to contract the largest amounts of debt ($374 billion and $452 billion respectively) despite their higher tax revenues; while no-income-tax states Florida and Texas also have contracted large debts ($107 billion and $313 billion respectively). Total debt seems to be much more correlated with overall population (the size of the tax base) than with tax rate, as states with higher potential income are able to borrow more freely.

Tax Incidence

As noted earlier, the progressive tax brackets in the United States income tax code (and many other countries' income tax codes also) shift the majority of the tax burden to the wealthier portion of the population. This makes sense to many Americans in the abstract; but the particulars are not so easy: just how much of the tax burden should be shifted to the wealthy? And what constitutes wealthy?

According to income tax data released by the IRS for the 2012 tax year, a little over 45% of American households had zero tax liability (and most of these were eligible to negative income tax through the Earned Income Tax Credit). In the years since then, this number has edged closer to 50%; so when we talk about protecting "the poor" from undue taxation, we must recognize that our current tax regime excuses nearly half of all Americans from the tax burden entirely. (Unfortunately, this is not the perception of many of those excused: because their negative income tax is termed a "refund," they image that they are receiving back their own money, instead of being given money by the federal government, so many net-tax-recipients continue under the notion that they are taxpayers, since they are aware that some amount is deducted from their paychecks, but not aware that a greater amount is being returned to them.)

But the shift continues: if we look at the top half of the top half, we discover that this quarter of American households paid about 86% of all personal income taxes in 2012. Narrowing our search further, we discover that most of these taxes even were paid for by the top 10% of households [making over $125,000 annually], who by themselves paid 70% of all taxes. Cutting that group in half, we discover the top 5% of households [making over $175,000 annually] paid by themselves almost 60% of the personal income tax burden. Looking finally at the hated 1% (e.g. the 1.37 million households in 2012 who earned $435,000 or more), we discover they paid 38% of the nation's personal income tax bill all by themselves.

Tellingly, politicians do not advertise this arrangement when they issue calls to make the rich pay their "fair share."

Ethical Considerations

Before considering our standard ethical dimensions for income tax, it is important to note that all of these are impacted by an additional dimension not yet discussed in detail: size. Size of tax was not selected as an agreeable ethical dimension, since people have wildly different opinions about how high tax rates can go and still be "reasonable" to them. Almost all of us agree that representative taxation is preferable to unrepresentative taxation; but a poll of any ten people might yield ten different answers about the appropriate size/rate for taxation in general. Significantly, such differences in opinion about tax rates are closely tied to differences in opinion about how much government is desired: a person who wants very limited government will only brook a small tax rate, while another person who believes in the value of larger government with welfare benefits (including social security, Medicare, etc.) will need a higher rate to pay for all of that. These two individuals are likely to argue with each other about the most ethical tax rate for a given tax; but truly they really are arguing about the most ethical size of government. However:

This text is *not* about resolving the size-of-government debate.

The exercise of this text is to help people consider taxation from an ethical perspective, and to motivate them to search for more ethical forms of taxation—using a framework that nearly all Americans can find some common ground and shared values, whether they support small government or large government, and no matter what their other political preferences.

But the size of the personal income tax presents us with a challenge: for should we discover that this kind of tax performs poorly on our ethical criteria, advocates of large government will be threatened. The small-government advocate will simply cite this as evidence in favor of a smaller government; but the large-government advocate depends upon some larger minimum amount of tax revenue being available to fund their ideal government—and therefore may find it psychologically difficult to consider that the primary means of funding that government has some ethical shortcomings. It *must* be ethical, you see, because the good government *needs* to be funded.

I therefore invite advocates of larger government to approach this section in the following manner: do *not* imagine all ethical criticisms of income tax to be criticisms of your ideal government, and do *not* reject them *a priori* as beyond consideration; but instead devote yourselves to imagining how the tax system might be reformed to alleviate the ethical difficulties. Perhaps some difficulties are insoluble—but others might have solutions within our power. Perhaps we can at least make incremental change toward a system more acceptable to all.

With this in mind, let us turn our attention to our first fundamental American principle of taxation, that taxation with representation is preferable to taxation without representation. How does the personal income tax measure up to that?

We are not off to a good start. Recalling what we learned about tax incidence, we must recognize that we are very nearly to the point that a simple majority of voters will be able to tell a minority of voters to pay all of the tax (although, this is an improvement over the situation in the early days of the income tax, when a supermajority of voters paid no income tax). And with more than 80% of the personal income tax being paid by only one-fourth of the voters, we [permanently?] have a situation in which the government that serves the whole of the people is supported by just a fraction of the people, always outnumbered by voters who can demand changes to the tax rates of the minority while bearing no consequence themselves.

But, one may object, the richer people have always had greater political access—that is, more representation—and in light of that maybe this situation is not so unbalanced as the numbers superficially suggest. Let us consider this statement to be true for the sake of argumentation: what further can we discover from this? First, we must note that this augmented representation does not apply to all tax payers, but only to the very rich, leaving a huge number of middle-class Americans and small business owners without this safety, and therefore vulnerable to both the voting bloc of non-taxpayers and the political power of the exceedingly wealthy—in Revolutionary terms, taxation without representation. Second, we must also recognize that for the very wealthy to maintain this representative advantage, they must divert considerable sums of their money to buying political influence—amounts which are not counted as "taxes," but which are still part of the cost of taxation (only these amounts do not fund good government, but rather line the pockets of politicians instead).

So long as the taxpayers vote in a single bloc (but of course they don't, because they do not agree on other political issues), the taxpaying citizens have some defense—they still make up the majority of voters. Politicians trying to fund the government (which is currently running a budget deficit) would face a difficult task if they attempted to raise all the income tax rates at once; but the progressive structure of the income tax allows them to raise tax rates on smaller populations at a time. This means there is perpetually the opportunity to combine the non-taxpayers with those in the lower brackets to raise the rates on the higher brackets; or to combine the voters on opposite ends to raise the rates on the lower tax brackets (which can actually generate more overall revenue, since there are so many more taxpayers in those brackets and a smaller Laffer Curve impact for those earners). In actual practice, this has been difficult at the national level, because it turns out that culturally, distaste for taxes is so common that even a great number of non-taxpaying Americans vote against tax increases. At the state level, several states have had greater success.

Meanwhile the whole contest (and it is a contest) impacts our Peace criterion badly—in that there is no peace. The politicians who attempt to rally the votes of the non-taxpayers to raise the tax rates on the wealthy ferment both envy and enmity among the populace, ever pitting the rich against the poor. Some among the rich pour lobbying dollars into the government to excuse themselves from portions of the tax burden; and then others among the rich recognize that they too must pour money into lobbying the government in order to protect themselves from having additional tax burden placed upon them. This incentivizes them to regard both the poor as their enemy (who vote to raise their taxes without bearing any consequence themselves), and the better-connected rich as their enemy also (who more effectively lobby government to shift the tax burden to other rich people—or to the middle class, who are less able to lobby). There is no peace in this process of trying to ensure that government is funded by other people. And—here is where the size of the government exacerbates the problem—the bigger the government (that is, the more tax revenue needed), the more significant the threat/burden. From the perspective of peace, the progressive tax system becomes increasingly problematic as tax rates go up and the number of tax brackets are multiplied.

The perpetual political contest has negative impacts for our Honesty criteria as well: for politicians are incentivized to hide from voters any information that could cost them re-election; so politicians hide and/or lie about tax increases that impact their own constituencies, and promise to raise taxes on *other* people who are not their primary constituency. Meanwhile they tirade about "loopholes" exploited by the rich—as if there are all sorts of accidental oversights in the tax code which could be closed, when in fact nearly every one of these "loopholes" is a specifically designed feature of the system, to count income/deductions in a specific way (often to serve specific constituencies, economic goals, or other political ends).

But one might point out that as politicians are similarly incentivized to lie about everything else, we cannot single out the personal income tax here; so let us confine ourselves to problems that are structurally related to the personal income tax:

First, there are the refundable tax credits (such as the Child Tax Credit and the Earned Income Tax Credit) which transfer money from taxpayers to non-taxpayers, but are termed "refunds," as if the non-taxpayers were getting back money previously collected from them. When a person's "refund" is greater than the amount they contributed, that makes them a net tax-recipient, not a tax payer; yet politicians from both major political parties call this a refund instead of a transfer payment or negative income tax—and when this "refund" is increased (most recently, with the Tax Cuts and Jobs Act), politicians call it a "tax cut" instead of a spending increase (although it is correctly identified on the official budget as a transfer payment administered through the tax code).

Second, there are the "temporary" tax provisions that get extended each time they expire—after lobbying funds are collected. Such tax extenders would be more accurately termed tax extortions, insofar as they require a lobbying fee just to maintain current law. Pay up, or we change the law to your disadvantage.

Structurally, personal income taxes are partially hidden from the public through the process of withholding. Now one might reasonably point out that a taxpayer can look at their paycheck to observe exactly how much was withheld, and can review their own tax documents to count exactly how much their government costs them in personal income tax each year—and this is strictly correct—but much of human perception is based upon felt experience, and the withholding process removes from the taxpayer the experiential awareness of the cost of their government, as people must budget from their net after-tax income, and use no mental effort to set aside savings for a tax bill—as people had to do in the early days of income taxation, before withholding was introduced. Paying the cost of government in installments like this made the overall price seem more bearable, thus enabling much higher rates.

Withholding also collects tax revenue from some who wouldn't owe any tax, since many poorer people who still get taxes withheld from their paycheck fail to reclaim these amounts by filing a federal tax return at the end of the year. If you wonder why they could possibly fail to do so, know that many simply do not believe it to be worth the hours of time and effort it would require to get some unknown amount of money back. And if you still wonder why anyone would fail to pursue not only their own money, but also the several thousand in refundable tax credits they might also receive if they just filed a return—then you have an ally in the local governments, who desperately want all their poor people to file income tax returns so that their "refund" money will be spent locally, promoting the local economy.

Helping the Poor Claim their Refundable Tax Credits

County and city governments are well aware that people eligible to refundable tax credits nevertheless fail to file their returns; so many launch advertising campaigns to motivate them to file, and even offer free tax preparation services in order to get more people to file returns. San Bernardino County in California, for example, diverts hundreds of its county employees every year from their normal jobs to instead prepare free tax returns for people who are likely to be net tax recipients. Yes, this is costly to the county—both in labor hours lost to other government activities, and because they hire additional help for this annual task, and pay overtime hours for it. But from their point of view, the millions of dollars in refundable tax credits make it worth it, because those "refunds" are spent on local businesses, promoting local jobs—and contributing to local sales tax collected.

Additionally, the withholding process has the added ethical problem that the government pays no interest to the taxpayers for withholding their money early for when their taxes are due. Had taxpayers the option to save for this bill, they could earn money at interest; and if the government feared that taxpayers would fail to save for this bill—and surely many would—it could alternatively require them to save for it, and let them earn interest on their savings. But instead, the government takes it and spends it immediately, before it is officially due, so the taxpayer is cheated of their interest.

Beyond the matter of withholding, one cannot ever say that the US income tax system is open, simply on account of the massive complexity of it. And the complexity is stupendous: 2,600+ pages of statues, 6,000+ pages of IRS regulations and revenue rulings, and 60,000+ pages of case law—so much law that not even the agents of the IRS can keep track of it. Literally: journalists have on multiple occasions decided to test the IRS agents on this by calling the IRS at different times, asking the same tax questions of different agents—and getting different responses. Which problem would be bad enough; but it is made Kafkaesque by the fact that a taxpayer can obey explicit instructions from an IRS agent, and then *still* be found to be in error, *and held liable!*

With the tax rules being so complex, and the multiple forms and schedules and several hours of research and paperwork required, many opt to pay the additional cost of hiring a professional. But the professionals also have trouble keeping up with all the rules and regulations and case law; and journalists have documented inconsistencies among their results as well. Still, hiring a tax professional is worth it to many taxpayers (particularly those who have multiple sources of income, or who wish to take advantage of more deductions), as it significantly increases their chances of their tax return being prepared correctly. But having to pay for a professional preparer is like paying an additional tax on top of your tax—and where else do we regard it as both normal and acceptable to have a law that requires people to pay extra money just so they can increase their still-uncertain-chances of understanding and obeying the law??

A simple error in a tax return which results in underpayment of tax (as calculated by the IRS auditors, who may or may not be correct) will first result in the IRS charging you *both* a late fee *and* interest on the amount owed; and if they determine (by their own judgment) that your error was the result of "negligence," they will add another 20% to your penalty. Failing to understand the law perfectly and correctly compute your tax liability is no joke: the IRS can take direct enforcement action, including seizing portions of your income or even seizing some of your property directly from your bank. (You can appeal their decisions, of course—to the Appeals Court *within the IRS.* Or try to take them to federal Tax Court, which can easily take more than year, during which time the IRS still holds your money without interest.)

Now the enforcement power of the IRS might be quite acceptable *if* the tax law was simple enough to understand and comply with; but allowing this power to an agency which often fails at interpreting its own rules is an egregious wrong. And giving it to an agency which presides over changing regulations (regulations change not only when Congress passes new law, but also when the IRS itself has to specify details, clarify, and issue guidance on that law; and also with case law resulting from court decisions) is a further problem, since Americans often must purchase this knowledge in order to comply with it (no individual can keep up with all the laws themselves, so they have to hire tax professionals and lawyers to do so for them—effectively, "purchasing" the ability to know and comply with the law). True, somewhat more than half of Americans do not need to make this purchase (either because they have no tax liability, or because their taxes are simple enough not to be affected); but is it ethical to require any portion of the citizenry to purchase the ability to understand and comply with the law—and then still hold them liable when that purchase is insufficient (because both the tax professionals and the IRS may make mistakes)?

If this was the end of our ethical examination, we would already have a significant case against the personal income tax (at least to reform it, for those people who are irrevocably committed to keeping it as a necessary revenue source); but we have some additional concerns yet:

Federal taxes—that is, nationwide taxes—under our current government run afoul of the appropriateness criteria (it is more ethical to tax the population receiving the benefits of the government than it is to tax another population). Now in the days of smaller, more limited government, this was not the case: a national tax provided solely for national services, such as the defense budget, the federal courts, and specific enumerated powers in the Constitution. And insofar as our national taxes continue to pay for these things, national taxes are entirely appropriate; however, the current government also does many other things which involve distributing specific benefits locally, or block-granting funds to states for them to spend locally: consequently, some states send more tax money to the federal government than they receive back to fund their mandated programs (such as education and Medicare/Medicaid), while other states receive more than they spend. Donor states (or "losers") include New York, New Jersey, Illinois, and Minnesota; the worst receive less than 70 cents back for every dollar they pay. Beneficiary states ("winners") include states like Kentucky, Mississippi, and New Mexico, all of which receive well over $1.50 for every dollar they contribute. But of course the big winner is Washington, D.C., which receives more than $4 for every dollar its citizens contribute. (Numbers change somewhat with demographics; you can check the most recent federal tax data from the Office of Budget and Management and the most recent spending data from the Consolidated Federal Funds Report published by the US Department of Commerce.)

Thus the federal income tax moves income from some states to other states, taxing some geographic populations to pay for others. And, of course, it moves a lot of that income to itself—6 of the nation's 10 wealthiest counties are suburbs of Washington, D.C.—and to important voting areas which can be swayed by federal projects. Now state income tax systems do this also, on a reduced scale; and we noted that in the discussion of sales tax. So we may say that this particular ethical problem is not intrinsic to the personal income tax, but rather intrinsic to the size and scope of the taxation—which we must acknowledge here, given that the federal income tax is by far the nation's largest tax in size and scope.

Being so large in size and scope, any economic harms created by the tax are amplified. But focusing specifically on elements that are intrinsic to the personal income tax, we note that as a progressive tax on production (income) as opposed to a flat tax on consumption (sales), the income tax actually discourages the production of wealth. This effect may well be entirely negligible at low rates; but as tax rates increase, additional work/income beyond what is necessary to meet needs becomes less valuable to the earner. The progressive rate structure amplifies this by raising the rates at multiple points of productivity; and people do avoid being bumped into a higher tax bracket by additional income, since that income is less valuable to them than what they are used to, and the effort to make that income competes with other uses of time and energy.

That said, the federal personal income tax in the United States is not as bad as it could be: a proposal from the 2019 governor of Illinois involved changing his state's flat tax rate (of 4.95%) to a progressive system which would include a rate of 7.95% for those making more than one million dollars annually that would apply to *all* of their income, rather than only to income earned above $1,000,000. Under his proposal, a person making exactly $1,000,000 would pay $70,935, but earning a single dollar more would raise their tax bill by more than $8,000, to $79,500. This type of progressive system is atrocious (in terms of economic consequences); immediately it would incentivize entrepreneurs and other highly-productive individuals to leave the state, and this loss would reduce the economic opportunity for all those that remain. (Such tax flight is not so big a concern at the national level, for the US federal government simply needs to make sure tax rates remain lower than its competitors— England, France, and any other country wealthy Americans might move to if threatened with high enough taxation—to reduce the danger of this economic harm.)

Finally, the progressive tax structure also turns the income tax into a potential weapon of punishment against the rich—although politicians prefer to avoid the word "punish." You have doubtless heard rhetoric that demonizes the wealthy. And while rhetorical demonization can be found everywhere, it is a particular problem when the "demons" belong to a specific tax bracket that can applied against their presumed evil.

Summary Report Card – [Progressive] Income Taxes

Representation/Participation   **Highly Problematic**

Since the tax burden is concentrated upon so few, a majority of voters get to urge their elected representatives to set tax policy for a minority of voters.

Honesty   **Flatly Unethical**

Politicians wantonly lie about income tax policies and figures. Cash payments which transfer money from one group of people to another are termed "refunds."

Openness   **Poor**

Collecting income tax through withholding of earnings disguises the price of government from the taxpayers.

Simplicity   **Stupendously Unethical**

The tax code is so stupendously complex that no one can understand it all, and even trained tax preparers—and IRS agents!—provide different answers. *The IRS may give you incorrect advice, then penalize you for following their instructions!*

Appropriateness   **Fail**

Income taxes are collected at a national level; but many of the benefits get concentrated in the most populated areas, or those areas where votes are most needed to win Congressional elections—and, of course, in Washington, D.C.
Some states gain from the national collection and redistribution; others lose.

Consideration   **Pass**

The poor are exempted from the personal income tax burden. So are many who are not poor—nearly half of the citizenry all told.

Minimizing Harms   **Fail**

Income tax has more negative economic effects than consumption tax; it reduces the incentive to produce wealth. Meanwhile the great number of deductions, temporary rules, and specific rulings distort market prices and cause instability.

Justice   **Problematic**

Some voters and pundits specifically call for higher tax rates on the rich to punish them. The progressive tax structure makes this possible.

Peace   **Flatly Unethical**

The progressive tax structure pits people against each other, so that different groups always have the promise of making other groups pay for tax increases. The poor are told they can make the rich pay for everything (their "fair share," and the rich feel constantly under siege from looters.

Flat Tax

It must be noted that income tax does not *have* to be structured in multiple tax brackets which get progressively higher as income increases: it could be based upon a single rate paid by all people, regardless of income. This would eliminate the ethical problems of representation and participation, because everyone would be voting on their own tax rate—trying to increase another person's taxes would increase one's own as well. Consequently, it would also settle the justice and peace issues as well, since every voter/taxpayer would be allied with each other in the same group, instead of pitted against one another. Such a task would easily pass the openness criteria—for everyone would know the tax rate—and also be the simplest form of tax, eliminating all the evils that stem from the incomprehensible complexity of the current code. And by keeping a constant rate, it would reduce the economic harms that result from progressively higher rates deterring the creation of wealth.

What about consideration for the poor? Theoretically, a flat tax could still allow a sizeable exemption of baseline income for necessities; for example, initial income up to the poverty line, or even twice the poverty line, could be exempt from taxation—although the higher the exemption, the more the proposal edges back into the ethical problems created by progressive tax breaks.

But if a flat tax rate is so superior—from an ethical standpoint—to the progressive rate, why is it not adopted?

Because any flat tax proposal faces a possibly intractable set of problems: price, and self-interest. For in order to generate the same revenue as the current system, a flat tax would have to be set upwards of 20%, currently around 25%, but probably higher given the current projected spending increases as the American population ages and more people retire. Such a rate would be a massive tax increase for most Americans, while the wealthiest 1% would experience a tax break. So for most Americans, it is simply in their self-interest to keep a progressive tax system; and for many Americans, it is simply unconscionable—not from a reasoned ethical calculus, but from a more primitive emotional reaction—that the "rich" should get any tax relief if the less rich have to pay more. So any flat tax proposal, despite all of its other economic and particularly ethical advantages, is practically impossible, given our current level of government spending, our current cultural attitudes regarding inequality, and our culture's current level of comfort with envy and class enmity.

But what if it were possible to maintain the government with a lower tax rate—say, 10%? Would a flat tax be acceptable to the American public then? Then we must recognize that consideration of the ethics of taxation requires us to consider the ethics of government spending as well.

8

Business and Corporate Income Taxes

The United States income tax code does not just cover taxes on individuals, but also on businesses, and much of the complexity of that code is specifically related to defining and evaluating business income. For what is business income—is it total revenue (amount of money received from customers), or is it gross profit (revenue minus costs of goods) or is it net profit (gross profit minus all other expenses)? If net profit, do all expenses reported by the business count, or only particular expenses allowed by the government—what, exactly, constitutes an "expense"? And do these definitions change from industry to industry? The income tax code addresses all of these questions and hundreds (or thousands) more—hence many of the 5,000 changes to the tax code made between 2001 and 2013—such as how depreciation is defined for buildings and capital equipment, and how losses in one year can be accounted for on the tax returns in subsequent years, etc.

Definitions are Difficult

Some self-employed individuals, and some small business owners, make little enough profit that they apply for public benefits, including cash aid (welfare), food stamps, and/or Medicaid. Interestingly, each of these programs have their own rules for determining a business's expenses and net profit—which don't agree with the tax rules.

It is not possible for voters to become well-informed about all of these decisions—about not only the tax questions, but also how answers might differ between one industry and another—to make this a voting matter when selecting a representative. Indeed, it is complex enough that even the elected representatives cannot always (or often?) make informed decisions about specific details in the tax code; so they must entrust themselves to others—staff analysts, experts from the industries in question (who are often, though not always, registered lobbyists), and members of party leadership—to determine their votes. But it *is* possible for voters to be concerned with the underlying *values* which drive these decisions, and make decisions about who to represent them based upon that.

Description and Purpose

Business taxation takes many forms; besides the taxation of income—which differs according to how the business is structured—several other types of tax are also levied on businesses at not only the federal level, but also at the state and local levels; and businesses are further required to collect taxes on behalf of state and local governments through the sales tax. Running a business requires the owner to be aware of and comply with all of these different tax policies, not only in their own city and state, but also in every region they do business with.

Dishonest Discussion of Business Taxes

Different businesses have different excise taxes they must pay on their various products (often goods, but sometimes services, too). These excise taxes, as discussed earlier, may be applied for all sorts of political reasons, from simple revenue collection to trying to change consumer/producer behavior to tilting a particular competition in favor of one's own constituents, and more. To keep up with them all (and to prevent one's own business from being disadvantaged), businesses hire lobbyists (if they can afford them) and lawyers. But sometimes, the excise taxes are not very clear, and the IRS has to create a new policy.

In the aviation industry, there is an excise tax on every domestic flight sold by an "aircraft management company" to a passenger—a "ticket" tax. But when this excise tax was created (it was set at 8% in 1972, later changed to 10%, and has been 7.5% since 1997), the law was not clear about whether or not it applied to companies who maintain and staff private jets on behalf of the jet's owner. Did these companies count as "aircraft management companies" subject to the ticket tax? They didn't sell tickets; and the passengers were the owners of the aircraft. Consequently, no ticket tax was collected from them.

Until March of 2012, when the IRS decided that it should have been collecting these taxes all along, and was ready to charge businesses for years of back taxes. This reversal would have been financially disastrous to many companies, so a five year lobbying battle was waged to clarify the law with the previous standard, until July 2017, when the IRS decided it would stop trying to collect these taxes.

In November of 2017, Congress introduced tax reform that, among many other things, officially codified this policy, ending the legal uncertainty and restoring the status quo of the past several decades. So how was that described by the press? As the GOP giving another tax break to the rich, of course—a "tax break for private jet owners." After all, anger-mongering sells more papers than does accuracy. Now sometimes, a newspaper article might acknowledge in the body of the article that the "tax break for the rich" indicated in the article's headline was in fact only codifying the IRS practice of decades; and voters always read the body of the article, don't they? Meanwhile snopes.com also acknowledged that there was no tax break here—no taxes were being reduced, only the longstanding IRS policy was being formalized in law—yet *still* rated the "tax cut for the private jet owners" claim as "mostly true," because the original legislation spared them a tax burden borne by ticket-buying passengers. Was the editor lying here, or just confused? Or maybe it was like Obi-wan Kenobi says: "true—from a certain point of view."

For businesses owned by sole proprietors, partnerships, and small corporations meeting particular criteria (termed S Corporations), income is taxed not as the income of the particular business, but as the income of the sole proprietor, the partners, or the shareholders of the S Corporation; this is what is termed *pass-through* business income. For larger corporations (more than 100 shareholders), and for all corporations in particular categories (e.g. financial institutions, no matter their size), their profit/income first gets taxed as the corporation's income, before being taxed again as the shareholders' income. Besides these income taxes, businesses are also subject to:

- Payroll taxes (addressed more specifically in a later chapter)
- Unemployment/worker's comp taxes (amounts vary by state)
- Excise taxes (varies by product)
- Local Income taxes (varies by city/state), and
- Regulatory fees (which are effective taxes, though not termed taxes)

Dividend Income

When a corporation pays dividends to their shareholders, it is paying them their share of the company's profits. Some countries allow certain businesses structures to deduct these payments from their profits before paying taxes on what is left (the retained income); but in other countries—like the United States—corporations are not allowed to deduct the dividends paid out prior to figuring their taxes; therefore the same profit gets taxed twice, first as corporate income at whatever the corporate income tax rate is, then again as dividend income at whatever separate rate has been established for dividends.

(Originally, the United States did allow dividends to be deducted, specifically to prevent double taxation of income; but this was changed in 1936, and that government has been double taxing this income ever since.)

The corporate income tax was first passed in the United States in 1909 for two purposes: to collect revenue (at that time, direct income tax was still unconstitutional, but the corporate income tax was counted as an excise tax instead of a direct income tax, so allowed), and to collect information on corporations to enable more effective government regulation. Today, he current tax regulations are complex enough to include various other purposes also at work—such as incentivizing certain economic choices, or trying to make a more "fair" field of competition, etc. (Meanwhile, given the complexity, one could be forgiven for imagining the purpose is to discourage new business altogether.) Again, many of these purposes and much of the complexity comes from how the regulations define income and expenses, as well as all the allowances, exemptions, and other accounting devices used to determine the final amount of tax.

A corporation's taxable income is frequently taxed at a different rate than personal income. In the United States, for example, the top corporate income tax rate as of 2019 is 21% (prior to the passing of the Tax Cuts and Jobs Act, it had been 35%); throughout the world corporate tax rates vary from nonexistent (about a dozen countries, all small) to 55%, with an average of about 23%. Like personal income taxes, corporate tax rates are often structured progressively, with higher rates applied as a corporation's income goes up. In some countries (like the United States), certain minimum rates are also set (the Corporate Alternative Minimum Tax) to stop deductions and tax credits from pushing a corporation's tax rate too low.

Most countries practice territorial taxation, in which they tax only the income earned within their own country. The United States, however, has had a longtime practice of global taxation, where it also collects tax revenues from multinational corporations on income they earn in other countries; this practice was modified recently, with the Tax Cuts and Jobs Act of 2017. Under the global tax system, multinational companies with operations in the United States would escape the extra layer of tax (on top of what they were paying to other countries for the business they did there) by re-investing profits overseas (with the funds re-invested, they no longer counted as taxable income under the US system); such businesses were often debt-heavy in the United States and cash-rich in other nations. But with the modifications made to how "foreign" income is taxed, those same corporations no longer have the same tax incentive to do that, and are now freer to make investment decisions based upon expected economic return. (Naturally, those corporations which had been most adept at navigating the prior tax regime did not welcome the change, as they lost their competitive advantage over companies injured by the prior tax law.)

Historically, corporate tax rates have varied considerably. The rate set in the United States in 1909 was only 1%; it was raised to 12% to finance WWI (afterwards only lowered to 10%). During the Great Depression, the top rate was raised to 15% (probably worsening the depression, as this certainly did *not* help to encourage job creation), and during WWII was hiked to 40% to finance that (and again, taxes enacted in times of war were not remitted in the following peace). In 1951, it was hiked again to over 50% (this time ostensibly to pay for the Korean War). In the 60's, it was briefly cut to 48%, only to be hiked back up to 52.8% to pay for the Great Society programs. That was its high point in the US: it was reduced to 48% under Nixon to fight a recession, reduced to 40% under Reagan, and again to 34% to fight recession in 1988. Under Clinton it was put back to 35%, remaining there until the reduction to 21% in 2018. Throughout this time, other countries have experimented with their corporate tax rates as well. In the United Kingdom, their rate was reduced from 52% to 34% under the leadership of Margaret Thatcher; and in the 21st century that country reduced it even further, to 28%, and then to 19% in 2010. On average, corporate tax rates have fallen worldwide since the changes began by Thatcher and Reagan.

The GILTI Tax

While the Tax Cuts and Jobs Act reduced the corporate income tax rate from 35% to 21%, making the United States much more tax-competitive in relation to other countries; 21% is still higher than the 0% in certain tax-free nations, and with the change from an extra-territorial tax system to a territorial one, certain businesses were anticipated to use intellectual property to shift profits from the United States to those foreign territories. Therefore a new definition of income was created for the tax code, known as the Global Intangible Low Tax Income (GILTI), and this income was given a top tax rate of 13.125% (still higher than 0%, but much lower than the 21% being dodged).

The particulars of the law are complex, and those who deal with the implications of the law debate whether it works as intended. But even this debate is about the details, rather than about the ethics—which is particularly interesting, given the ethical statement made by the title: GILTI, as in, a company is "guilty" of wrongdoing for trying to reduce its legal tax liability to a particular country.

Economic Effects

In a tax-free environment, every business makes production and investment decisions based upon expected return: what allocation of resources will yield the greatest profit? Different entrepreneurs will make different decisions upon their individual values—one will direct their business with an eye on short-term profits, while another focuses on long-term gains, with greater investments in capital goods; one attempts to acquire the highest-quality labor force, while another chooses to specialize in goods and/or services which can be produced by even unskilled labor; and so on. Business taxes alter these decisions by introducing new expenses to consider, de-valuing some sets of decisions and incentivizing others. In order to maintain the highest level of profit, businesses may alter investment and growth strategies to reduce their tax liability, whenever and wherever that option has a greater predicted payoff than other options for investment. The more complicated the tax laws governing business, the more numerous the changes and adjustments businesses have to make—the more they deviate from the most productive opportunities.

For multinational corporations, one way to reduce tax liability is to shift business activity and income from a high-tax jurisdiction to a low-tax jurisdiction. Some corporations will move their headquarters entirely from one country to another, sometimes merging with another company in the desired country to make such transition possible, since escaping to a lower tax rate can mean the difference of millions of dollars annually. From the perspective of low-tax nations, this is a great benefit, as it tends toward more jobs and more overall wealth being created in the low-tax country; for nations with a higher tax rate, this results in capital flight, loss of jobs and overall wealth production, and less tax collected than expected (since the emigrating companies no longer pay). Governments with higher corporate tax rates *hate* this, and often call for international tax harmonization, urging other countries to increase their rates so that everybody can maintain a higher rate. (In private business, the collusion of companies to charge a uniform higher price is termed cartelization; in international politics, it is discussed as a legitimate goal. But such hoped-for harmonization is not likely to happen so long as lower-tax nations prefer to reap all the benefits of attracting business which they get from their lower rates.)

Race to the Bottom?

The reductions in corporate income tax rates made under Reagan and Thatcher upset many in other countries, who saw immediately that multi-national businesses had a tax incentive to shift business activity and/or move their headquarters to the countries that had the lowest tax rates. This tax competition motivated many countries to lower their rates as well even though they were not initially inclined to. Some pundits observed this and predicted there would be a "race to the bottom," as the tax competition forced corporate tax rates to nothing or nearly nothing; and these pundits lamented the loss of tax revenue, expecting dire consequences for governments getting increasingly short on cash, and being forced to raise personal income and/or sales taxes to compensate for the loss.

Since the 1980's, corporate tax rates internationally have declined on average, but not to nearly 0% as feared. For while tax competition provides a downward pressure on tax rates, the need for tax revenue from sources that are popular with voters provides a counterbalancing upward pressure.

A second way businesses reduce their tax liability is by changing how they raise additional investment funds or make investments themselves. In the United States, for example, paying interest on debt is a countable business expense (interest is paid before taxes), while paying dividends is not (dividends are paid after taxes); consequently, if a corporation needs money it is less costly for them to issue bonds than it is to issue shares. This incentivizes investments in assets more readily financed by debt (like buildings, which can be used as collateral for the debt), dis-incentivizing investments more readily financed through sale of stock (like research and development, or the purchase of specialized capital equipment); and it results in established companies gaining additional advantage over new companies (since newer companies and start-ups lack the assets needed as collateral). These effects make innovation and entrepreneurial activity more difficult, slowing economic growth.

Corporate taxes also change the risk/reward calculations corporations make when considering where to expand their business, innovate their processes, and develop new technology. Investments always involve some level of risk—the new expansion, innovation, or invention might actually cost money instead of earning it—so businesses estimate their possibilities of success against the cost of their investments, and act accordingly. For example, imagine a corporation considering a $10 million investment, estimating a 50% chance of making $20 million dollars or more: mathematically, if they make multiple investments like this, they expect to profit overall. But if the anticipated taxes reduce the expected profit to less than $20 million, then they will avoid such investments, because after repeated investments they are like to end up losing money overall. The higher the corporate tax rate, the more it impacts such investment decisions, with higher rates discouraging the exploration of new (i.e. risky) ideas—and thus slowing economic growth.

Another way for businesses to reduce their tax liability is to lobby for changes to specifics in the tax code (not the overall rate, but rather the definitions and rules which govern how income and expenses are calculated); effective lobbying can result in obtaining some advantage over competitors by making sure that one's own business and accounting practices can take better advantage of the tax code than one's competitors. Meanwhile, as long as the code remains complex—and subject to change in all the minutiae—a business must divert some amount of its funds to hiring corporate tax lawyers and accountants. Meanwhile the time it takes to file all forms is time not spent on other productive business activity, resulting in an opportunity cost of nearly 3 billion hours annually in the United States alone.

Because businesses react to changes in tax laws and tax rates, increases (and decreases) in the rate frequently result in revenues quite different from what the government anticipated at the time it made the change. As tax increases result in businesses leaving a country (or just shifting assets and investments to another country), and in less overall development/growth, total tax revenue is negatively impacted—and at some point, absolute revenue actually declines. Meanwhile, when a tax cut results in more growth, and an influx of business from other countries, tax revenue is positively impacted—and in some (by no means all) cases, absolute revenue can actually increase. More commonly, however, increase in overall economic development have more latent effects: initial tax revenue may be reduced by the lower rate, but future tax revenues may be increased due to the larger, richer tax base. However, there is no way to satisfactorily determine how much economic growth is caused/stifled by any change in a tax rate (as we cannot run a parallel Earth with all other variables held constant, and compare results), so there is no universal agreement among economists about final effects. Meanwhile it is easier—and more effective for polemics—to assume a linear relationship between tax rates and revenues, and therefore argue that such-and-such reduction in rates has "cost" a nation so much in lost revenue. In truth, any such assertion of revenue losses are fantastical, based upon the assumption that businesses would have behaved in exactly the same way regardless of the differences in taxes levied upon them.

Similarly, one may read complaints that many businesses "escape" corporate income taxes by filing as S Corporations; but such complaints ignore some very significant facts: first, a business which structures itself as an S Corporation cannot raise revenue from issuing stock (they cannot have more than 100 shareholders), which tends to limit their size and growth; second, the owners still pay taxes on the their corporations' profits through the personal income tax; and third, the taxes they are "escaping" are a double taxation of the same income (since after paying the corporate income tax, they would still be liable for personal income tax for their share of the corporate profits).

Attracting Local Business

Tax competition exists not only at the international level, but also between states and between counties within states. One of the ways local governments compete for new businesses is to offer tax breaks or credits to companies considering a move to the area—build here and we'll forego taxing you so many millions of dollars—to make sure the business chooses one location over a neighboring option. From the standpoint of local politicians, this is a way to increase local business (adding jobs to the local economy—and through those jobs, people spending money subject to local sales taxes) without cost, since they are not spending any money on the enticement, but only foregoing potential revenue which would not be received anyway if the company chose to locate somewhere else. Of course, that doesn't stop critics (most frequently public sector unions, but any group which is seeking money from the county's budget) from dishonestly complaining that the county "gave" millions of dollars to the businesses enticed, or pretending that the county could have spent the [nonexistent] tax revenue on other things. How do you spend tax revenue that you never receive because the business never came to your jurisdiction? But whether those who make such arguments are knowingly lying and taking advantage of voters' naiveté, or they themselves are truly that economically ignorant (if we take them at their word, they believe that the enticed businesses would have made the exact same decisions without enticement), who can tell? Either way, economic ignorance is a major problem.

Tax Incidence

Many economics effects of corporate income taxes are difficult to measure, as they vary according to how the tax burden is distributed—and economists are not in uniform agreement about that. Recall that excise taxes and tariffs are distributed between the buyer (through higher prices) and the seller (through reduced profits), and the division between those two is impacted primarily upon the product's elasticity of demand: when buyers are less price-sensitive (such as when they perceive a need for the product and do not have or value many alternatives), they end up paying the bulk of the tax through higher prices; and when buyers are more price-sensitive (such as when they have many other alternatives available, including the alternative of simply not buying the product), the seller may end up paying the bulk of the tax through reduced profits (or, may stop selling the taxed item altogether, if the profit margin becomes too low). But a corporation typically sells many different products, and besides has many other variables impacting business decisions; and the multiplicity of variables multiplies the difficulty of determining the exact impacts of a tax, or of a change in tax rate.

However the tax burden is distributed, it is important to remember that in the end, it is *people* who pay taxes. Corporate income taxes are taxes on people; the question is simply, *which* people specifically? Is it mostly the rich CEOs and shareholders? Or is it the poorer consumers and employees? Economists may differ about how exactly the tax burden is distributed, but they virtually all agree that the tax burden is distributed among all of these groups, not simply very rich.

Meanwhile, the average voter naively assumes that corporations pay corporate income tax, and the cost stops there. Simultaneously, owners and managers often assume that the bulk of the tax is passed along to consumers in the form of higher prices—which may or may not be the case, with different businesses having different results. While this confusion and uncertainty is a headache for economists, and a very real concern for the most attentive business owners and managers trying to maximize their business, it is—from the perspective of the politicians—not a bug in the system, but an attractive feature. For so long as the tax is *perceived* to be paid by someone else, there is no great opposition to it. (As the 17th century French Minister of Finance Jean-Baptiste Colbert once said, the art of taxation "consists in so plucking the goose as to obtain the largest possible amount of feathers with the smallest possible amount of hissing.")

Since most voters are comfortable with taxes paid for by other people, the corporate income tax is pretty popular insofar as taxes go. But might they vote otherwise if they had more knowledge about how much of those taxes are paid not by other voters, but by themselves?

We know that some portion of the tax gets passed along to consumers in the form of higher prices; but we cannot provide an estimate for this which applies to all corporations, as each business is different in its power to change prices. Generally, the less competitive industries will be more able to shift prices to consumers than the more competitive industries; so the consumer portion of the tax burden is distributed unevenly among the population, with those consumers with fewer economic alternatives (generally, the poor) bearing a greater portion than those consumers with more economic alternatives (the not so poor).

The other portion of the tax burden would reduce profits—but as people like to protect their profits (their income, and the very existence of their businesses and livelihoods), owners and business managers may be able to change expenses within their business to protect their profit margin. One way they might be able to do this is by reducing the cost of employees (by reducing wages, reducing the value of benefits, laying off employees, or at the very least slowing the rate of wage growth). Industries with the greatest need for high-quality labor in a competitive market are least able to do this (the supply of labor is low enough relative to the demand that each business bids up the price of labor to get the best workers); industries able to use unskilled labor are most able to do this (since paying less for the less-effective workers has a smaller or even negligible economic cost to overall production). So the employee portion of the tax burden is also distributed unevenly—and the least-skilled employees (generally from the poorer segments of the population) bearing a greater burden.

Finally we come to the portion of the corporate income tax burden born by the owners/shareholders—probably less than half (though again, this number varies across industries, and in a particular business may be as low as a quarter or as high as three quarters). Their profits have been reduced, resulting in a lower return on their investments. But since investments are only made by the very rich, the majority of voters don't care—except, no, investments are not made by only the very rich: the middle class invest also, for their retirements, for their children's college education, and for trying to improve their own futures in other ways. Lower returns impact everybody who invests.

Lower investment returns in the corporate sector leads to some additional economic effects. People who invest seek the highest returns on their investments, so when the value of returns declines in the corporate sector, investors shift money to the non-corporate or tax-exempt sectors of the economy. This reduces the amount of investment capital available to corporations, reducing their ability to raise funds for growth; and increases the supply of capital for the non-corporate sector, with this increased supply applying a downward pressure on prices (returns). Prices equalize, and we discover that returns on investments in both the corporate and non-corporate sectors have been reduced to pay a portion of the corporate income tax burden.

Ethical Considerations

In the 18th century, corporations were frequently chartered by the government, and were granted special privileges—particularly monopoly and/or exemption from particular laws. One could easily make the ethical case in the 18th century that corporations should pay for these special privileges through a tax. However, no such privileges are afforded today's corporations: today, corporations are founded through private contract. So what is the grounds *today* for taxing corporations?

As with most taxes, the grounds is without ethical consideration: the justification is simply, the government needs revenue, and here is a potential source for revenue. It is perceived by the voting public to be an acceptable source, so we tax it. And in the United States, we tax it twice, first as corporate income tax and then again as personal income tax when the money is distributed form the corporation's account to the shareholders' individual accounts. And why do we tax it twice? Because in 1936 politicians decided that they wanted/needed the revenue, and this option was acceptable to the majority of voters, since the majority of voters would not be subject to the double taxation. These are very secure grounds for a tax from a political perspective; but from an ethical perspective, they are exceptionally weak.

In the 21st century, many more people (not just the very rich) invest in corporations; so theoretically, the tax actually does better under the criteria of representation and participation now than it did in 1936. Investors do have the ability to respond to the tax through voting; and because the burden of the tax is distributed between both the shareholders and the consumers, once could say that the whole of the population participates in this tax, albeit unevenly. Unfortunately, the lack of knowledge about how this tax is distributed, and the great variability between industries in its distribution, make both representation and participation problematic: voters cannot make *informed* decisions about this tax, and instead are directed by misinformed *perceptions* of who pays the tax.

And the perceptions are greatly misinformed. Politicians in search of tax revenue have great incentive to describe excise taxes on businesses and corporate income taxes as taxes upon the very rich—and they do. A whole class of politicians use the faceless nonperson corporation as a kind of villain and natural target for taxation, to curb "unfair" profits and inequality in income, always neglecting to disclose that attempted taxation of these profits raises consumer prices and lowers employee wages (and when their political opponents do point out these effects, the effects are just cited as further proof of corporate greed). This perpetual political hoax also means that corporate income taxes do poorly under the criteria of peace: corporate income tax rhetoric is a means of fueling class strife.

Demonization of Corporations vs. Tax Competition

If greedy, faceless corporations are so readily demonized, and voters so keen to tax other people, why aren't corporate tax rates much higher?

In the past, corporate tax rates were much higher—even being supplemented with "excess profits" and "war profits" surtaxes during both world wars—and having a highest peacetime rate in the United States of 52.8% under Lyndon Johnson. And as long as other countries had similar preferences for high tax rates, this seemed to work fine. But not every country had high rates, and as international trade increased and the economy globalized, the differences in tax rates started to produce profound economic consequences. Corporations started leaving high-tax countries in favor of low-tax countries; corporations that remained where they were still shifted income and investments to other countries. And the countries with the highest rates began to observe a resultant drag on economic growth and job creation.

Thus some political leaders saw that reducing the corporate tax rate had economic advantages—they would bring business and investment back into their country—and began promoting that. And as some countries began lowering rates (the United States and United Kingdom in the 1980's), many other countries did so also, to prevent businesses from leaving their territories.

In many countries, one political party has advocated the lowering of corporate income tax rates in order to promote economic growth, while another party continues to use the "tax the rich" rhetoric to advocate increasing it (although often they maintain the rhetoric without actually increasing the rate, a hint that maybe they recognize the economic effects but continue with contrary rhetoric as a strategy to garner votes). So the rate in any given country may move up or down depending upon which party has been more successful in their rhetoric— and is actually interested in following through with that rhetoric.

If the political rhetoric matched economic reality, one would think corporate income taxes do very well in terms of consideration for the poor, since the poor do not own corporations. But as the reality is that some [unknown] portion of the tax gets passed down to the poor through higher prices and worse employment opportunities, we cannot be so confident that these taxes are considerate to the poor at all. Maybe in some industries the middle class and the rich bear most of the burden; and in some industries the poor do. But we cannot make a satisfactory judgment on this criteria in light of the fact that economists have such great disagreement regarding the final tax incidence.

Now we return to the issue of tax complexity. As discussed earlier regarding the personal income tax, the complexity of the United States tax code is stupendous. Whether a business is paying corporate business taxes, or whether it is small enough and/or structured such that the owner/partners are paying personal income taxes, in either case they are accountable to a tax code so large and so confusing that even professional tax preparers do not compute the same results. And every dollar a business spends on hiring tax lawyers to navigate this code is a dollar diverted from productive (wealth-producing) activity. How many productive jobs are lost because businesses need to pay for tax lawyers just so they can obey the law? Furthermore, the tax code is complex enough that IRS agents themselves arrive at different answers—yet businesses are held liable to their inconsistent results.

Finally, we cannot mention the IRS in a book about ethics without addressing a specific problem related to IRS powers (although this is not about the tax policy per se, but rather about how the enforcers of the tax code abuse their power): civil asset forfeiture. First, banks are legally required to notify the IRS every time there is a transaction—such as a bank deposit—over $10,000. Second, avoiding such reporting requirements by breaking transactions into smaller chunks (called "structuring") is also illegal. Thus when the IRS notices a business making multiple deposits beneath this threshold, they get suspicious—is this tax evasion? money laundering? income from drug deals? Third, based upon their suspicion only, without having to obtain any evidence of criminal activity, the IRS may seize from the bank the assets of the suspicious business. They never have to charge the person with a crime. Fourth, they get to keep for themselves a portion of the money seized—incentive for them to be more suspicious, and make more seizures.

Unfortunately for small businesses, there are many reasons that it is appropriate to make multiple deposits under $10,000: perhaps their customer traffic results in a daily banking deposit of less than that; perhaps their insurance won't cover more than $10,000 cash loss in a robbery; perhaps they were told by an unwise teller that it saves the bank paperwork to make deposits less than $10,000. In any of these cases, they may discover that the IRS has gone to the bank after them and seized the entirety of their funds there—even hundreds of thousands of dollars' worth—on suspicion of structuring.

Now the IRS got enough bad press on this topic a few years ago for them to decide to reduce the frequency of seizures, and to establish a process by which wronged business could appeal forfeitures. But then the IRS declared that as of 2/8/17 that service was no longer available. So every year, some unlucky small businesses have their cash stolen from them by the IRS on suspicion of structuring; and some get it back after legal action, while others do not, or even go out of business while fighting a long and difficult legal battle to recover their stolen money.

Summary Report Card – Corporate Income Taxes

Representation/Participation | **Problematic**

Voters cannot make informed decisions about this tax because we cannot accurately determine the tax incidence. Inaccurate perception dominates.

Honesty | **Unethical in Practice**

While corporate income taxes are not *necessarily* dishonest—theoretically they could be described more accurately—in practice they are described by politicians as taxes upon the rich, and/or as taxes that are not placed upon people.

Openness | **Unethical**

Corporate income taxes and taxation of shareholder dividends effectively tax the same income (the profits from a business) twice, under two different names and at two different rates. This allows us to pretend the tax rate is lower than it actually is, hiding the true cost of the taxes from shareholders and the larger public.

Simplicity | **Stupendously Unethical**

Same as with personal income tax: the tax code governing business income and expenses is so stupendously complex that no one can understand it all, and businesses must spend millions of dollars upon tax lawyers to navigate it. And the IRS can *change interpretations of the law, and then pursue "back" taxes!*

Appropriateness | **Fail**

Corporate income taxes are not collected for any purpose relating to corporate business activity, but only to serve the general fund.

Consideration | **Unknown**

We cannot accurately ascertain the tax incidence; but it is likely that the poor, who have fewer economic options, likely suffer more from the portion of the tax burden passed on to consumer through higher prices and to employees through lower wages and fewer employment opportunities.

Minimizing Harms | **Unknown**

Effects are difficult to measure, and variable between industries. There is some unknown amount of reduction in entrepreneurial activity and economic growth.

Justice | **Catastrophic Failure on One Particular Front**

The IRS may seize a small business's money (sometimes hundreds of thousands of dollars) without ever charging them with a crime.

Peace | **Problematic**

As long as voters imagine corporate income taxes to be taxes upon the rich, politicians will court that ignorance to stir up class strife.

Postscript: Windfall Profits Tax

Typically, competition in markets brings profits down (grocery store profit margins, for example, typically range from 1% to 3%). But sometimes there is a sudden shift in the market that results in an unusually high profit margin for a company or an industry for a period of time. This can be the result of the introduction of new technology, of disruptions in international trade, of sudden reductions in competition or supply, or other factors. But even as the owners of profiting firms rejoice at the increase in profits, governments may decide that the new higher profits are "excessive" or "unfair" and propose a special Windfall Tax to take some share of those profits. Typically, such taxes are applied to a specific industry (which makes sense when it is an entire industry that is benefitting from the market fluctuation—but sometimes it is also more expedient politically to tax an entire industry even if it is only a particular firm or set of firms that is reaping the profits), such as the oil industry or the banking industry.

However, while the tax is supposed to target "windfall" profits, in practice such taxes tend to outlast the market conditions that create the windfalls. For example, when Iranian oil production fell significantly at the end of 1978, triggering the 1979 oil crises, domestic oil producers in the United States started reaping higher profits; so the Carter administration levied a new Windfall Profits Tax on the oil industry to make sure the oil industry "paid its fair share," and to "combat" the transfer of wealth from energy consumers to energy producers that resulted from the higher prices. Though termed a Windfall "Profits" Tax, the tax was not applied to the profits, but rather to the difference between the market price and a legislated base price (the price the government thought was fair). Furthermore, although it was created to address "windfall" profits, the tax remained in place for several years after the price of oil continued to fall (in 1986, the market price even fell below the legislated base price, resulting in zero windfall profit tax collected for that time). By the time it was repealed in 1988, total revenues collected over its lifetime were only a fifth of what had been originally anticipated.

No windfall taxes have been enacted in the United States since 1988, and none have been enacted in Great Britain since the late 1990's, when they taxed "excessive" profits in the utility industry. But they do get proposed from time to time in both countries, as remedies against perceived profiteering and greed in unpopular industries. The historical track record has shown windfall taxes to be highly disruptive of economic activity and underperforming in terms of generating revenue; but historical facts are easily forgotten by voters (if they were ever informed of them in the first place), while rhetoric calling for a "fairer" distribution of "underserved" profits will always be persuasive to some portion of the legislature and the electorate, so such taxes will continue to be proposed from time to time as "windfalls" are perceived.

9

Capital Gains Taxes

The income tax code describes many different types of income, including wage income, business income, rental income, interest income, dividend income, and capital gains. This last category, capital gains, needs to be considered separately, as it has its own particular set of economic effects; and consequently, is subject to a different tax rate. This distinct rate is a point of great political contention, particularly in regards to class considerations: for the capital gains tax is paid primarily by wealthier people, so Americans tend to have a visceral reaction to the fact that its tax rate is set lower than the highest rates for wage income (recall Warren Buffet announcing that his secretary paid a higher tax rate than he did, and the perpetual outrage over that since then). But in the midst of such emotional reaction, voters frequently forget to investigate: *why* is the rate set differently? (No, it is *not* because rich people buy the Congress.) What *economic* reasons exist for taxing this particular type of income differently from wage and other income?

Description and Purpose

Capital gains are the profits made from selling capital assets, such as stocks, bonds, and real estate (capital is money, land, or equipment that has the ability to produce other goods; stocks and bonds are capital assets, as they represent money used to start/grow a business). If I buy one share of stock for $100 today, then sell that share a year later for $120, I have a $20 capital gain, subject to taxation; conversely, if my sale price is instead $80, then I have a $20 capital loss, which I can count against my taxable income.

This is all very easy to calculate if I make a single investment, with only one initial purchase and one final sale; but it does become more complicated as I continue to buy and sell capital assets. For example, over the course of one year, I may buy stock several different times, at different prices (let's suppose 20 shares at $100, followed by another 20 shares at $105, followed by 10 more at $115), and also sell multiple times at different prices (let's suppose I sell 30 of those shares at $110, buy another 30 when the price drops to $100, and then sell 10 of those when the price goes back to $110). How shall I calculate these gains for the purpose of taxation? Which shares got sold at which time? Do I count them as First In, First Out (FIFO); or Last in, First Out (LIFO); or do I calculate the dollar average of my purchases; or can I specify which individual shares were sold at which times? In the United States, I actually may choose between these options (and if I do this a lot, it may behoove me to trust my stock broker or even to hire an accountant to keep track of all the different investments and compute for me the most tax-advantageous way to account for them); while in other jurisdictions, there may be a single standard basis for counting the gains (and losses), such as using FIFO. But even this is only the simplest kind of example; other events further complicate the tax.

Under the United States income tax rules, these considerations are also taken into account when computing capital gains taxes:

1. Inherited capital assets are re-valued (or "stepped up") when inherited, so when sold their gain is computed as the sale price minus the value at the time of inheritance, not time of purchase.

2. Capital losses can be carried over to future years—except this does not apply to the sale of personal property, such as a residence.

3. When a business buys a property and then sells it, it can be taxed at the capital gains rate; but if they develop the property and then sell it, this is counted as ordinary income rather than capital gains income. (Exactly when to treat it as a capital gain and when to treat it as ordinary income is delineated in the court decision *Byram v. United States*.)

4. Short-term capital gains (assets held for less than 1 year) still get taxed as ordinary income; an asset has to be held long-term (more than 1 year) to get the lower capital gains tax rate. (The definitions of short-term and long-term has varied over the history of the tax, from 6 months to 10 years.)

5. Like ordinary income, capital gains taxation is subject to different tax brackets; but in this case, there are fewer brackets: 15% and 20% (plus an additional 3.8% Medicare tax on all investment income over $200,000).

Historically, the capital gains tax rate has varied over time, but has almost always been lower than the ordinary income tax rate (it was briefly the same in the 1980's). Political negotiation to raise or lower it has often been managed by balancing changes in the ordinary income tax rate (i.e. trading an increase in one rate for a decrease in the other). For several decades now, debate over this tax rate in the United States has been divided along partisan lines, with the Democratic Party favoring a higher rate and the Republican Party a lower rate. The political rhetoric of the Democratic Party says the lower capital gains tax rate is a "tax break" for the rich that enables them to avoid paying their fair share; and some even try to count the foregone revenue (or more accurately, the amount of revenue they anticipate has been forgone, on the contrary-to-reality assumption that the same economic transactions would have been made at a higher tax rate) as a tax expenditure—a payment to the rich. But while this is the rhetoric, it is instructive to note that even when the Democratic Party controlled both houses of Congress and the Presidency (four years under Carter, two years under Clinton, and two years under Obama), they did not raise the capital gains tax rate to the same level as ordinary income (although Obama did raise it from 15% to 20%). Why not? Possibly because of some significant economic effects:

Economic Effects

Since investments in capital assets are made mostly by wealthier people, this kind of tax could be said to target the wealthy; and based upon this, one might expect it to be a natural place to increase taxes (and if one took political rhetoric seriously, this is what one would predict). However, capital gains income is different from ordinary income in several important ways which have significant impacts upon potential tax revenue:

1. Capital assets do not have to be sold at a particular time; they may be held for a more opportune time. Whereas ordinary wage income is fairly consistent, and less responsive to changes in tax rates (a wage-earner must continue working enough hours to pay expenses, even when their tax rate goes up), income from capital gains is irregular, realized at the discretion of the [wealthier] individual who can more easily postpone when they receive that income (the fact that they had money to invest in capital assets is an indicator they had wealth in excess of their daily needs, so they are not under the same pressure to collect that income immediately). Consequently, the Laffer Curve for tax revenue on capital gains has a revenue-maximization point at a much lower tax rate (below, left) than the Laffer Curve for tax on wage income (below, right). A revenue-seeking government, taking this into account, will pursue a lower tax rate on capital gains than on ordinary income if it wants to collect the greatest amount of revenue.

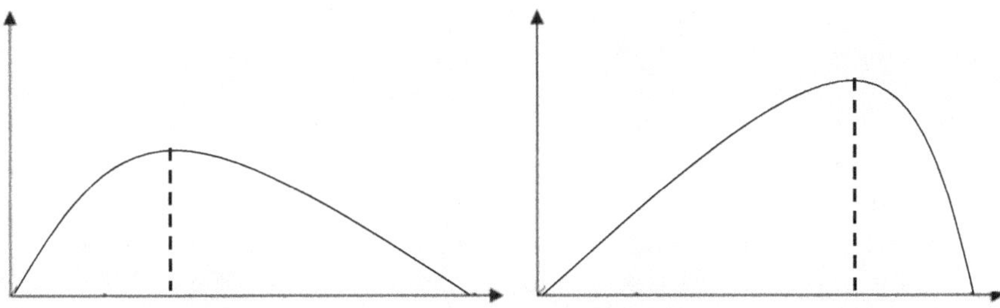

Consequently, while it may be politically advantageous to call for a higher capital gains tax rate, the economically-informed politician will go against their own rhetoric and still refrain from raising the rate as high as they promise—although economically-uninformed politicians might try to do this, until prevented by the noncooperation of others in their own party (although using "uninformed" here is charitable: the information has been presented to them many times, but still some politicians dismiss claims of Laffer Curve effects—that is, they dismiss the basic premise that real human beings change their behavior in response to their environment).

2. Capital gains income results from putting capital (savings) to productive use (when the use is non-productive, there is no gain, but rather a capital loss), such as when investors provide the capital an entrepreneur needs to start or expand a business. Putting savings to productive use through investment in capital assets is a major driver of economic growth. Capital is one of the fundamental factors of economic production; economists on both the political right and the political left (and even Marxists on the farthest left!) agree that having more capital available (both to existing companies already equipped to make use of it, and to entrepreneurs to create new products and/or innovate new methods and means of combining capital and labor) encourages growth.

   But increasing taxes on capital gains makes investment in capital assets less profitable; consequently, people respond to this by spending incrementally less on capital investments—making capital less available to businesses and entrepreneurs. Thus this particular type of tax has direct consequences for the creation of new business and economic growth; raising the tax does not simply extract more tax revenue from the rich (in the short term), but reduces the overall amount of investment made in new business and job creation.

   Again, politicians recognize that taxing a thing results in getting less of that thing— that is their explicit logic behind excise taxes. The same logic is true for capital investments: raising taxes on it results in less investment than would otherwise have been made; therefore so long as a government wants investment (wants economic growth), they should want to encourage capital investment rather than discourage it through excessive taxation.

3. Economic growth (growth in the production of goods and services) means also the growth of real income—which in turn increases ordinary income tax revenues (and the Congressional Budget Office anticipates some amount of increase in tax revenues every year resulting from economic growth). Consequently, slowing that growth reduces future tax revenues; therefore the government which depends upon ordinary income taxes has this additional reason to favor capital gains with a lower tax rate: for a significant increase in the capital gains rate will have a negative impact upon ordinary income tax revenues in the future.

4. The availability and improvement of capital correlates with real wage rates. Capital increases worker productivity (a worker with the right machine can produce a great deal more than a worker with a mediocre machine—or no machine at all), and worker productivity directly correlates with worker pay. (Pay rates change according to supply and demand, but there is a higher demand for more productive workers; and the production of wealth is what gives us the means to pay for anything else, including the labor of workers.)

Capitalism depends upon capital. The more capital available, and the more freely capital may move, the more opportunities for the production of real wealth. Stock prices reflecting the free movement of capital provide market information (as all prices in a free market provide information) about relative supply and demand, enabling individuals in a larger economy to shift resources from less-productive uses to more-productive uses. But the larger the tax, the less freely capital moves, and the less efficient/productive the economy.

How to Make a Tax Even Worse

Capital gains are taxed when the gain is "realized;" that is, when the capital asset is sold, and the seller can compute how much they have profited. Unfortunately, the United States tax code does not consider inflation when assessing the tax on capital gains, so sometimes the nominal gain is in fact a real economic loss. For example, if one had purchased stock for $1000 in the year 2000, and then sold that same stock in 2010 for $1200, that would be a nominal gain of $200; but because of inflation, $1200 in 2010 dollars is equivalent to a little less than $950 in 2000 dollars—the investor has *lost* $50 worth of purchasing power, yet is being taxed on an apparent "gain."

At least the investor is not required to sell; and if the value of the investment increases faster than inflation in the future, the investor may yet experience a profit. Unless Senator Ron Wyden gets his way:

Wyden has proposed to tax *unrealized* capital gains on an annual basis, by computing how much assets would be worth *if* sold, and then assessing tax based upon that (and at the ordinary income tax levels to boot!). If this were to pass, investors would have to pay money every year they held their investment—and if they didn't have enough cash on hand to pay that (this can easily be the case if one has stored the bulk of their wealth in capital assets), then they would have to sell off their assets. And since the Wyden plan also does not account for inflation, this means that assets growth which is outpaced by inflation would be taxed every year, despite the fact that the real value of the asset is going down. And if the market value of the stock crashes after unrealized gains have been taxed for several years, then the stock owner will have paid years of taxes on an overall loss.

Naturally, Mr. Wyden advertises his tax proposal as making the rich "pay their fair share." But he might as well be advertising that he wishes to see a drastic reduction in capital markets, as investors would be highly incentivized to withdraw from much of their current investments to avoid losses to this tax.

Tax Incidence

Capital gains are collected from those individuals who make capital investments; and such investments are made predominantly by the wealthy. But many middle-class individuals also make capital investments; in fact any middle class household that attends a financial management workshop or who reads, listens to, or otherwise consumes material on money management and pursuing wealth likely spends some amount of their disposable income upon capital investment, deferring some of their current consumption for the promise of a greater future income. And while the bulk of capital gains tax is paid by the wealthier individuals (because more of their income comes from capital gains), less-wealthy middle class taxpayers constitute the greater *number* of individual capital gains taxpayers.

Retirement Tax Trap

The middle class also invests in capital for the purpose of saving for retirement. Now as the government wants to encourage saving for retirement, it offers some incentive to do so by deferring all taxes on capital gains and dividends which get re-invested in the account—but this comes with one big drawback: when the funds are finally withdrawn from a traditional Individual Retirement Account (IRA), they get taxed at the *ordinary* income tax rate, instead of the lower capital gains rate.

But these are the direct payers of the capital gains tax; are there any who pay the tax indirectly (as we have observed in most other kinds of taxes)?

We do find one important cost borne by another population; the cost of the tax is not directly transferred to them in the form of higher prices (as with tariffs, excise taxes, and sales taxes), but nevertheless reduces their buying power another way:

As noted above, capital investment correlates significantly with real wage growth. This does not surprise the economist: capital makes it possible for workers to be more productive (that is, more wealth-producing), making their labor more valuable to employers. Final wage rates will be impacted by overall supply of labor (for example, some capital machinery requires a higher level of operator skill than others; jobs which require more skill will see the greatest increases in wages, as there are fewer workers—a more restricted supply—to meet employers' demand); but the overall market effect tends toward wage growth. The upshot of this is that when capital gains taxes are high, and capital investment is consequently reduced, growth in real wages is also reduced: thus workers (who do not invest directly in capital assets) pay for higher capital gains taxes in the form of lost wages.

Ethical Considerations

The simple ethical justification for taxing capital gains is that the government needs revenue, and would like to collect that revenue from the portion of the population most capable of paying it; as capital gains income is enjoyed most by this population, it seems to be a natural object for taxation. Unfortunately, high taxation of savings and investment discourages savings and investment—but the government would like to promote savings and investment (since that promotes economic growth which results in more real wealth to be enjoyed in aggregate); consequently, it also makes sense for a government to limit the tax rate for capital gains, which in turn limits the amount of revenue that can be collected from the portion of the population that makes this their primary source of income.

If human beings were not involved, this would be a very interesting puzzle, and economists and legislators would set themselves the task of determining what balance of trade-offs is most preferable when setting the capital gains tax rate (for there are no perfect solutions, only trade-offs between different alternatives). But because human beings are involved, this is not simply a puzzle; rather, it is an uncomfortable contest between different values and expectations. Yes, we want economic growth that produces jobs and increases in real wage rates; but something just *feels* wrong about taxing a wealthy population at a lower rate than a less-wealthy population. Investor Warren Buffet has famously made this point by declaring that he pays a lower tax rate than his secretary (he pays a magnificently greater amount of total taxes, but because almost all of his income is from capital gains, while hers is ordinary income, she pays a higher top marginal rate).

Many politicians agree with Buffet, and argue that we should close this "loophole" in the United States income tax code. (This is dishonest rhetoric here: for there is no "loophole," but a distinction in the tax code made by design, specifically for considerations of economic growth.) Many do not understand why the capital gains rate is so low; others understand but nevertheless disagree with the logic. Many argue that this preferential rate "costs" the government a great deal of money (although this too is a bit of deceitful rhetoric, making it sound as if the government is paying for something, and depending upon the assumption that the government has a natural right to all such income in the first place).

But raising the capital gains tax rate is not the only way to resolve this tension; theoretically, it could also be resolved by lowering the ordinary income tax rate. But such significant tax reduction would require a much, much smaller government, and probably the end of the established entitlement system. Alternatively, both the tax on savings/investment and the tax on productive labor could be replaced with an equal tax on consumption—but most people don't want to do that, either.

Thus we have an aspect of the income tax system doomed to be unsatisfactory to some significant portion of the population, whether the rate is set high or low. This makes for a tax policy that foments conflict rather than peace; and in the absence of widespread economic knowledge among voters, encourages impassioned demagoguery and outright deceit among one wing of politicians vying for votes (the opposing wing has decided to promote low capital gains tax rates), rather than careful consideration and debate of the trade-offs involved.

Ideally, we would commit to careful economic analysis to estimate economic effects. Revenue-hungry governments would want to know the shape of the Laffer Curve, and in particular the tax rate that would maximize revenue collection; while more future-oriented governments would want to estimate the trade-offs between each dollar spent through government as opposed to being spent through further investment (if the effect of government spending is less productive than the effect of private investment at a particular tax rate and size of government, one might want to lower the tax rate to even below the revenue-maximizing point on the Laffer Curve).

And given that we cannot ever have perfect economic models (we cannot run an experiment with a second Earth using two different tax rates), we might commit to making small, incremental changes in the tax rate rather than drastic ones. Unfortunately, investors' knowledge that the tax rate will change in the future has a direct impact upon their decisions (i.e. they will often choose to wait until the rate is more favorable before realizing their income), so even a policy of incremental changes is fraught with drawbacks. If investors anticipate a lower rate in the future, they will be more inclined to hold on to their investments until they can take advantage of the lower tax rate—thus reducing liquidity in capital markets, slowing investment. On the other side, if investors anticipate a higher rate in the future, they will be more inclined to realize investment gains before that time—but in anticipation of the higher rate, some portion of those gains will *not* be re-invested, but rather spent on other purchases (luxuries, entertainment/leisure, and like consumption); and this would also reduce the amount of investment capital available to new and expanding businesses.

Meanwhile the best option for economic growth is to abolish this tax altogether; but that returns us to the fiscal problem of reduced tax revenue and higher deficits, as well as the social problems that result from sparing the wealthiest people from the tax burden. We might resolve the economic, fiscal, and social challenges by trading all income taxes for consumption taxes, eliminating the tax dis-incentives for productive behavior—if only we could surmount the population's objections to a national sales tax or VAT. No solution would in the end be perfect, of course; for there are only trade-offs between alternatives. Now if only voters could become aware of the alternatives available to them and start considering which package of benefits and disadvantages they most prefer.

Summary Report Card – Capital Gains Taxes

Representation/Participation   **Problematic**
A minority of voters pay this tax; they can vote on it, but are always vulnerable to a majority that could impose new rates unilaterally.

Honesty   **Unethical in Practice**
Many politicians rail against the preferential capital gains rate as if this rate were a favor to the rich, instead of acknowledging the real economic reasons capital gains are taxed differently from ordinary income.

Openness   **Good**
Capital gains tax rates are published and identifiable.

Simplicity   **Needs Improvement**
While simpler than the rest of the income tax code, there is still enough complexity (e.g. distinguishing between short and long-term gains, deciding which accounting basis to use, etc.), to warrant paying for a tax professional.

Consideration   **Pass**
Capital gains taxes are levied upon those who are able to defer current consumption (people whose basic necessities are already met).

Minimizing Harms   **(Currently, in the United States) Pass**
Capital gains in the United States are taxed at a lower rate than ordinary income in order to promote economic growth through capital investment. Countries which have high, investment-hampering rates would fail this metric.

Justice   **Fair-ish**
Capital gains taxes in the tax code are passed to generate revenue, not to pursue punishment. Unfortunately, the political rhetoric of many demagogues does explicitly call for punishing the rich.

Peace   **Problematic**
The lower rate applied to capital gains is a point of great contention for those who do not accept the economic arguments in favor of this tax preference; taxing different parts of a population at different rates fosters conflict between those groups—exacerbating the already-present conflict narrative of rich vs. poor.

Note: it appears this tax cannot pass both the *peace* and *minimizing harms* criteria simultaneously—but this is only true for higher tax rates. At a low enough tax rate, ordinary income and capital gains could be taxed at the same rate, satisfying *peace* and avoiding the economic harms which result from discouraging investment.

Postscript: the Financial Transaction Tax

In addition to capital gains taxes, some politicians in both the United States and the European Union also advocate for a Financial Transaction Tax (FTT) to be applied to particular financial transactions, such as the purchase/sale of stocks, bonds, debt securities, and other financial assets, and sometimes also currency trades as well. Though a kind of sales tax, it is useful to consider here since it is proposed to target the same taxpayers that the capital gains tax targets—although while the capital gains tax will only tax profits, the financial transaction tax will apply to all transactions of stock, whether they bring profit or loss.

There are a variety of different forms and proposed forms for this kind of tax, with differences regarding the specific kinds of transactions being taxed and the specific rates. Typically, the rates range from .1% to .5%, but a few countries have even higher rates (Belgium has 1.32% on purchases of stock in investment companies, and Finland has a 1.6% rate on certain securities there). These might seem to be low rates: but recall that these are in addition to any capital gains taxes, and also will be assessed twice when changing one investment to another (for if you sell one stock in order to buy another, you get taxed on *both* the transaction of selling the first stock and the transaction of buying the second stock). In response to these additional costs, investors change their trading behavior, pursuing larger returns—or taking their investments to other jurisdictions not subject to the tax. Consequently, the Laffer Curve for this tax is something severe, with an extraordinarily low revenue-maximizing point: one analysis by the Tax Policy Center estimated that a .5% tax brought in no more revenue than a .1% tax, so the revenue-maximizing point (according to that analysis) would be between there. Meanwhile higher FTT rates can even result in *negative* revenues for the government, as the consequent reduction in trading volume (as investors move to other markets to escape the tax) means that less money is collected from capital gains taxes. This is part of the reason why Sweden and Germany both abandoned their FTT in 1991, and Japan abandoned theirs in 1999 (the United States had abandoned its 1914 FTT decades prior in 1965).

In addition to failing to collect much (or any) revenue, the FTT also fails in its goal of reducing volatility in the stock market: although trading volume is reduced, speculative trading can still result in bubbles—with greater frequency even, since the slowed trading volume reduces price discovery (the rate at which new information is communicated through changes in market prices). Slower price discovery results in greater mismatches of knowledge between buyers and sellers, increasing chances of drastic price fluctuations as the information catches up with the market. Meanwhile every dollar collected by an FTT reduces the capital stock of a country, slowing GDP growth. All told, the negative economic consequences of the FTT tend to greatly outweigh any benefits gained from the [small, if at all positive] revenue collection.

10

Payroll Taxes

Because of the exemptions and credits available, only about half of adults in the United States pay income taxes; but income taxes are not the only taxes withheld from a worker's paycheck. Nearly all workers, rich and poor alike, have an amount deducted from their checks for payroll taxes. In the United States, these include state and federal unemployment taxes, and much more significantly, Federal Insurance Contributions Act (FICA) taxes. Other countries likewise use payroll taxes to fund similar programs (old age/pension, health and disability insurance, and unemployment insurance). These taxes are particularly interesting to consider because unlike most other taxes, they are tied to specific government expenditures. Our income tax funds everything from the military to welfare to corporate and farm subsidies; but our FICA taxes are supposed to fund the specific programs known as Social Security and Medicare. Because the spending projections for Social Security and Medicare directly impact this tax, any discussion of the payroll tax policy necessarily involves discussion of these programs as well.

Description and Purpose

Payroll tax was inaugurated in the United States in 1935, with the passage of the Federal Insurance Contributions Act (FICA) to fund Social Security (passed in the same year). Initially, the tax was 2% (split between employee and employer) on a worker's first $3,000 in earnings; but these amounts have gone through numerous increases over the years. By the mid 1960's, the rate for Social Security was 7.7%, and an additional 0.7% was added to pay for the new Medicare program. Both of these rates continued to increase until 1990: since that year, the Social Security rate has remained at 12.4% (6.2% deducted from the employee's wages, plus another 6.2% of the employee's wages paid by the employer) and the Medicare rate at 2.9% (also split). As of 2019, the Social Security rate applies only to a worker's earned income up to $128,400 (which amount is adjusted each year to account for inflation); whereas the Medicare tax applies to all earned income. After personal income tax, payroll taxes make up the largest share of all tax revenues; meanwhile, government spending on the Social Security and Medicare programs together exceeds the total discretionary spending on all other government programs (including the military) combined.

Social Security, aka OASDI (Old Age, Survivors, and Disability Insurance), aka RSDI (Retirement, Survivors, and Disability Insurance—which perhaps makes more sense, as it seems odd to buy insurance against so certain a thing as old age) is currently so fixed in the societal landscape that most Americans assume it to be normal, and cannot imagine the feasibility of an alternative system, let alone no such government system at all. So many Americans rely on this program—or expect to rely upon it when they retire—it is often referred to as a "third rail" of American politics: as touching the third rail in an electrical rail system will likely result in death, so challenging Social Security is seen as death for any politician.

This is problematic, as the Social Security program was designed in a way that was mathematically unsustainable, and this has never been fixed. For while the program collects payroll taxes throughout a taxpayer's career, it pays out a lifetime pension at retirement that is not based upon the amount that was collected, but rather upon a formula that results in a benefit far exceeding the amount collected (for a person with an average lifespan). Currently, the Social Security Administration estimates a person retiring at 67 years old will live for another 16.5 years. Now, in order for 45 working years to carry a person through 60+ years of adult life, a person would have to save about 25% of their income if they wanted the same net income during retirement, or about 15% if they were willing to have retirement income of about half their working income (and experience zero inflation, or have all savings earn interest such that they would match inflation). So of course the original legislation set the mandatory savings rate (i.e. the tax rate) at... 2%. Today, it's 12.4%, which is closer, but still not quite high enough—assuming that one's savings were actually, well, saved, and that they earned enough interest to match inflation.

> **Social Security Benefit Formula**
>
> Social Security benefits are paid based upon your average monthly earnings for your best 35 years of work, adjusted for inflation. They then pay:
>
> 90% on monthly earnings up to $926
> 32% on earnings from $927 to $5583
> 15% on earnings from $5584 to 10,700
> 0% on earnings above that

However, Social Security taxes are *not* saved by the government to pay for future Social Security benefits: instead, they are immediately spent by the government on other expenses, requiring retirement benefits to be paid not by their own [forced] savings, but by the taxes of younger workers. This is part of the design of the legislation: despite common misconceptions that one has some sort of "account" with Social Security, no such individual accounts exist; individuals do not "get back" what they have paid into the system, but instead are paid benefits out of current workers' contributions—and on average, receive significantly more in benefits than they ever paid in taxes. Now this was very easy to promise in the initial decades of the legislation, when there were very few beneficiaries and very many working taxpayers, because you can pay a generation more than they saved if each subsequent generation is bigger (and therefore contributing more in taxes). But then lifespans increased, and family sizes shrunk, and the original unsustainable math got even worse. From the mid 1970's to about 2005, there was a fairly consistent proportion of about 3.3 workers paying taxes into the system for every 1 retired person collecting benefits, but by 2013 there were only 2.8 working taxpayers for every beneficiary, and the Social Security Administration expects that number to be somewhere between 2 and 2.3 by 2034. There simply are not enough new workers to pay the benefits promised to retired workers, and that shortage is only expected to get worse.

But wait, you ask: what about the Social Security Trust Fund? Isn't there a Trust Fund full of people's savings which funds benefits? Unfortunately, the answer is there is a "trust fund" in name only, not in actual practice. For the Social Security legislation requires that all surplus payroll taxes (taxes collected in a year in excess of the amount of benefits which must be paid out) be used to buy "Special Interest Securities" from the US Treasury—effectively a kind of nontransferable savings bond—at which point the federal government then spends the money on other budget items. The Special Interest Securities are simply IOUs issued by the federal government (and this description of them as IOUs is *not* a partisan preference: nonpartisan entities like PolitiFact and virtually all independent economists describe them the same way). Later, when Social Security needs to redeem these "assets" (the Social Security Trustees Report terms these savings bonds assets), the IOUs are paid by the federal government out of current tax receipts.

Since Social Security began in the United States, it has collected more in new payroll taxes than it has had to pay in benefits, so the "Trust Fund" appears to be fairly large, at almost $3 trillion dollars (in IOUs from the federal government); but because payments are expected to exceed tax receipts in 2020—and every year thereafter—this "Trust Fund" is expected to be exhausted by 2035 or so. But 2035 is not the important year; 2020 is—because that is the year that Social Security payments can no longer be funded by payroll taxes, but must instead be paid out of the General Fund as it redeems the Special Interest Securities—that is, paid out of other taxes (personal and corporate income tax, etc.).

The balance of tax revenues versus expenditures for the Medicare portion of the tax (currently 2.9%, of employee wages, also split between employee and employer, but with no cap on income) is even worse, on account of the significant medical expenses incurred at end of life. The good news is that people live longer, and have access to better medical care than they did 50 years ago; the bad news is that involves many more years of many more dollars spent on old age—and particularly end-of-life—medical care, and a 2.9% tax simply isn't enough to fund the level of benefits promised in the current Medicare system. So those benefits too are funded by other taxes.

Social Security and Medicare expenditures—dubbed "entitlements" in the federal budget, because the payments may not be adjusted through the discretionary budget process—are expected to continue to grow, both in absolute terms and as a share of the federal budget. If current trends were allowed to continue without change, spending on just these two items would eventually cost more than the government collects from all tax revenues, leaving nothing left to pay for defense spending, other welfare programs, courts and law enforcement, or anything else.

Is the Social Security payroll tax regressive?

Income taxes in the United States are *progressive*, meaning the rates increase as income increases. A *regressive* tax is the opposite: the tax rate gets smaller as income increases. Alternatively, a *flat tax* is one which has the same rate at all levels.

The payroll tax for Social Security is set at a flat rate of 6.2% (plus another 6.2% paid by the employer) on all wages up to $128,400. Since wages above that are not taxed, many people dub this a regressive tax, arguing that having a 0% rate on wages above $128,400 results in the wealthiest Americans paying a lower overall tax rate: for example, a person earning $200,000 annually pays 6.2% on only the first $128,400 of their income—$7960.80—effectively only 4% of their total income.

However, this description is misleading, because Social Security benefits are *not paid on the untaxed income*. As a tax specifically to fund these payments, the tax rate is a flat rate; it could only be considered regressive if this tax were to finance additional benefits. In other words, so long as we pretend that the Social Security tax funds the taxpayer's Social Security benefits, we must admit that it is a flat rate; only when we decide that Social Security taxes pay for *other* people's benefits (not just Social Security) and for government generally can we argue that it is "regressive."

Meanwhile the benefits that are paid go down as income goes up, so poorer people receive a much higher proportion of their earnings than do richer people. Here are the expected benefits for retiring in 2019 at full retirement age:

Average Monthly Earnings (adjusted for inflation)	Expected Monthly Social Security Benefit	Percentage of Average Earnings
$900	$810	90%
$2,000	$1154	58%
$4,000	$1817	45%
$6,000	$2386	40%
$8,000	$2686	34%

With poorer people getting a much higher return on their Social Security contributions, one could justifiably dub the Social Security tax-benefit schedule *progressive*, not regressive.

Economic Effects

The most significant effect of the entitlement systems funded by the payroll tax is how it has reshaped our cultural conceptions of old age and retirement. Additional effects follow from its structure as a payroll tax specifically, but let us consider first the larger effect of this tax/benefit program.

From an historical perspective, "retirement" is an interesting concept, for throughout most of history human beings did not have any conception of "retirement" matching what we take for granted today. Historically, people did not retire: they worked, and when they could no longer support themselves through work, they were supported by their children. (This is one of the reasons that children were so important economically: for the childless man or woman had no one to provide for them in their old age, and consequently was likely to suffer more and die sooner.) But after the explosion of wealth and other social changes wrought by the industrial revolution, more and more people gained the economic capacity to save from their current earnings to provide for themselves in the future. Old people could rely on the fruits of their former labor to sustain them economically, instead of relying upon their children.

But how does one save for retirement? One could set aside silver and gold, but such a person would have the problem of keeping that safe. But savings could be kept safely (it was supposed) in banks, or invested in businesses to gain interest and increase in value. Unfortunately, the events of the stock market crash of 1929 and the subsequent Great Depression demonstrated that neither of these avenues was certain: the contemporary equivalent of about $400 billion dollars in invested savings was lost in about a day, and afterwards systemic bank runs and consequent bank collapses wiped out the "safer" savings of many more Americans. Old people who had saved no longer had savings, and their children often did not have the economic capacity to satisfactorily provide for them ("satisfactorily" being a necessary term here: we must acknowledge that this is a subjective value appraisal, *not* an objective description). Social Security was the Depression-Era solution to this calamity: this system, modeled on a system previously implemented by Otto von Bismark in Germany, addressed the felt needs of voters with a promise of a safe retirement.

This "safe" retirement quickly become a bedrock social expectation/norm for all the countries that implemented it, and citizens growing up in those countries grew up with the expectation that they would work until old age (generally 65-70), at which time they would retire, supported by a continued income provided through the government. To most people in these countries, "retirement" is normal, and government-sponsored retirement is normal—even unquestionable. This is simply what good governments *do* (the fact this required redefinition of the General Welfare clause in the US Constitution is inconceivable to most Americans today).

Yet it is important to consider that a nation has alternatives to a mandatory government retirement/pension system. To begin with, people could be left free to save for their own retirements. True, those who choose to invest everything in the stock market would still be susceptible to loss; but no one need mandate that they invest there (and if the government simply stopped inflating the money supply, people wouldn't feel compelled to invest in stocks to keep pace with inflation). Meanwhile the government has decided to insure bank deposits, so people no longer have to fear bank runs destroying their savings. So let us compare this alternative with the current system:

Government Mandated Social Security	Individual Responsibility for Retirement
Workers are taxed to fund it, lowering wages and reducing economic options available to people in the present	Workers enjoy higher wages; they choose how much to enjoy now and how much to set aside for the future
A fixed percentage is removed; workers may not adjust social security savings to account for immediate needs	Workers are free to adjust their retirement savings up or down to meet current and unexpected needs
No investment of retirement savings	Investment of retirement savings in wealth-producing businesses
Workers have no property rights to their retirement: the amount they get is determined by law, subject to change	Workers have property rights to all the money they have saved
If a retiree dies young, their family has no property rights to their retirement (although there are Survivors benefits for certain situations as defined by law)	Worker's families inherit all savings in accordance with established property and inheritance rights
If legally-established benefits exceed payroll taxes, benefits are paid through other tax revenues (collected from the younger generation)	People receive back their own property (which includes interest and investment earnings) and nothing more

The Individual Responsibility alternative has the value-advantage of greater freedom, while the current Social Security system has the value-advantage of security; different people will come to different conclusions about which of these values they prefer. As for the economic advantages, the Individual Responsibility option provides a much greater capacity to adjust for changes in economic conditions—both on the individual level and on the national level—increasing the overall efficiency (wealth-producing ability) of the larger economy. The investment of savings in businesses (as opposed to IOUs from the treasury) increases the amount of capital available to create new firms and technology, expand and improve existing firms, and increase overall wages (recall that all economic theories note the importance of capital for real wage growth).

Now some economists and most politicians argue that the federal government also makes investments in economic growth (for example, by building roads and funding scientific research). So the question becomes: which type of investment, government spending (allocated according to political processes) or private spending (allocated according to the profit motive), tends to produce greater wealth? This question came up earlier, when we noted that the income tax made possible a much larger government; it comes up again here, because the payroll tax to fund Social Security forces a significant transfer of spending activity from the private sector (where people spend their own money on the things they want, considering costs and quality) to the public sector (where political actors spend other people's money on things for other people, with less consideration for cost or quality). Government may indeed get credit for investing in roads and scientific research; but it also "invests" in military spending, bank bail-outs, pork-barrel spending to reward constituencies and lobbyists, and many other things generally considered to be waste. Perhaps, as implicated in the Rahn Curve, some amount of initial government spending can net a larger return than the same amount of private spending; but after these initial investments are made, further government spending tends to be less effective than private spending in terms of promoting economic growth.

Drivers of political spending	Drivers of private spending
Popular constituencies	Consumer demand
Private constituencies (donors, lobbyists)	Stakeholders' profit motives
Logrolling/vote-trading to garner support from other political actors	Self-interest, coordinated with the self-interest of others
Bureaucratic inertia, insulated from competitive pressure	Large business inertia, vulnerable to competitive pressures

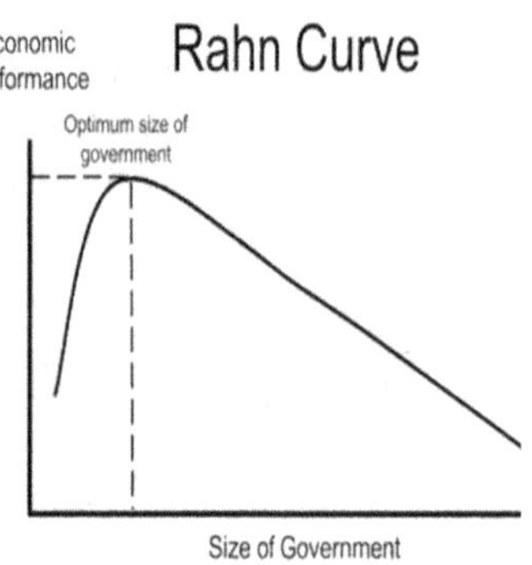

Of course, one may still prefer the mandated Social Security program over an alternative of total Individual Responsibility, despite the inefficiencies in cost— perhaps because under a program of total Individual Responsibility, many people would simply fail to save enough on their own (and/or fail to purchase insurance against disability), and therefore end up destitute in old age and incapacity. But if that is one's value proposition, there is still an economic alternative to mandated Social Security: for the government could instead allow individuals to designate their Social Security taxes to fund the retirement and disability insurance options of their own choosing, instead of the state's program. This would transfer the spending choices back to the consumers, and drastically increase wealth-producing investment.

Unfortunately, allowing workers to allocate their payroll taxes to investments of their own choosing has one major economic drawback: major budget deficits for the government, since it is depending upon current workers' payroll taxes to pay for the benefits of those who have already retired (because it already spent the retirees' payroll taxes years ago, instead of saving or investing them). Nevertheless, the very large short-term deficits created by such a change (which will vary between countries, according to their own Social Security programs and promises, and according to their own demographics) may still be less costly over the long term than current unsustainable Social Security programs. Consequently, several countries are considering just such a transition; and about 30 countries already have some form of private social security system, so we have some practical examples.

Chile's Retirement System

Chile introduced a social security system funded by payroll taxes in 1926. Unfortunately, payments into the system had little correlation with benefits paid out, and by the 1970s, the system's pension funds were running out. But in 1980, they reformed the system such that workers no longer had to pay into it, but instead paid 10% of their earnings into private investment funds. Such funds must be government-approved; and any fund which failed to deliver a minimum return is liquidated and the collected assets are transferred to another fund; also the government guarantees workers a minimum return, making payments in case of a particular fund going bankrupt. Under this government-regulated private-investment structure, Chile has maintained a fully-funded retirement system wherein retirees rights to their invested property and reap the returns of interest.

Being funded in this manner did mean that those who did not pay much into the system would not get much out; therefore in 2008 the system underwent some reforms, including adding a government benefit to supplement the poorest retirees. Some argue that the Chilean system pays too little in benefits, and complain that those who do not pay into the system receive no pension at all (which to supporters is a feature rather than a bug); but all recognize that the benefits are funded, and will continue to be funded, even as many other countries (including the United States) are projecting major budget shortfalls, without any operable plan to pay for the benefits their systems promise.

But while the primary economic effect of the payroll tax is to transfer retirement and investment choices from the market (individual Americans) to the government (a very small subset of elected Americans, with very different interests), it must be noted that the amount of tax used to force this transfer is yet insufficient to pay for the program it is supposed to fund. And because this tax is statutorily linked to a specific set of programs, we might also consider the larger costs of those programs also.

In the United States, and many other countries besides, payroll taxes are grossly insufficient to sustain the social security benefits promised by current law. For these countries, the most significant economic effects may be in the future, as social security benefits take up an increasing share of a nation's government budget. The Social Security Administration's Trustees' Report projects that benefits will exceed payroll tax revenues in 2020, and every year after that; by 2035, payroll tax revenues will only be able to pay about 75% of scheduled benefits. The difference will have to be made up by general fund revenues (from other taxes)—or promised benefits will have to be cut (and remember, although they are termed "entitlements," the federal government and the Social Security Administration in particular have made it clear that no recipient has a property right to any benefits, but rather the government may reduce benefits by law at any time). To finance the same amount of benefits, the federal government will have to choose between making huge tax increases, cutting spending on discretionary programs (which the government almost never does), or contracting massive additional amounts of debt (which adds even more expense each year to pay the interest on that debt). Such massive budget shortfalls are inevitable because the Social Security program is structured as a defined-benefit pension, and the payroll taxes used to finance it have never been enough to pay for those benefits, but have always depended upon payments from younger workers.

Meanwhile the Medicare potion of the payroll tax (which pays for the original Medicare program, Part A; Parts B and D is paid for by a combination of premiums and general funds) is even more imbalanced: average lifetime Medicare benefits far exceed the amount of Medicare taxes one pays in their lifetime, being double, triple, or even quadruple (depending upon lifespan and medical needs) the amount of tax collected. As with Social Security taxes, this imbalance is not immediately felt, for as long as workers (payroll taxpayers) outnumber retirees (Social Security and Medicare beneficiaries), the imbalance on any given year is reduced. But while Social Security was able to run an annual budget surplus (which Congress spent on other things) based upon the worker/retiree ratio—until 2020, that is—Medicare has been losing money from its trust funds (that is, its store of IOUs from the federal treasury) for several years. Even with the additional Medicare surtax applied to higher-income earners as a result of the Affordable Care Act, Medicare payroll tax revenues are insufficient to cover costs, and money from the general fund (other tax revenues) are applied to make up the difference. And like Social Security, this budget shortfall also only gets worse as people live longer, and spend more on medical services—services which are increasingly seen as a right, whether the nation's collective payroll tax contributions are sufficient to cover the expenses or not.

An Interesting Social Consequence

As noted before, the concept of retirement, and the expectation of retirement being a normal part of the life cycle, are relatively new concepts in human history. Prior to the industrial revolution and prior to the development of an economic environment that made savings/investment more possible and more rewarding, most people had not the means to retire. Older people no longer able to work and disabled people unable to work largely depended upon their families for support; consequently, the economic and social value of marriage and childrearing was much higher; and the economic and social costs of living apart from one's family of origin and without any children also that much greater. Failing to marry and beget children left one without any certain means of support in old age. There might be charities or other social networks available, but depending upon one's community, there might not.

A government-secured pension entirely changes this economic calculation. With the government promising to maintain a minimum level of income to retired workers, it becomes economically safe to be single and childless. People become free to choose a lifestyle previously unthinkable to most. And with the necessity of marriage and child-rearing removed, the meaning of those institutions changes also: people may become more selective in their choices, and make choices to wed and raise family with greater consideration for other values than economic prudence. On a national scale, one consequence of this new option is a drop in the overall birth rate (although there are other factors also contributing to the drop in birth rates).

Social Security was not created to change family and social realities; but that is one of the interesting consequences of the program. And with these changes have come re-evaluation of cultural values, wherein some of the values associated with family have been reduced in emphasis, while some of the values associated with the individual have gained in importance. What is normal has changed in an extraordinary way; but minds confined to their own lifetime only are not even aware of this.

Tax Incidence

Nearly every country splits payment of the payroll tax between the employee and employer. However, as with other taxes, the person or entity who nominally pays the tax is not necessarily the person or entity who bears the tax burden: in the case of payroll taxes, the "employer" portion of the tax is largely born by the employee in the form of lower wages. Exactly how much of the tax burden is shifted to employees in this manner is subject to some debate, and it appears there is some variance between countries and markets; but in the United States, one can expect somewhere between two-thirds and nearly all of the employer tax to be shifted to employees in the form of lower wages, with the biggest shifts occurring in jobs with the largest labor supply.

For from the employer perspective, the cost of hiring a person is not just that person's wages, but also that person's benefits, administrative costs, and all taxes associated with that person; so the employer portion of the payroll tax is already considered in the price of labor when shopping for new employees. We may term the other benefits (health insurance, etc.) as part of an employee's total compensation; but all of it—benefits and taxes together—are part of the cost of labor. Absent the payroll taxes, employee wages would move up, as businesses in labor-competitive industries could bid up the price of the best employees until they reached their price points.

But split payroll taxes between employees and employers is very useful to governments, in that it disguises the full cost of the tax. Workers who examine their paychecks can only see their portion of the tax (they may see the employer contribution, but they have no way of knowing how much of that employer contribution reduced the employer's profits, versus how much it reduced the employee's own wages); so they estimate the full cost of the tax (to them) to be much less than it is.

Meanwhile there is an additional tax incidence which appears at some delay: for the inadequacy of one person's payroll tax to cover that same person's benefits requires future workers to make up the difference. Now at a ratio of 3+ workers to every retiree, the current payroll tax rate appears sufficient; but with that ratio now below 3:1 (and projected to continue approaching 2:1 in the future), the current payroll tax rate is by no means sufficient to cover payments to beneficiaries— beginning in 2020 the program runs at a loss, with every subsequent year being worse than the one before. Therefore in order to maintain the same level of social security and Medicare benefits (and politicians are deathly afraid of even considering the possibility of reducing those benefits, because retirees vote in large numbers), the payroll taxes will likely be raised for the younger workers still paying in (as has happened before). Future workers will bear a greater share of the tax burden.

This is the direct tax incidence; but because payroll taxes are designated for specific government programs, we might also consider the distribution of those benefits also. For Social Security and Medicare benefits are not distributed equally: but since they are paid to beneficiaries for the remainder of their lifetime, longer-lived individuals receive far more in benefits than shorter-lived individuals, irrespective of how much was paid into the system through payroll taxes. So who has the longest and shortest lifespans? Generally, wealthier people tend to have healthier lives, better medical care, and less physically demanding or risky labor, so live substantially longer than poorer people. Thus the payroll tax, being re-distributed through Social Security and Medicare, transfers money from poorer people to wealthier people.

The Correct Payroll Tax Rate

Selecting the "correct" rate for payroll taxes will depend upon one's conception of the programs it funds. Let us start with Social Security: is this program

    A) a means of securing each worker's own retirement, or
    B) a means by which younger and more able people
       provide for those older and less able?

The difference matters, because under Option A, one can structure the program such that a worker's taxes fund their own pension, while under Option B the program can be structured to transfer money from some people to others. Under Option A, one establishes a rate based upon estimating an individual's working life (40-45 years) against their retired life (10-20+ years)—which has increased significantly since the beginning of the program, destroying the usefulness of the initial calculations. Under Option B, one establishes a rate based upon the ratio of those working to those no longer able to work (through age or disability)—and this rate has also changed significantly, trending towards fewer working people to support the nonworking population, once again destroying the usefulness of initial calculations.

Americans were sold Option A, but were actually given Option B.

To be entirely accurate, the rhetoric of American politicians at the genesis of the Social Security Act and throughout the years since then has not been at all uniform; and one can find many examples of honest description of the program among the numerous dishonest ones—and perhaps many more descriptions which are confused or unclear enough that one cannot quite evaluate the honesty—and many other descriptions would claim both purposes.

Nevertheless, throughout the decades politicians and voters alike have maintained the fiction of Option A, thinking of retirees as receiving "their" tax dollars back to them; and because benefits paid out are correlated with taxes paid in, it appears to most that people are saving for their own retirement (and insuring against their own disability). It is only when one notices that the benefits paid out have historically been much greater than the benefits paid in that one realizes that we cannot possibly be merely saving our own tax dollars for retirement, but in fact are transferring dollars from current workers to pay for those retired—in actual practice we are operating, and have always been operating, under Option B. And sometimes politicians admit that. (And many voters may approve of that—while other voters do not; and the cunning politician would like to keep the support of both groups, so a little obfuscation here is expected.)

Selecting the correct payroll tax rate for Option A is both difficult and ethically problematic. Because Social Security Retirement is a defined benefit lasting until death, instead of a refund of contributions plus investment earnings, the government runs the double risk of either overpaying the worker or underpaying them. Charge too high a tax rate, and the worker gets back less than they contributed, upsetting the workers/voters who were forced to take a loss on their retirement savings; charge too low a tax rate, and the workers gets back more than they contributed, requiring the government to borrow the money or take from other tax revenues to make up the difference. This is a risk run by any private defined-benefit pension plan, too; but in the private market the business can go bankrupt if it pays out more than it takes in, while the government faces no such risk so long as it can borrow money and levy additional taxes.

Selecting the correct payroll tax rate for B is a little easier, because the overcharging issue is altered: the taxpayer is isn't paying for their own needs, but for the needs of older people and disabled people, so as long as they accept that premise, they can only be "overcharged" if the retirement/disability benefits were considered excessive. Currently, most Americans think Social Security benefits are emphatically *not* excessive, even referring to them as "inadequate," or "parsimonious"—descriptors that make no sense under Option A, but which may be considered meaningful (if debatable) under Option B. Option B is also more attractive because so long as there is a large enough workforce, the tax rate can be set substantially lower than it could under Option A. Of course, there is still the possibility of undercharging—of setting the tax rate too low to cover costs—and that is in fact the situation beginning in 2020.

Setting the correct payroll tax rate for the Medicare program is similar; and again, the actual practice is Option B, using the tax contributions of current/future workers to pay for current beneficiaries. As with the calculation of retirement lifespan (and probability of disability) and worker/retiree ratio for Social Security benefits, Medicare also needs to take these into consideration, along with the changes in costs for end-of-life medical care—which has increased significantly since the program's inception. Partly we spend more on end-of-life care because we live longer, and partly because of new medical options for care—and partly for a host of other reasons involving the economics of the medical industry and the governments involvement in that industry, which are beyond the scope of this book. But within the scope of this book is that the Medicare portion of the payroll tax (2.9% of the employee's gross pay, matched by an equal portion from the employer) levied on the working population is nowhere near enough to pay for the amount of medical services received by current retirees: in 2018, $272 billion dollars of Medicare payroll taxes were collected for a program that spent $740 billion, with the rest of the funding coming from other sources, including Medicare premiums (about 15%), and general tax fund revenues (about 43%).

Ethical Considerations

Since an old age pension and disability/survivors' insurance program is a direct response to losing one's ability to work, it makes some sense to fund it through a direct tax on labor like the payroll tax. A payroll tax designated specifically for the Social Security program (and the additional payroll tax to fund Medicare) escapes the multiplication of tax rules, definitions, deductions, and other arcana built into the income tax code; it makes sure that all workers contribute; and it—theoretically—indicates the cost of the program it funds, so taxpayers can directly experience the cost and compare it to the value of the program. Unfortunately the reality of the tax does not measure up to the theoretical ideal, because the tax rate has not been set at the level needed to actually fund the program (it has always been funded by future tax revenues, and beginning in 2020 the Social Security program must be funded by other sources of current tax revenue, re-introducing the complexity of the income tax system).

The tax/benefit structure has direct implications for several of our ethical criteria, beginning with representation: future taxpayers cannot vote on today's policies. The very structure of the program pushes costs from one generation to the next; every generation is incentivized to minimize their own tax liability at the expense of the next. Politicians aware of the budget shortfalls in the Social Security and Medicare programs know that changes need to be made if the program is to continue to be funded; but they are also aware that demanding higher taxes from today's voters may cost them their careers, so to preserve themselves they leave the problem alone for those who shall come after them. Meanwhile the voters of today who become aware of the programs' financial situation know that they themselves have been cheated, so why should they be made to pay more to fix the system for the future? Shouldn't the next generation be equally cheated? And it shall be, because the future generation cannot yet vote.

Now there are some politicians who are scrupulous enough to recommend changes; but they must compete for votes with other politicians who have no such scruples. Paul Ryan, for example, spent many years advocating for reforms; and his opponents ran national television ads depicting him throwing his own grandmother off a cliff. Though his local constituents continued to elect him, he could never rally enough support from the rest of Congress to actually pass any significant reforms—few elected officials are willing to allow voters imagine them throwing the elderly over a cliff. Perhaps you wonder that such [mis]characterization of a person could ever be taken seriously—but enough voters take it very seriously, so fearful are they of losing promised benefits. Consequently, it is in politicians' interest to lie about the state of the program, and to lie about their opponents trying to save the program.

But lying is not new to politics; and it is certainly not new in the histories of the Social Security Act and the payroll tax. Both the program and the tax was founded in dishonesty, with the advocates of the program creating propaganda to create a public demand for the program. (Despite the travails of the Great Depression, the majority of Americans at the time were skeptical of turning over such an amount of freedom to the federal government; remember, what is normal to us today was to them very new, and uncertain.) The government promised the people that the payroll tax would never exceed 3% (it passed that rate in 1954), promised them that social security numbers would not be used for identification purposes (the cards actually had printed on them "For Social Security purposes—Not for Identification" until they changed that in 1972), promised them they were making "contributions" (the taxes were mandatory) to their "secured" retirement (in fact the retirement amounts are not "secured," but subject to change by law, and by 2018 had $122 in unfunded liabilities—an unsecured amount 6 times the size of the annual gross national product).

An Honest(?) Mistake

One of the economic justifications for Social Security was couched in the Keynesian theory of economics. A 1937 Social Security pamphlet, after noting that most people do not save enough for hard times, puts it thus: "spending… is necessary to hold up the fabric of trade and industry on which the living of the Nation depends. When a large part of the population cuts down spending, that fabric sags, and workers and others feel the weight of hard times." Under the Social Security Administration's interpretation of Keynesian economics, Americans *can't* save for retirement: "The safety of all of us now depends also on the general streams of earning and spending." They reasoned that if the whole population saved more of their money, demand for goods would decline, lowering employment and depressing the economy. But their solution to this [imagined] catastrophe was to have the government collect payroll taxes and immediately spend them instead of saving for retirement, forever using younger people's taxes to pay for older people's benefits. This last part, however, they did *not* advertise in the 1937 brochure.

Was it an honest error of economic theory to argue that encouraging Americans to save for retirement would *harm* the economy? The same theory continues to be advanced today to claim deflation (a decrease in the money supply) would harm the economy, and to recommend the government promote some amount of positive inflation. But other schools of economic thought regard these arguments as entirely incredible, and empirically discredited. You can consult many books on both sides of this debate. Perhaps in 1937, it was still a relative unknown. Or perhaps it was already a known sham for selling the program.

Meanwhile the dishonesty continues, with every mention of the Social Security and Medicare "Trust Funds" which have in them no assets other than IOUs which must be made up from future taxes. The $2.85 trillion or so in "reserves" the Social Security Administration claims it has are Special Interest Securities and Treasury Bonds: their *only* value comes from the government's ability to collect taxes and spend that tax revenue. Economists point out that the "trust funds" are full of IOUs, and that the result is the federal government spends the excess payroll tax revenues on other things (at least until 2020, when there will no longer be any excess); and the Congressional Budget Office plainly records these funds "borrowed" from Social Security in its annual computation of the federal budget and budget deficit. Based upon these facts (we should be able to call the CBO's data factual, no?), many people describe this as the federal government "raiding" Social Security ("borrowing" is the technical, factual term; "raiding" the emotional descriptor) and spending the money—but the Social Security Administration itself argues on its website that it is a "myth" that the federal government has spent the Social Security taxes on anything else!

In addition to the historical dishonesty associated with the sale and promotion of the Social Security program, there is the obfuscation built into the payroll tax structurally. Splitting the tax between employee and employer disguises the cost of the tax from Americans, encouraging them to imagine that richer employers pay their portion of the tax out of their lavish profits; but any economist knows that the employer's portion of the tax involves a reduction in the worker's wages. When the benefits payments start to exceed the payroll taxes collected, the federal government is likely to raise the rates again, trusting they can continue the disguise: but more information is available to Americans now, and perhaps this time they will see the impact upon their wage growth.

Lying, or Really Confused?

It's not only the SSA that makes such bizarre claims: you can find non-government parties also claiming that it is a "myth" that Social Security has been raided, citing its "reserves" as evidence the money is still there. It seems to me that describing an IOU (an I-will-pay-you-using-future-tax-revenue) as proof the money previously collected has not been spent is either rank dishonesty or amazing incredulity. The federal government's accounting fiction would be recognized as fiction in any private business: if, for example, the East branch of my business was making a profit while the West branch was losing money, and I moved funds ("borrowed") from my East branch to make up the deficit, no one could claim that my East branch had any real-money "reserves;" one could only note that it had a legal claim on the future profits of the West branch. That is the state of the Social Security program: its own funds were spent, and now it has $2.85 trillion in claims on future tax revenues.

So the payroll tax does not do well by either our honesty or our openness criteria, and it cannot pass either the representation or appropriateness criteria as long as it transfers today's costs to future generations. Its projected insolvency, and the unwillingness of politicians to proactively resolve these problems, means that it also fails the criteria of minimizing harms. But what can positively be said about the tax?

Well, it's mostly simple: the payroll tax itself is mostly uncomplicated, aside from the splitting between employer and employee, and the effect this has on self-employed individuals (they must pay both halves, so they are given a tax deduction for the employer half, to make their tax burden more equal to other workers, who do not pay taxes on the employer contribution). Also, it passes the participation criteria, in that nearly the whole of the population is subject to the tax. (There are some people who get exempted from the tax—mostly government employees with other pension programs, the reason being that their retirements are already secured by these other means. Unfortunately, the vast majority of these pensions have also been over-promised, resulting in both the federal government and many state governments having billions of dollars in unfunded liabilities here, also.)

Interestingly, despite all of the problems noted above, the payroll tax does seem to pass the peace criteria, in that it does not pit groups of Americans against each other. (In fact, it pits current Americans against future Americans, but the children and the unborn are unable to argue the matter.) One might expect more argument between older Americans and those younger Americans just starting to pay the tax—with 40 years of payments ahead of them and little hope for just recompense—but it appears that the vast majority of Americans agree that the Social Security and Medicare programs are necessary, and must be preserved, even if that means younger people must pay more. Or maybe it only seems that we have so much agreement: for much larger percentages of older Americans vote than do younger Americans, so it is possible that many younger Americans are not so happy about this arrangement, but have not yet made themselves heard on this issue as a voting bloc.

Maybe the agreement on this issue stems partly from the unwillingness of politicians to face the problems with the program, and provide alternatives: for without alternatives to consider, the voting public's only perceived options are to keep the status quo or... what? eliminate the program and the tax? To most that would be unthinkable. Most Americans recognize a moral obligation, an ethical duty, to provide for our elderly and disabled. Of course they do: this value has been part of the human race as long as we have records—and much longer than we have had the Social Security and Medicare programs. But how did we come to the conclusion that this ethical duty requires us to use this particular method? Perhaps we never did; but our current generation was born into a world where this was the established custom, so it gets the assumption of being ethical. But should it?

Prior to the Social Security and Medicare programs, and prior to the payroll tax, how did people meet—or attempt to meet—the ethical obligation to provide for the elderly and disabled? To begin with, the obligation was framed differently: it was not that "society" had a duty to provide for the elderly and disabled, but that families had a duty to provide for *their* elderly and disabled. Of course, this does mean that the elderly and disabled without families are not provided for—nor the elderly and disabled with destitute families, or "bad" families (families who did not attempt to live up to this obligation). So collectively, a society which wanted *all* of their elderly and disabled to be provided for might do well relocate this obligation from the family unit to the larger community—even to the national government. But if it does make ethical sense to make the obligation to care for the elderly and the disabled a function of the national government, it does *not* logically follow that every option for doing so is therefore ethical. The current system was *not* the only possibility before us in the 1930s; nor is it the only possibility open to us now.

Unfortunately, the proposal of any alternative is met with great hostility from some quarters; amidst fear and insecurity, we accuse reformers of callous disregard for the needy, and by doing so raise the social cost of proposing effective, sustainable reform.

We must recognize both the economic and ethical costs of our current program, and begin to imagine alternatives to weigh them against. Some of the costs of our current system include the reduction of people's freedom to make their own savings and investment decisions (which for many means actually reducing their standard of living in retirement, if they could have made better savings and investment decisions than the mandatory federal retirement program), the reduction of the poor's ability to meet their immediate needs, and the pushing of increasing costs upon future generations (and while our culture acknowledges than children have an obligation to their elderly and disabled, it also acknowledges that each generation has some responsibility towards their children and further posterity). Questioning the current program is *not* questioning the value of the old and infirm, though it may involve an attempt to balance the needs of today's old and infirm against the needs of tomorrow's old and infirm.

Discussion of possible alternatives to the current Social Security and Medicare systems warrants a book of its own; this unsatisfactory chapter can only introduce us to the issue. Hopefully, such consideration can advance the discussion (or lack thereof) from its current state to a point that we may actually be able to consider—and evaluate—alternatives at a national level, without accusing people of trying to throw grandma off of a cliff.

Summary Report Card – Payroll Taxes

Representation   **Unethical toward Posterity**

Since the beginning of the Social Security system, benefits had to be funded by taxing younger and future workers; but future workers cannot vote, and therefore have no say in their share of the cost. Each new generation of workers gets to inherit the unsolved problems and obligations of the system.

Participation   **Pass, with one Exception**

The payroll tax is applied to the whole of the working population—except certain classes of people (mostly government employees) who are exempt, since they participate in other pension systems (which, on average, are in even worse financial shape than Social Security).

Honesty   **Flatly Unethical**

The Social Security and Medicare programs were passed under false pretenses (there were never individual retirement accounts, and payroll taxes were never saved for retirees) and is supported by a fiction (a "Trust Fund," which in fact contains only government IOUs financed by future taxes).

Openness   **Fail**

Nominally splitting the payroll tax between employees and employers disguises the full cost of the tax from the employees who bear the tax burden.

Simplicity   **Pass**

Appropriateness   **Declining**

Theoretically, the population being taxed (workers) is the population which receives benefits (those who have worked); but this only passes if taxes and benefits are commensurate over time: with solvency declining, the population being taxed today will not enjoy the full benefits in the future.

Consideration   **Somewhat Problematic**

The Social Security and Medicare programs funded by the payroll tax transfer some amount of money from shorter-lived poorer persons to longer-lived wealthier persons.

Minimizing Harms   **Total Fail**

Politicians do everything they can to avoid addressing the harms created by Social Security and Medicare's absolute unsustainability and looming bankruptcy.

Peace   **Pass?**

The vast majority of Americans appear to be in agreement that the Social Security and Medicare programs are necessary, and also in agreement that benefits for the elderly should be maintained even if that does cost younger generation more.

11

Real Property Taxes

Property taxes are one of the oldest forms of taxation, even predating money itself, since ancient governments could collect the tax in the form of a share of crops raised from the land (the oldest tax records we have describe such a tax five thousand years ago). Property is a rather obvious kind of wealth, making it an easy target for taxation. But how property is taxed has varied quite a bit over the centuries; and we have discovered better and worse methods of doing so.

Description and Purpose

Property taxes are applied as a percentage of the value of property; most frequently they are applied to "real" property (real estate, including land, buildings on the land, and "fixtures"—immovable property connected to buildings/land, or property that would cause damage if moved); however, some governments also tax personal property as well. As taxes on Real Property are far more common, impacting far more voters on a more significant scale—and as the differences between property tax options are particularly instructive—we will be focusing on taxation of Real Property.

Throughout the world, property taxes are levied against the owners of property (the exception being Great Britain, which has a Council Tax levied against the *residents* of a property, rather than the owners), generally on an annual basis (although some jurisdictions levy the tax, or an additional tax, at the time of transfer of property). In the United States, property taxes are not [currently] levied by the federal government, but are by state and local governments. As of 2019, state rates range from 0.27% in Hawaii to 2.44% in New Jersey (where the average homeowner pays more than $7,000 a year on this tax). Property owners may also pay county and/or city property taxes in addition to these state rates (and in California, additional "special district" Mello-Roos property taxes to cover bonds and other local expenditures).

Taxing Personal Property

Personal Property taxes can apply only to Tangible property (equipment, furniture, etc.) or also to Intangible property (stocks, copyrights, patents, etc.). Not all states tax personal property; and of those that do, most tax Tangible Personal Property only. Almost every state exempts household items from this taxation (only a few counties in Oklahoma try to tax that); instead they levy the tax on motor vehicles, personal watercraft, and business property (including vehicles, capital equipment, and, depending upon the jurisdiction, inventory). Thus most individuals are not much impacted by such taxes; but for businesses it can be a considerable expense: depending upon the jurisdiction, such taxes may be assessed at anywhere from 5-15%, and must be paid even when the business is failing to make any profit, annually eroding their capital.

Since property taxes are generally levied as a percentage of the value of property, the government which collects them must establish some means of assessing the value of property. A government tax assessor establishes the taxable value of the property, often by reviewing the sale prices of like properties in the area—or through whatever other method has been established by legislation. These assessments may or may not reflect the actual (or perceived) values of the properties; in many jurisdictions, property owners may challenge their government's assessment in the courts. Such assessments may be undertaken annually (Or however often the government desires), to revise the tax values in light of changing market prices. Since property values can be impacted not only by a property owner's own development, but also by the development of neighboring properties, a property owner with an older, less-developed property may still find their taxes increase as their nearby community grows.

Property taxes may or may not be equal throughout a jurisdiction: for the taxing body may establish separate rates for different kinds of property (such as one rate for business property and another for residential); they may involve multiple tax brackets (for example, having an additional surtax on "mansions" valued over $1 million dollars); and/or provide various exemptions for particular groups (such as veterans, farmers, and non-profit organizations). Property taxes may also be assigned based upon the *effects* of property: for example, Maryland, Illinois, and New Jersey have a special tax on property determined to generate excess water runoff (these are called stormwater fees by proponents and "rain taxes" by those who oppose them)—which tax also requires a special assessment by the governing body according to both legislated rules and the interpretations of those rules by the delegated bureaucracy.

Property taxes are often levied to fund the state, county, or city government generally, but may also be levied across smaller jurisdictions to specifically fund schools and other specified public goods. Funding the building and maintenance of local schools, parks, roads, and utilities is often supplemented by additional Impact Fees levied on new developments; these nonrecurring Impact Fees can vary widely according to the local jurisdiction (in some areas of Texas, these may be $1,000 per home; while in California they can range from $20,000 per home in some areas to more than $150,000 for a home in Fremont).

In the vast majority of jurisdictions, property taxes are assessed based upon the total value of both the land and the buildings upon that land. However, some jurisdictions have taxes upon the value of the land only, irrespective of its development. These taxes, termed land-value taxes to distinguish them from the more normative property taxes which count buildings also, have profoundly different economic effects, which we shall consider below.

Assessing Property Values

Since property taxes are levied as a percentage of a property's value, the government needs some means of assessing the value of that property. Therefore the government employs tax assessors to determine the value of each and every property within the taxing government's jurisdiction, generally—but not necessarily—by looking at the sale price of the property at the most recent sale, and adjusting that price according to current prices. If the property in question has not sold in some time, tax assessors may—not must—compare it to similar properties (as the tax assessors define similar) in order to estimate the property's value if it were sold. You may immediately perceive a problem with such a structural arrangement: since the government collects more taxes the higher the property is valued, government agents are always incentivized to overestimate the value of the properties they assess. Thus government tax assessors frequently determine the value of a given property increases every year, even during recessions and other times when nearby similar properties are being sold for less money. Now there may be a legal way to dispute the government's tax assessment—by appealing to another government bureaucrat, of course, which usually involves paying fees, completing paperwork, and providing one's own assessment based upon market research that took some amount of time and money to compile, and which has no certainty of convincing the government agent being appealed to. Property owners with significant holdings (for example, multiple apartment complexes) may find themselves appealing their tax assessments every year; but many smaller property owners (such a simple homeowners) just endure the slight overvaluation of their tax assessment each year.

Meanwhile the government which depends upon property taxes for its revenues has a vested interest in keeping property values high; so it is more likely to pass other laws to promote increases in property value. Typically, they sell these laws as "benefiting homeowners" and "propping up the housing market;" but they may have more to do with propping up the government's revenue stream.

Economic Effects

Most taxes increase the immediate price of goods and services, as the cost of the tax is added to (or transferred to) the price of the product. But taxes on real property can actually reduce the [immediate] price of land, since businesses and investors must take into account the ongoing cost of the property tax when computing their expected return on investment. Suppose for example that a piece of real property is expected to yield an income of $20,000 annually: if the average market yield for long-term investments were 5%, then I would want to pay no more than $400,000 for this property ($400,000 x .05 = $20,000)—at any higher price, I would make alternative investments, which would net me a better return. But if that property were subject to $4,000/year in property taxes, then the net income from that property would be only $16,000 annually, and I would therefore not want to pay any more than $320,000 for it ($320,000 x .05 = $16,000)—and I would pay even less than that, if I had any suspicion that property tax rates would be raised in the future.

Businesses, landlords, and other investors have to make similar calculations regarding any improvements to the property they own, wherever property taxes apply to buildings and fixtures (and in some cases, livestock). When considering any addition and/or improvement to one's rental housing units (or warehouses, factories, farms, etc.) one must estimate the amount of income that will be lost to property tax when calculating expected return on investment; and if the end result is a lower rate of return than alternative investments, then the addition/improvement will not be made.

As we have noted with other taxes, taxing any item or behavior tends to result in less of that item or behavior, as raising the price makes the item/behavior less valuable to people than other alternative uses of their money. Thus the power to tax is easily the power to destroy, if the tax rate is set high enough. Now land itself is not produced, so one might be tempted to imagine property taxes escaping this pattern; but since property taxes apply to all the improvements upon land (buildings, fixtures, etc.), the same rule applies: high property tax rates result in less development of land, insofar as the development of land becomes less profitable in comparison with alternative uses of limited resources.

Consequently, the tax policies of local governments can have significant impacts upon the development of cities. Areas with low and/or stable tax rates attract investment: houses, apartments, commercial businesses, factories, warehouses—and with all of these, people and jobs. Meanwhile places with high and/or rising property tax rates are more prone to decay, as upkeep and renovation become less profitable than alternative investment. Unprofitable buildings can be left to rot, since attempting to improve them only results in them losing more money when the property gets reassessed for the next year's taxes.

Property taxes affect homeowners, also; but because a home does not provide an annual income, single homeowners may not calculate return on investment, unless they are looking to sell soon. But like investors and commercial businesses, they may calculate impacts upon making home improvements: that new deck, new pool, or additional bedroom won't only cost $30,000 up front, but also an extra $300 every year (at merely a 1% property tax).

Economic Effects of Further Legislation

When housing prices increase, homeowners find themselves paying more each year in property taxes as the value of their homes gets reassessed. So in order to protect themselves from having their property tax bills increase too quickly, in 1978 Californians passed Proposition 13, which limited new tax assessments to 2% annually, until the property was sold and could be reassessed at its full market value. Thus when people's homes appreciate faster than the 2% limit, they end up paying much lower taxes than new owners of comparable homes. This brings with it a new set of economic consequences: homeowners who benefit from this have a strong dis-incentive to move, since moving into a similarly-priced house results in a drastic increase in their annual property tax bills. Consequently, many people with homes that once housed large families keep ahold of their homes even after all the kids have moved out, though they no longer need the space. It just makes more economic sense to them to retain their over-large homes than to move into smaller ones. Meanwhile the new families discover a smaller supply of homes available to meet their needs—raising the price of homes for them accordingly.

In addition to these direct economic impacts upon land development, the government's interest in property values motivates legislators to pass laws that encourage home-buying and to prop up existing real estate values. This constant intervention in the housing market (which significantly favors single-family homes over apartments and other multi-family units) to alter prices—the carriers of information—reduces the ability of developers and entrepreneurs to interpret price information and allocate resources to meet the people's real demands. Extra resources get allocated to build higher-priced single-family homes instead of multi-family homes, leaving some areas with a shortage of lower-priced homes and apartment buildings.

Now government involvement in housing development—including zoning, permitting, subsidizing, and half a hundred other policies—and these other policies also may result in surpluses and shortages in the housing market, and many have much more significant impacts than the tax issue noted above. These policies are beyond the scope of this work; but they must be mentioned here to indicate that the effects noted above are only a part of a much larger and more complicated picture. So even if we solve for the tax issue, we'll still have many other policies impacting our results.

Economic Effects – Land-Value Taxes

The economic impacts considered above result from property taxes applied to both land and the developments upon that land; but there is an alternative means of assessing property taxes, which would have very different economic consequences. This is the land-value tax—a tax upon the market value of the land only, leaving all buildings and other developments upon that land untaxed.

To generate a similar level of revenue to the more common property tax, the land-value tax would be set at a higher rate. For example, a $400,000 home on a $100,000 parcel taxed at 1% under normal property tax would net the government $5,000 annually ($500,000 x .01 = $5,000); so a land-value tax on the same property would be set at 5% to net the same amount ($100,000 x .05 = $5,000). If we were to replace the property tax with a land-value tax like this, homeowners could be minimally impacted, with most homeowners paying about the same amount as before.

But future development would change significantly.

Under the normal property tax regime, we observed developers must calculate future taxes when considering future construction, and overall this results in less construction, whenever the tax rate reduces the expected rate of return on investment to a level below other opportunities in the market. But under a land-value tax structure, no such tax considerations need to be made, as the new construction will not be taxed. The land—which cannot be produced—gets taxed the same whether it is empty or developed; meanwhile the productive activities of building, renovating, repairing, cultivating, etc. are unhindered. Under this system, landowners actually have a greater incentive to develop their lands, because undeveloped land only costs them money. Land would be used more efficiently (with the caveat that governments will still interfere through other means, including zoning regulations, height restrictions, and other means), and existing buildings would be more frequently improved (or replaced).

Additionally, land speculation and urban sprawl would be reduced. Under the current system, investors buy up parcels of land around cities and then hold on to them without developing them, waiting for others to develop the neighboring land first, at which point the empty parcels can be sold for a higher amount. They can do this profitably now because the low tax rate on empty land allows them to hold on to the empty land for many years and still recover that cost. But under the land-value tax, the empty land is taxed at a higher rate, increasing the cost of holding it long-term. Thus several localities have specifically implemented land-value taxes to combat their urban sprawl.

Tax Incidence

We already noted how property taxes reduce the price of investment properties (properties expected to turn a profit): the buyer, calculating the tax's impact on their anticipated return, offers the seller a lower purchase price. If the property owner then has any tenants (whether residential tenants in an apartment complex, or commercial tenants at a shopping center), they will try to shift whatever costs they can onto the renters, being more or less successful depending upon the ability of their tenants to move elsewhere. So if property taxes are raised, the owner of an apartment complex will try to raise rent in order to cover that raise; and if all nearby apartments are subject to the same property tax increase, then each may transfer all or nearly all of the cost of the tax increase to their tenants' rent, since those tenants won't be able to find a better deal elsewhere. In contrast, if the apartment complex is on the border of a tax jurisdiction, and is subject to a property tax increase while its nearby competitors are not, then less of the cost may be passed along to the renters, since they may be able to move to a cheaper dwelling—until the competitor raises their own rents in response to this new demand.

But while landlords will seek to transfer as much of the tax burden as they can to renters, they will not always be able to do so. In some jurisdictions, rent control laws will prevent it; in other cases, the market of renters may not be able to bear the new price, and respond by choosing other living arrangements (such as moving in with other family, since they can no longer afford rent). In either of these scenarios, an increase in property tax reduces the landlord's profits (and in the case of rent-controlled neighborhoods, can reduce it below zero, so the landlord is losing money so long as they own the property). When profits are reduced, landlords may respond by cutting expenses for maintenance, beautification, renovation, etc.—so the tenant bear the cost of the tax increase in terms of poorer housing.

**Combining Bad Policies:
High Property Taxes and Rent Control**

Local governments may raise taxes to generate revenue while at the same time passing rent control to "protect" renters from high rents. But when rent control prevents a landowner from being able to make a profit, the landowner may abandon the property, leaving it to decay ownerless. As the housing unit falls into disrepair, no other housing units are built for that price range, since they too would be unprofitable. So the total stock of available housing units gets reduced—further raising rents on nearby units not subject to rent controls. Meanwhile the apartments which barely make a profit are kept in a state of disrepair, since that reduces their market value, and therefore the ongoing cost of their property taxes.

Renters also bear the unseen cost of foregone renovation. For any improvement made to a rental property may invite a new tax assessment, and higher property taxes; so landlords will only improve their properties when they anticipate a higher profit resulting—that is, when such improvements may command higher rents from new tenants. This reduces the overall level of improvement made to existing apartment buildings, making the overall housing quality decline relative to newer developments. Significantly, jurisdictions which rely on land-value taxes instead of regular property taxes do not have this problem: for improvements and maintenance in those jurisdictions can increase profitability without incurring additional taxes.

Meanwhile homeowners bear the entirety of their property taxes, as they have no one to shift the burden to. To manage the burden of the property tax, many homeowners have escrow accounts set up with their banks to pay a portion of their property tax each month along with their mortgage payment; then when their property tax bill is due the amount is pulled from their escrow account instead of requiring them to write a large check. Many homeowners may prefer making monthly payments on their property tax instead of paying them annually or semi-annually; but wealthier homeowners who regularly make investments may prefer to put their money where it can earn more interest for them; for these people, living in a jurisdiction that requires an escrow account for property taxes is in effect paying an additional amount of tax equal to the foregone interest they might otherwise have earned.

Tax incidence upon homeowners can vary considerably according to how property taxes are assessed, and how many jurisdictions (state, county, city, and Mello-Roos special jurisdictions in California) are assessing such a tax. Wherever laws (such as California's Prop 13) limit how much tax assessments may increase each year, newer property owners bear a greater tax burden than established owners—the tax difference between two similar properties may be several thousand dollars annually.

Ethical Considerations

Historically, the justification for property taxes has been quite sample: wealth comes from the land. Since economies have transitioned from being based upon agriculture to being based more on manufacturing and trade, income and sales taxes have become more important; but property taxes still make intuitive sense to many, as property owners tend to be people who can afford to be taxed. The current reality is not so straightforward as that, of course, with property taxes being passed along to renters; but as a local tax property taxes still make intuitive sense: the local government is collecting revenue explicitly from the people who live in and have investment in the local community, and who are the direct beneficiaries of local government services, like schools, police, and fire departments.

Being a local tax, property taxes do well on the representation criteria: for even if taxpayers do not vote in political elections, they may choose where they live—if a voter finds their local property tax too onerous, they may "vote with their feet" and move to another jurisdiction. Now moving to another jurisdiction may involve foregoing many benefits of the local area, including parks, city centers, and various civic improvements supported by property taxes—which fits our appropriateness criteria quite nicely, as the primary beneficiaries of the local government are the local property taxpayers themselves.

Property taxes are also fairly straightforward (although this varies between jurisdictions: a local government is quite capable of complicating their property tax laws with split tax rolls, multiple rates, sundry exemptions, and other lows). And to homeowners and businesses, they are fairly open: the taxpayer knows (or can learn with minimal effort) what amount they are paying—though it must be noted that renters do not have this same knowledge (since they do not pay property tax directly, and it is not communicated to them how much of the tax gets passed on to them).

However, there is one practical disadvantage that comes from the local government's dependence on property taxes as a primary revenue source, which in turn presents some ethical difficulties. This is that a local government short on revenue must consider decisions in light of potential property tax revenues, and this can be a disservice to their community: particularly, it means that local governments become

Combining Bad Policies: Property Taxes and Eminent Domain

Eminent Domain is the power of the government to take private land (paying whatever compensation the government decides) for public purposes, such as the construction of roads, government buildings, and utilities. In the United States, however, the government has asserted "public use" to include taking private property from one person and giving it to another private person, if the new owner promotes "economic development" by creating jobs and *increasing local tax revenues*. This gives local governments, already hungry for increased tax revenues, the legal authority to take land from poorer neighborhoods (paying less taxes) to give to richer developers to create richer neighborhoods (who will pay more taxes).

Such legal theft was officially sanctioned in the 2005 Supreme Court decision Kelo v. City of New London. Yet after that case was decided, the developer failed to follow through: thus people had had their homes confiscated and demolished to become nothing more than an empty lot—which quite failed to produce the $1.2 million in annual tax revenues that had been anticipated!

easily biased against allowing low-income housing, family-dense apartment buildings require more schools to be built and more police and other services. For even if the people living in low-income housing units had less need of police, fire, sanitation and other services than higher-income people, the per-capita property tax contribution from households living in apartment buildings is lower than the per capita tax contribution from people living in single residence homes. Consequently, many towns and cities zone the vast majority of their residential areas for single family units, discouraging the building of costly (for the city) multi-family apartment buildings.

The additional negative economic effects of taxing the buildings and permanent fixtures upon land also run afoul of the Minimizing Harms criteria—particularly since there is a readily-available policy alternative here, since governments do have the option of taxing the value of the land only. Land-value only taxes absolutely minimize economic harms, since no productive activity is being taxed. The economic efficiency of land-value taxes is acknowledged by economists on both sides of the political spectrum. The free market economist Milton Friedman—renowned for lecturing on the failures and shortcomings of government—acknowledged that so long as people desire certain government services (such as police, legal courts to enforce contract rights, etc.), tax revenue must come from somewhere, and land-value taxes with the best option for that, insofar as they had the least impact on productive economic behavior. Meanwhile pro-government (and pro-tax) economists on the opposite side of the political spectrum, like Paul Krugman, have likewise acknowledged the economic efficiency of land-value taxes—the point of contention between them is only that the large-government economists believe that we need more revenue than what can be generated from land value taxes alone, so they argue for additional taxes to supplement that.

However, despite the moral virtues of land-value taxes, and to a somewhat lesser extent, the virtues of regular property taxes, taxpayers themselves seem to have a different opinion about their ethical value: 40% of respondents to a 2005 Gallup poll, for example, identified the property tax as the "least fair" tax, worse even than income taxes. Why is that? Possibly they are unpopular because the property tax is the last tax that people still have to write out a big check for (recall the importance of tax withholding for changing public perception of the income tax). But there is an additional reason: property tax assessments go up even when homeowners do nothing to improve their homes, but the surrounding neighborhood had improved, raising the value of their home. Homeowners like seeing their home's value go up—particularly if they are thinking of selling, or needing to take a loan out from their home's equity—but they hate seeing their tax bills go up at the same time, when they themselves have taken no action to increase the taxable value of their property. Meanwhile the taxpayer cannot take any action to reduce their tax liability—short of moving, of course.

Summary Report Card – Real Property Taxes / Land-Value Taxes

Representation — **Good / Good**

Property taxes fund local government, and property owners have the choice to participate in local votes or "vote with their feet" by moving to lower-tax areas.

Participation — **Pass / Pass**

While property owners are not the whole of the population, the tax incidence on renters effectively means the entire population in a jurisdiction is being taxed.

Honesty — **Vulnerable / Fair**

There is a structural vulnerability in that the party interested in maximizing the tax revenue is also the party which assesses the value of the property.

Openness — **Good / Good**

Property taxes rates are publicly available, with no structurally inherent deceit.

Simplicity — **Pass / Good**

Some complexity results from multiple jurisdictions assessing taxes on the same property at different rates, as well as with regulations covering escrow accounts to pay the taxes. Jurisdictions which assess property taxes on items beyond land and buildings to include livestock, vehicles, and intangible property would get something less than a Passing result; but jurisdictions which tax the land only get a higher mark on this criteria.

Appropriateness — **Some Issues / Some Issues**

Property taxes are assessed to support local government services, but the level of government services provided does not match up with the taxes collected in each area; instead wealth is transferred from some neighborhoods to others.

Consideration — **Debatable / Good**

The negative economic consequences of regular property taxes fall mostly upon people who live in lower-income rental housing. These same negative economic costs are absent in a land-value tax.

Minimizing Harms — **Problematic / Excellent**

Significant economic harms result from property taxes on buildings and other improvements. But land-value taxes eliminate all of these harms: by taxing only the land, which cannot be produced, land-value taxes are the most economically efficient (that is, they result in the least loss of productivity) of all tax options.

Peace — **Problematic / Excellent**

The biggest threat to peace comes from combining government dependence upon property taxes with the government's power/abuse of Eminent Domain laws; but the incentive to use Eminent Domain laws for the purpose of obtaining additional tax revenues is absent under a land-value tax.

Postscript: Wealth Taxes

Taxing real property makes a kind of intuitive sense: a government which rules over an area of land and provides services to that area of land has some right to support from the owners of that land. However, some people leap from the advantages of taxing real property to the idea of taxing *all* property, including savings, business assets, investments in stocks and bonds, fine art, and every other kind of asset. Such people reason: we want to tax the wealthiest people, so why not tax the wealth directly? Such a tax currently does not exist in the United States, but several politicians support such a proposal. Unfortunately, taxing the whole of a person's wealth presents some additional problems:

To begin with, taxing total wealth as opposed to total income is an easy recipe for leaving the governed worse off than they were before. For when we tax income, we take only a portion of a person's *improvement* in life: the taxpayer still gains by their labor, and can budget for their needs based upon their remaining income. But applying a similar tax rate to a person's wealth can leave them each year with less than they had before, until the majority of their wealth is plundered. This is particularly the case for new businesses owners, who after investing great amounts of wealth in a new business often go several years before turning a profit: under a wealth tax, they can easily be taxed out of business before the profits come. Or consider a person who has the bulk of their wealth in the form of stock in a company (maybe a company they helped start years ago). In order to pay the wealth tax, they need cash; but to get the cash, they have to sell some of their stock (incurring additional capital gains taxes on the income from selling the stock), leaving them with less stock than before—and then again the next year, and the year after that. Wealth taxes literally plunder people wherever the tax rate is higher than the income generated from the taxed assets: so for every business with a low profit margin (grocery stores, for example, often run a profit margin of about 2%; and as noted before, many businesses have initial periods of losing money before they become profitable), wealth taxes force the owners of the business to sell off assets, shrinking their business until it is no more. Likewise, if a taxpayer's retirement savings earns less interest than the wealth tax [plus inflation], they can also find themselves losing retirement savings every year. People subject to a wealth tax would have to stop making safer, low-interest investments and move their money to higher-interest investments to stay even—except those investments tend to be riskier. This is true even for "small" wealth tax rates of 1-2%.

Significantly, *the same wealth is taxed every year*; repeated taxation of the same amount of wealth only reduces (plunders) its value—even if "only" a few percent at a time. At least with income taxes, money is taxed only once (sometimes multiple times, in the case of certain incomes, like dividends); but wealth taxes never end.

But suppose a wealth tax were applied only to the "very wealthy," (one proposed plan would levy a 2% rate on fortunes above $50 million, and an additional 1% on fortunes over $1 billion). This would still have several negative effects for the non-wealthy in the same economy, including:

1. Wealthy people would move their investments to other countries to avoid the taxation, reducing the amount of capital available to new and growing businesses in the domestic economy.

2. Existing investment assets would shrink, further reducing the amount of capital available to new and growing businesses in the domestic economy.

3. A reduction in available capital results in both slower job growth, and less growth in real wages (both free-market and Marxist economists agree that capital formation is a major component of wage growth. Depending upon the rate and duration of the wealth tax, the nation could easily see *reduced GDP, reduced wages, and reduced employment.*

The whole nation bears these economic costs, although the politicians promise the tax will afflict only the very wealthy. Such disastrous economic costs may be the reason why most of the countries who have tried the wealth tax in the past have abandoned it (more than a dozen European countries used to have wealth taxes, but now only Norway, Spain, and Switzerland do). Those nations that retain the tax have significant collection costs (assessing all the property each year requires a significant investment of government resources) to collect less revenue than originally anticipated.

Alternatively, sometimes politicians suggest a one-time wealth tax instead of an annual tax; such proposals tend to suggest much higher rates, since it would only be a "one time" tax. But proposals for a "one time" wealth tax are quite dubious: for if any government discovers that it can, by popular vote, extract such a portion from their wealthy citizens, who shall believe that they will not do it a second time? Especially if the justification of such a "one time" tax was to redistribute wealth or reduce inequality, or to resolve the national debt or some other emergency—for would not all these reasons be repeatable in the future? (Even if a national debt were paid off, certainly politicians would not restrain their spending after discovering such a solution!) Any person subject to such plunder on one occasion will consider how to protect themselves from a second incidence—in this case, by moving to a less rapacious country and taking their wealth with them, to be used as capital in that economy and promoting that economy's growth.

12

Inheritance Taxes
(aka Estate Taxes / Death Taxes)

The use of the term "death taxes" to describe estate taxes and inheritance taxes is a meaningful—and for some people, contentious—decision. For although the terms "death tax" and "estate" tax in the United States may denote the same thing—a tax upon a person's property assessed after they have died—each term emphasizes a different aspect of that tax, and people have different emotional responses to the two terms. "Estate tax" emphasizes the target of the tax—wealthy people with magnificent estates—while "death tax" emphasizes the occasion of the tax—an unhappy event common to all people. Polls and focus groups have consistently shown that people are more likely to oppose a "death" tax than an "estate" tax: about two-thirds of Americans oppose the estate tax on polls, while about three quarters of Americans oppose the same tax when the poll question refers to it as a death tax). So when discussing this tax, people of opposite opinions may first argue over what to even call it. Which term is more proper, or fair? For the purposes of our discussion, I argue that we must keep in mind both terms/emphases, and recognize that each term/emphasis triggers a different set of ethical considerations (or at least reflexive responses, which have not yet risen to the level of intentional consideration).

Terminology Matters

Though proponents of higher estate taxes may argue that the term "death tax" is unfair, note how they themselves will often be careful to advocate "strengthening" the estate tax when they could more straightforwardly advocate "raising" the tax. They know that people consider "weakness" to be undesirable; calls to therefore "strengthen" the tax ask us to assume that raising the rate is more desirable, instead of asking us to analyze that very question.

Description and Purpose

Death taxes may refer to estate taxes or to inheritance taxes, or to both collectively. The difference between estate and inheritance taxes is that estate taxes are assessed prior to dividing a deceased person's assets between their heirs (the government takes a portion of the estate), while inheritance taxes are assessed after such division (the government takes a portion of each individual's inheritance). Some countries choose the one method of taxing the wealth distributed at a person's death, while other countries select the other. The United States federal government chooses to tax the estate, prior to it being divided among heirs; twelve of the fifty states (plus the District of Columbia) levy their own estate taxes in addition to those of the federal government, while six states choose to tax at the point of inheritance—Maryland, however, has both taxes, essentially taxing the same transfer twice under two different names, taking one share before a dead person's property is divided, and then taking an additional share from each inheritor.

To pay the estate tax in the United States, the survivors of the deceased (actually, their tax lawyers), inventory all the deceased person's assets—including cash, securities, real estate, insurance, trusts, annuities, business interests, works of art, etc.—and report them on IRS form 709, which as of 2019 was 29 pages (and may require additional supporting forms and documentation) with a set of official instructions exceeding 50,000 words. The current fair market value of all assets has to be determined, and the value of all gifts the deceased gave before their death must be added up (the tax regulations need to consider such gifts in assessing the estate tax to prevent taxpayers from dodging the estate tax by giving away their property in life). Then the value of assets above the exemption level ($11.4 million in 2019) is subject to the tax, on a progressive scale (like the US federal income tax) with marginal rates ranging from 18% (for the first $10,000 of taxable assets) to 40% (for all taxable assets after the first $1 million). Finally, an additional amount of Generation Skipping Tax is calculated for all assets passed to grandchildren (or any other person more than 37.5 years younger than the deceased), because the government would otherwise be missing the opportunity to tax these assets twice (if passed from deceased to child, then from that parent to child, instead of from the deceased directly to grandchild).

While everybody dies, not everybody pays the death/estate tax, as the exemption level in the United States is high enough that only a fraction of the even the very wealthy pay the tax—that is, less than a fifth of one percent of the American public in 2018. This exemption rate has not always been so high: back in 2004 the exemption was only $1.5 million dollars, impacting a much larger share of American estates. The fact that the exemption level has been raised multiple times since then to its current level makes one wonder just what the purpose of the tax is.

As we have noted before, the primary purpose of most taxes is to raise revenue for the government, so that it could provide services and wage war. But some kinds of taxes are designed for other purposes also, or even primarily: for example, tariffs are designed to privilege domestic businesses over foreign competitors, and excise taxes are created to discourage the population from purchasing "bad" products. Historically, the purpose of and justification for estate taxes has been not simply (or even primarily) to fund government, but to redistribute wealth and reduce inequality. The idea was that uninhibited inheritance would concentrate wealth and capital among the few, depriving the many of the bounties of the earth.

Exemption Level by Year	
2004	$1,500,000
2006	$2,000,000
2009	$3,500,000
2010	$5,000,000
2012	$5,120,000
2013	$5,250,000
2014	$5,340,000
2015	$5,430,000
2016	$5,450,000
2017	$5,490,000
2018	$11,180,000
2019	$11,400,000

Now a top marginal tax rate of 40% on estates at death quite supports a plan to redistribute/deconcentrate wealth—but an $11.4 million exemption that leaves the majority of estates intact does not. Meanwhile the high exemption also reduces the tax base so far that the tax fails to generate much revenue for the government, so it's not doing much to meet that purpose, either. Now it must be noted that advocates of the estate task propose reducing the exemption in order to better meet both of these purposes, and hearing such explicit advocacy we may accept that at least some people want this; perhaps the existence of so high an exemption without total repeal of the tax simply represents the compromise between one group who would do away with the tax entirely, and the opposite group who desires the tax—with one of those factions simply having had the upper hand for the last 15 years.

Economic Effects

With so small a tax base for the estate/death tax, one might expect [relatively] small economic effects. As it turns out, the scope and significance of the economic impacts are rather contested, with a wide range of estimates about their dollar value. We will not be able to solve for the exact numbers in this debate; but we may at least consider the different kinds of effects.

One direct effect is the expansion of the estate planning industry, as wealthy individuals hire tax lawyers and consultants to help them arrange and dispose of their estates in such a way as to avoid some amount of the taxes. The higher the rate, and the lower the exemption, the more significant this planning industry is. The consequence of such estate planning is to move economic capital away from some [wealth-producing] uses to other [generally less wealth-producing, but tax-evading] uses. Such re-allocation (or misallocation, in terms of pure economic efficiency) of economic capital reduces overall economic growth not just for the wealthy individual, but also for the entire economy that individual's $12+ million net worth is involved in. This loss is in addition to the amount of capital directly removed through taxation (which, theoretically, is returned to the economy through government activities, albeit at some reduced level of efficiency).

Another effect of high marginal estate/death tax rates is that they encourage retirement over sustained self-employment. Retirement, it should be noted, is perceived very differently by business owners/entrepreneurs and laborers: for the laborer who earns money from the sweat of their brow declines in productivity with age, so retirement—if secure—is the anticipated time of life to reduce or stop working; but the entrepreneur may still be highly productive at the same age, and for many years to follow. Consequently, wealthy business owners and entrepreneurs, as a population, tend to have much longer careers, working well into the "retirement" years; however, an anticipated 40% tax on their estates comes into consideration as the business creator/developer approaches the exemption limit, changing their cost-benefit analysis of retiring vs. continuing in their productive enterprises.

Taken together, the reduced economic productivity of wealthy individuals plus the reduction of capital available to other new and growing businesses slows overall economic growth (both job growth and growth in real wages, which is linked to capital growth). How much it slows economic growth is debatable—for we cannot run parallel Earths with all constants held equal except for the estate tax—but we may infer that this economic cost increases as the tax rates go up and the exemption levels go down.

Ethical Considerations

As noted in our consideration of the purpose of estate and inheritance taxes, advocates of such taxes frequently advance them on [what is to them] moral grounds: these taxes promote the good of society by reducing inequality, by preventing wealth from accumulating in the hands of a few, providing some counterbalance to the gross unfairness of some people starting life with such significant wealth, while the majority must start out with relatively little. Such moral imperatives, however, are certainly not universally held (hence the ongoing debate to repeal the death tax); and in fact, they run into some conflict with some of our more commonly held ethical guidelines. So let us consider first how this kind of tax stands against the guidelines we have been using, and then return to analyze the independent merits of this moral demand to tax.

Immediately we observe that this tax, being levied on such a tiny minority of the population, does not fare well under the criteria of representation, participation, appropriateness, and peace. Those subject to the tax certainly may vote on it, but are outnumbered by those not subject to the tax by a margin of several hundred to one. Meanwhile the revenues collected from this tax are explicitly collected to transfer wealth from the taxed population to the untaxed population. For most such taxes in a representative government, the only recourse for the taxed population is to invest heavily in lobbying elected officials—an additional cost on top of the tax that diverts money from productive economic use to lining the pockets of politicians, undermining the credibility of the representative system. In this case, however, less direct lobbying is needed (at least in the United States): for the majority of Americans dislike the death tax (and a majority still dislike it when called simply an "estate" tax), even though they do not have to pay it. But this is an attribute of the voters, not of the tax: structurally, the tax invites contention rather than peace.

The estate/death tax fares better under the criteria of consideration, honesty and openness. The high exemption level not only excludes the poor from the tax, but also small businesses and farms (in the past, small family businesses and farms were injured by this tax, but the exemption level in the United States has been raised considerably, in part to accommodate these taxpayers particularly). The tax itself has been advanced forthrightly (arguments over popular terminology aside), and the operation of the tax is not hidden or disguised in any way. While it is true that most Americans are not aware of the details of this tax, that has more to do with the fact that they do not need to concern themselves with paying it than anything else.

As for simplicity, 50,000+ words of instructions indicate that this is *not* simple. Estate/death taxes require the evaluation of all assets (including the definition of which assets are taxable) at current market prices (which is another expense the taxpayer is subject to, on top of the actual tax). Additionally, computation of the estate/death tax requires computation of all gifts given by the deceased during their lifetime, as well as a special tax computation for any assets subject to the Generation Skipping Tax. The complications introduced by the Gift Tax and the Generation Skipping Tax were created to recover revenue lost to legal tax avoidance; and as this battle between tax collector and taxpayer never ends, we might predict such a tax to only grow in complications in the future.

In order to minimize their tax burden (that is, in order to maximize the amount of gifts a dying person is able to pass on to his/her own children and other heirs), wealthy people employ tax professionals to help them allocate their wealth. Such tax-minimization activity (typically termed "tax avoidance") may involve the creation of certain kinds of trusts, moving to another jurisdiction, and other decisions regarding capital investment and [re-]allocation. Unfortunately, many of these decisions involve moving capital from more economically productive uses to less economically productive uses—because a 40% tax rate has a higher cost to the individual than losing an investment which gains anything less than 40%. Unfortunately, this means national economic growth is reduced—an unseen cost generally ignored by the government collecting the tax.

Ethics of Tax Avoidance

When the government decides to tax a particular behavior (such as with an excise or luxury tax), it expects people to change their behavior. But people cannot change the fact that they will die; but they can change how they allocate their assets in life and death, in order to minimize their tax burden according to the established tax regulations. Such legal activity is termed *tax avoidance,* and some (pro-tax) people regard it as immoral—although the same people regard it as *desirable* when people avoid cigarette taxes by smoking less. Why, exactly, is *legal behavior change* regarded as immoral? Maybe because when the purpose of a tax is to confiscate wealth, those who want to plunder that wealth don't like it when the victim defends themselves.

Now let us return to consideration of the moral claim for taxation of property transferred at death—or more accurately, the taxation of some people's property transferred at death. For the proponents of estate taxes do not want to tax every person's assets at death, but only the assets of the wealthy—those who own "estates"—for it is their mission to spread wealth around, reducing the inequality between the endowed wealthy and the un-endowed poor. Similarly, those states with inheritance taxes also have exemption amounts for inherited assets ($25,000 in Iowa, for example), so that poorer heirs may enjoy the full benefit of their parents' labors for them, while richer heirs must share their parents' labors with the larger society (via the government). We just need to distinguish between the poorer people who have a right to transfer property without taxation and richer people who do not have that same right.

Thus it seems the moral imperative to reduce inequality through estate taxation immediately creates a moral conundrum: for by definition we must decide that one group of people has a right that others do not; or to put it another way, that one group of people (the descendants of those who bequeath an amount of assets below the exemption level) have a right to the property of another group of people (the descendants of those who die with assets above the exemption level). And wherever we set that defining line (the exemption level), we will find it absolutely arbitrary; indeed we will find it quite impossible to justify that dividing line to the people immediately above and below it.

Those subject to death/estate/inheritance taxes may naturally wonder why Bob may give his own property to his son, while Todd may only give a portion of his property to his son. And perhaps those not subject to the tax naturally wonder this, too: for despite the fact the estate tax in the United States is applied to less than half of one percent of the US population, it remains unpopular with the majority of voters (even when referred to as an "estate" tax instead of the even more despised "death" tax). It seems, at least at present, that it is a majority value in the United States that all people have a natural right to give gifts to their children without the interference of the taxman.

But to that minority which asserts a right to tax assets at death in order to combat the [perceived] unfairness that some people are given more than others: indeed, some parents do have more than others—but whether they have that wealth fairly or unfairly is a question for each individual, rather than a fact to be assumed. If a wealthy person's wealth was obtained through plunder, we might be just to plunder it back; but if it were obtained through hard work, enterprise, and intelligent use of private resources, we might be more just to let it alone, and rather celebrate the actions which created the wealth. But I would not assume that all who have wealth have obtained it unfairly, nor would I tax based upon that assumption.

Summary Report Card – Estate Taxes (Death Taxes)

Representation/Participation **Problematic**

A [tiny] minority of voters pay this tax; they can vote on it—and they can spend money on lobbying (which is itself problematic)—but are always vulnerable to a majority that could impose new rates unilaterally.

Honesty **Pass**

Whenever and wherever estate taxes are passed, those passing tend to forthrightly declare they are taxing the estates of the very wealthy.

Openness **Pass**

Information about the tax is readily available to the public.

Simplicity **Fail**

Complications abound amidst the many regulations and decisions regarding what assets to count, how to count them, and how to rebut the tax collector's evaluation of them, as well as the further complications introduced by calculation of gift taxes during life and accounting for generation-skipping taxes.

Appropriateness **Debated**

Estate tax revenues are raised explicitly to transfer wealth from one group to another. While most people accept this as unethical between groups of economic equals, many people make an exception when it comes to transferring wealth from a wealthy population to a poor population.

Consideration **Pass**

The poor are exempted from this tax. Exemption levels in the United States are currently high enough to exempt the vast majority of small businesses and farms.

Minimizing Harms **Fail**

Estate taxes are promoted quite independently of any consequences, as if the economic costs (including the re-allocation of economic capital to minimize tax liability) did not exist.

Peace **Mitigated Fail**

Estate taxes tend to be advocated from a rich vs. poor standpoint, contributing to the class warfare mentality and incentivizing richer people to invest more in lobbying government to protect themselves from excessive taxation—which in turn further exacerbates the resentment of the poor toward the greater political power of the rich. However, Americans' aversion to "death taxes" is currently great enough that the majority of non-wealthy people side with their wealthier fellow citizens in opposing this tax.

A summary of Class Warfare Taxes

By this point, readers may have noticed some tension between the ethical principles of consideration (it is less ethical to tax the poor to fund necessary government than it is to tax the rich to fund necessary government) and the principles of appropriateness (when raising revenue for a particular service, it is more ethical to tax the population being benefited, than to tax a separate population) and participation (any tax applied to the whole of the voting population is more ethical than a tax applied to only a minority of the population). I say tension instead of opposition, because we can easily imagine a tax that meets all of these criteria, such as general sales/consumption taxes, or land-value taxes, or even a flat income tax with some universal exemption level that relieves the poorest (but *not* the majority of people) of the tax burden. But tension becomes outright opposition in the following situations:

1. We define "the poor" to mean half or more of the population; or
2. We use taxation to fund more than just necessary government (i.e. use it for the purpose of transferring wealth from one segment of the population to another).

Any time we limit the tax base to a minority of "wealthy" citizens (however we want to define the term—the top quintile, the top decile, the 1%), we invite a majority of the population to dictate terms to a minority of the population. The wealthy minority then must choose between accepting whatever terms the majority would impose upon them, or trying to negotiate better terms by persuading the electorate (through rational argument or through lies, or even through both) and by persuading the elected legislators (generally by spending large sums of money to purchase influence through legal lobbying and quasi-legal showering of monetary benefits not technically classified as lobbying). And any time we use taxation for the purpose of transferring money from one segment of the population to another, we frankly and openly invite political combat between those segments, as each faction seeks to get more government benefits while making the other faction(s) pay for them.

Such a framework engenders animus and enmity between segments of the population. Such animus and enmity tends to be further developed—or propped up— by ideology that borders on mythology: for the poor, the myth is that the rich have attained and continue to maintain their wealth through injustice, so it is only right for the poor to take a share of that through taxation/government redistribution; for the rich, the myth is that the poor are entirely undeserving thieves who seek to plunder wealth through taxation because they are not hardworking and intelligent enough to create wealth for themselves. In both myths, the hero is virtuous and the enemy is evil, justifying the hero's action—that is, justifying their pursuit of their own self-interest.

Fortunately, not everybody accepts these myths. Those that do accept these myths probably won't read this book, because their ethical framework is already established, and their course of action already decided: tax other people more. Unfortunately, the myths are pernicious enough that even those who don't fully subscribe to them can be emotionally impacted by them; and even when entirely immune to them we must negotiate with other voters who are not so immune. Which is why it is so important that we call these myths to public attention, and unmask them, and ask our fellow voters: Do we really want a government and a system of taxation based upon these ideas? Do we really want to continue demanding more government services—to be paid for by someone else? Do we really want to continue electing politicians who promise us that they will make somebody else pay for the things we want?

Of course, such questions go beyond the ethics of tax policy, to the ethics of government itself. And for some citizens, the answers will be yes. Those citizens will continue to pursue estate taxes and wealth taxes and luxury taxes and progressive income taxes and corporate income taxes and any other taxes they can conceive of to fund the government services they want. But those people will also have chosen to be continuously fighting, and continuously pitting different portions of the population against each other in fighting.

But for those who would avoid such continuous combat, there are alternatives. One alternative would be to reduce the size and scope of government services, so that they could all be funded by lower tax rates across a broad tax base. But even if you prefer a larger government offering more services, there are alternatives to class warfare: for broad-based consumption taxes and flat[ter] income taxes can still be deployed—just with higher rates. Then if the voters disapprove of the higher rates—that is, they do not wish to pay so much for their government services— that may be interpreted as a sign that they desire less in the way of government services, rather than as a sign they would like other people to pay for them.

For those who object that the entire point is to make rich people meet (pay for) the needs of poor people—recognize that this philosophy of government has an extraordinary ethical challenge, which cannot be dismissed by the simple assertion that the wealthy "should" provide for the poor. Perhaps they should; but to compel them to do so through taxation is unavoidably using force or the threat of force to confiscate wealth—the phrase class "warfare" is not mere rhetoric when men with guns can take you to prison if you refuse to contribute what the people (through their elected representatives) have decided. So you have your own very substantial ethical questions to answer here: how much may they people decide to confiscate? Are there limits? If so, how do we determine those limits? And if the people exceed those limits, is it just for the taxpayers to defend themselves with force of their own?

13

The Individual
Shared Responsibility Payment
(the Obamacare penalty)

We now come to a tax that many people are loath to call a tax: the Individual Shared Responsibility Payment, a financial penalty imposed upon United States citizens who did not purchase "minimum essential [health insurance] coverage from 2014 to 2018. A core component of the Patient Protection and Affordable Care Act (sometimes just referred to as the Affordable Care Act, or ACA, and popularly known as Obamacare), this payment was proposed not as a tax, but as a "financial penalty" [administered through the tax code and by the Internal Revenue Service] for not complying with the Individual Mandate to buy qualifying health insurance; but when the ACA was challenged as unconstitutional and brought before the Supreme Court, the Court determined that the law was valid under the government's power to tax:

> *"The Affordable Care Act's requirement that certain individuals pay a financial penalty for not obtaining health insurance may reasonably be characterized as a tax. Because the Constitution permits such a tax, it is not our role to forbid it, or to pass upon its wisdom or fairness."*

Because the ruling legal authority in the United States has determined that such financial penalties may be laid upon the American people as taxes, we must consider such taxes here. For although the Individual Mandate with its Shared Responsibility payment has since been abolished, the legal possibility remains for similarly-structured taxes in the future. So long as we may pass them, we must consider, should we?

This discussion will be difficult, because currently the only example we have of this kind of tax is the Individual Shared Responsibility Payment that was part of the Affordable Care Act. Since the ACA was and still is such a politically divisive piece of legislation, we are likely to bring very strong opinions into any such discussion. Now it is beyond the scope of this text to discuss all the merits and demerits of the larger Affordable Care Act: we are interested only in the novel tax it created. What can we say about this tax—quite apart from the rest of the law—and its particular economic and ethical implications?

Description and Purpose

The goal of the ACA was for all Americans to have health insurance—whether they wanted it or not. That last part may seem like a snide joke, and an unfunny one at that, since of course everybody wants health insurance. Except not everybody wants health insurance (though perhaps it is true that everybody wants health care), which is why the law included a penalty for all those people who chose not to buy insurance— or more specifically, who chose not to buy a level/type of insurance that met the lawmakers' approval ("minimum essential coverage"). The lawmakers' reasoning was that overall health care insurance premiums would be lower if all healthy people (who would not use as much health care services) were included in the same insurance risk pool as less healthy people (who use more services); in other words, some of the cost borne by the more needy could be transferred to those less needy. The plan was sold based upon its benefits to the needy (as all political proposals are sold based upon their benefits); less advertised was this transfer of costs (as all political proposals tend to downplay their costs).

The financial penalty, known as the Individual Shared Responsibility Payment, was assessed each year through the tax code. Information on health insurance coverage was reported to the IRS (forms 1095-B and 1095-C), then the IRS counted all months in which the non-exempt individual did not have Minimum Essential Coverage (MEC)—or did not have such for their dependent children—and assessed a penalty. In 2018, the last year of the penalty, this was the greater of 2.5% of an individual's income above the tax filing threshold in 2018, or a flat amount of $695 per adult and $347.50 per child up to $2,085 for the family. The payment was supposed to be onerous enough to motivate uninsured people—particularly healthy, young, single people—to purchase health insurance, adding themselves to the larger risk pool. However, $695 annually was still only a fraction of the cost of qualifying health insurance (which by law, had to include mental health and substance use disorder services whether the customer wanted those or not, as well as maternity care and pediatric services, even for single men who had no children and were certainly not pregnant), so individuals who made too much money to qualify for government-subsidized health insurance and who didn't expect to need to see a doctor might still prefer a $695 penalty to a $3,000+ insurance plan.

Since the goal of the ACA was to get everybody insured, it is evident that this financial penalty/tax was not intended to generate revenue for the government: the ideal amount collected from the tax would have been $0, if everyone who would have been liable opted to purchase qualifying health insurance. Other taxes associated with the bill (such as a proposed levy on "Cadillac" plans for the rich and an excise tax on tanning salons) were expected to generate revenue, but the Individual Shared Responsibility Payment was supposed to change consumer behavior. To many, this financial penalty was always a simple fine and never a "tax."

And here we come to an issue that extends beyond tax policy, to government policy in general: what is it that the government may do? The traditional American perspective is that government may only do what it has been authorized to do by the United States Constitution (either explicitly, or implicitly according to what is "necessary and proper" for exercising its enumerated powers); but a competing perspective is that the government may do whatever is good, whether that has been explicitly authorized or not. The history of American government has seen a considerable expansion of its powers and aims, sometimes through Constitutional

Amendment, but more frequently through unchallenged legislative action and court decisions which afterwards approved legislative actions which had been challenged. Today, many voters and legislators simply assume that government may do whatever the people will it to do through their elected representatives.

Yet even as the powers and aims of government have expanded, the Supreme Court has (in most cases) made some reference to the original authorization in the United States Constitution, particularly through [re]interpretations of the General Welfare and Commerce clauses. Congress's Constitutionally-authorized power to regulate interstate commerce, for example, has been re-interpreted by the Supreme Court (in *Wickard v. Filburn*, 1942) to include the power to limit a farmer's production of wheat for his own household, although the wheat never entered commerce, let alone interstate commerce (but, argued the Supreme Court, it potentially could have entered interstate commerce, and the act of growing wheat for oneself still impacted the price of wheat commercially by lowering overall demand, so Congress can still regulate it as interstate commerce). When the ACA was passed, supporters argued before the courts that such legislation was permissible under the established interpretation of the Commerce clause, and several lower courts agreed; but the Supreme Court (in *National Federation of Independent Business v. Sibelius*, 2012) disagreed, stating that the ACA could not be upheld under the Constitution's Commerce Clause—it could, however, be upheld under the power to tax:

> *"[T]he Constitution does not guarantee that individuals may avoid taxation through inactivity. A capitation, after all, is a tax that everyone must pay simply for existing, and capitations are expressly contemplated by the Constitution. The... Constitution protects us from federal regulation under the Commerce Clause so long as we abstain from the regulated activity. But... the Constitution has made no such promise with respect to taxes."*

With this decision, the Individual Shared Responsibility payment is legally a tax. Although this particular tax was repealed as of 2019, the United States government still has the authority to pass a tax on a person for not buying a particular kind of product. Whether that authority will ever be used again is up to the nation's legislators, and ultimately, its voters. And if it is used again, what might it be used for? Perhaps we could tax people who choose to not buy other insurance options, like life insurance. Perhaps we could tax consumers for not buying a certain minimum of healthy foods for themselves and their children. Perhaps we could tax parents who choose to not use the public schools (that is, parents who either homeschool their children or send them to private schools; currently, there are already state laws that fine and/or jail parents for allowing their children to be truant from all school activity). Whether these proposals are politically feasible [at this time] or not is debatable; but they are all legally possible taxes, at least in the United States.

Tax Incidence

Americans with incomes below the tax filing threshold were exempt from the Individual Shared Responsibility Payment; furthermore, low-income individuals and families could receive Minimum Essential Coverage through the federal Medicaid program (this program had an optional expansion under the ACA, allowing single individuals without dependents to receive aid so long as their taxable incomes were below 138% of the Federal Poverty Level; 37 states opted in to this expansion). Households without employer-based health insurance and income between 138% and 400% could receive some of amount of federal subsidy to purchase health insurance (this was also administered through the tax code, as the Advanced Premium Tax Credit, or APTC); and some states issued further tax credits beyond these income levels. Ideally, all of these lower-income individuals would have access to affordable health insurance, and would not have to pay the Individual Shared Responsibility Payment.

Theoretically, the penalty tax would be paid by those with higher income levels who chose not to purchase health insurance for themselves. However, with the high price of health insurance, many people who qualified for some amount of subsidy still found the remaining premiums to be too expensive for them, so even people within the 138% - 400% FPL range might find themselves subject to the tax.

Since the Individual Shared Responsibility Payment was applied only when the taxpayer did not purchase health insurance, there is no consideration of how much of the tax was born by the buyer and how much by the seller, or how it impacted prices—it fell entirely upon the [non]consumer. Of course the rest of the ACA legislation had quite a considerable impact upon the prices in the health insurance market, and we may consider the increases in health insurance premiums caused by the various ACA regulations and requirements a kind of tax incidence upon the consumer—but such legislative analysis is quite beyond the scope of this work. In this chapter, we are looking at the Individual Shared Responsibility Payment only, not at the larger legislation, nor the other excise and payroll taxes which were also included in the Act.

Taxes and Credits
In addition to creating a new kind of tax, the ACA also created a new kind of tax credit: the Advanced Premium Tax Credit (APTC), which was issued to people to help them purchase health insurance. The advanced issuance of the credit made it easier for people to pay their health insurance premiums, but it could backfire: for if a person ended up making more money than they had anticipated during the year, then upon filing their taxes they would discover that they had been over-issued their tax credit, and were then liable to pay it back—sometimes thousands of dollars.

Economic Effects

Determining the economic impacts of the Individual Shared Responsibility Payment is difficult, since we only have a single tax to look at, instead of several species in a class of taxes. Additionally, the larger Affordable Care Act had such an extraordinary impact upon the economy, and upon the health care sector particularly, that economists could write several volumes just investigating and debating those. But what impacts can be specifically linked to the penalty tax, the Individual Shared Responsibility Payment? And what economic consequences might we be able to anticipate from a similar kind of tax?

As noted before, the very purpose of the penalty tax was to change consumer behavior. In this case, it was to motivate healthy uninsured people to join an insurance risk pool which included less healthy individuals. The tax penalty was part of a carrot-and-stick approach (the Advanced Premium Tax Credit being the carrot, and the tax penalty the stick) to fundamentally change the health insurance economy from a more individualized model (where insurance premiums were based upon individual risk factors) to a collective model (where health insurance premiums and risks were generalized across a larger population).

Meanwhile other parts of the ACA eliminated the individual's option to purchase a health insurance plan tailored to their own needs (for example, a plan that only covered catastrophic needs, or at least one that didn't include mental health and substance abuse services); after removing Option A from the consumer, the new tax further penalized them if they did not turn to Option B. To accomplish this purpose, the tax had to be made high enough and onerous enough that even an expensive Option B would be preferable to paying the tax. (Though as it turned out, the rate—or perhaps the very existence of the tax—was onerous enough that the taxpayers voted for representatives who repealed the tax outright.)

According to US Census data, about 13.3% of the American populace was without health insurance in 2013 (prior to the Affordable Care Act taking full effect), dropping to 7.9% by 2017. However, most of that change is attributable to the expansion of Medicaid rather than to the implementation of the tax penalty (and also other factors unrelated to the ACA, as evidenced by the fact the uninsured rate had already been declining for 5 straight years prior to 2013). Meanwhile insurance premiums climbed each year after the act passed (though some Americans received subsidies that reduced their personal costs); but this too is more attributable to the other aspects of the ACA (such as the MEC requirement) than it is to the tax penalty (although one could anticipate, all other things being held equal, any increase in demand for health insurance would result in higher prices in the market).

It may be impossible to satisfactorily separate the economic effects of the penalty tax from the economic effects of the larger ACA. The question is further complicated by the fact that one encounters very different data according to one's news sources—apparently the economic picture is complicated enough and murky enough that different parties can look at the same records and extrapolate very different sets of results. Amidst all this confusion, are there any results—or at least any anticipated results—which are shared by people on opposite sides of the political debate?

Fortunately, there are. Both sides agree that the tax penalty increases the cost of being uninsured, and both agree that this will motivate some (exactly how many is debated) people to purchase health insurance when they otherwise would not have. Both agree that people with health insurance are more likely to use health services than people without health insurance; therefore both sides agree that there is an increased demand for health care services.

The tax penalty alters market demand for health insurance and consequently health care services; however, *it does not alter supply* (e.g. the number of doctors, nurses, hospitals, clinics, and other providers). If supply is not increased, this would tend to increase costs—but other provisions of the ACA also affect costs, and people do dispute the impact on costs. Meanwhile it would also tend to increase wait times or have other reductions in service (e.g. less patient time with each doctor), as the same supply of providers is stretched to serve a greater demand. Such reductions in service will not be spread evenly across the health care system, but be most concentrated in those areas that have the largest increase in demand relative to the available providers. Now this reduction in service will be perceived as a loss to all those who already had health insurance and were used to better service; meanwhile new customers will have no baseline for comparison, and therefore interpret the new level of service to be the norm.

Net Benefits

When debating government policy, legislators and economists often consider the "net benefits" of the policy: does the policy, overall, produce more benefits than costs? However, it is important to recognize that benefits and costs are not distributed equally, so in many cases one portion of the population experiences the benefits, while another experiences the costs. "Net benefits" for other people may not be valued or even recognized by those who bear the greater costs. This is one of the factors which complicate our ability to read data: depending upon our direct experiences of benefits and costs, we will be biased toward noticing the data that most accords with that experience.

Theoretically, an increased demand for a product would be followed by an increase in price, which is in turn followed by an increase in supply, as new suppliers move into the market in pursuit of the profits available there. However, several factors interfere with this market process when it comes to health insurance in America. First, price information gets distorted through the system of regulation, third-party payments, price controls (both statutory price controls, and the mandated payment schedules from government programs like Medicare), and subsidies that characterize the health insurance market. Additionally, the supply of health care services depends not only upon entrepreneurs but also upon the number of medical professionals—doctors—available, and it takes a long time to train a doctor. Even in a system of perfect price information, the supply of doctors can lag behind the demand.

Consequently, the varied economic effects of the Individual Shared Responsibility Payment will not all generalize to similar tax penalties which may be enacted in the future. We can anticipate that any similar tax penalty will incentivize a change in consumer behavior; but many of the effects of such a change will be highly variable, depending upon the economic activity being affected. And if any such future tax penalty is passed as part of a larger law (like the ACA), then prediction is even less possible, as the economic effects will be wildly different according to the other aspects of that future law.

That caveat made, we can still anticipate a few general effects, even if we cannot pin down exact numbers. To begin with, we can say that any future tax penalty passed to require consumers to make a particular kind of purchase (like health insurance) will result in more of consumers' money flowing to the providers of the required product. (Whether the increase in money turns into a similar increase in profits will depend upon the other particulars of the law.) This money will have to be withdrawn from other consumer purchases—exactly which purchases cannot be anticipated. Thus there will be a visible economic benefit for some (the providers of the required product) and an invisible economic cost to many others. The politicians promoting the new tax will be able to tout these visible economic effects; but those opposing the tax will never be able to identify all of the invisible sufferers who have less business because their customers were forced by a tax penalty to divert their money to another purpose.

Meanwhile we can expect the beneficiaries of the new money will probably be less responsive to customer needs—because so long as the government is forcing customers to buy from them, they will have less fear of losing customers through bad service. Overall product quality is likely to decline—as in any noncompetitive market—but we can probably count on such declines to be taken as evidence that the government needs to take even more action to fix those problems as well.

Ethical Considerations

With established sources of tax revenue, we tend to assume that the government has the right to collect that revenue. We know the government will collect taxes, so we allow them income taxes, payroll taxes, sales taxes, property taxes, death taxes, luxury taxes, excise taxes, tariffs, and... everything else the government asserts a right to tax? At least the legislators in the government seem to think as much, given that they invent new taxes when the existing sources are not deemed to be enough.

Although in the case of the Individual Shared Responsibility Payment, the legislators were not seeking new revenue: instead, they were creating a means of altering the people's economic behavior. Apparently, they assumed—and the voters who supported them assumed—that the government has the right to do this; and the United States Supreme Court confirmed that it did indeed have this right, through the power to tax. Which was all very novel: for never before had a government asserted the right to tax a person for *not* purchasing something. Or maybe it wasn't altogether novel: for many governments in the past have asserted the right to dictate economic decisions to its population under the threat of force (and I am not referring to totalitarian governments only: for even the United Kingdom once dictated to its citizens who were coal miners that they could not change occupations, or government officials with guns would imprison them). But nevertheless, this idea was novel as a tax.

As a new kind of tax, it should be given a little more rigorous examination, for we cannot give it the benefit of doubt accorded to long-established practices. Fortunately, since the tax was repealed, we the voters have a new chance to examine the tax, and ask ourselves if it is really appropriate to create this new type of tax, instead of just assuming it to be so. For the Supreme Court's [5-4] decision that the government may pass such a tax does not end the discussion: voters may still ask themselves if they *want* this new kind of tax or not. Do they—do we—*want* to confirm our government's right to tax economic *in*activity? And if we do want to confirm the government's right to tell us what we must buy under the penalty of taxation, on what grounds do we confirm that right?

During the course of the debate over the Affordable Care Act, advocates of the act and of the financial penalty (during the debate, they generally did not refer to it as a tax) argued that they had not only a right, but a responsibility, to pass the act, in order to provide better access to health care to more people. A laudable goal, certainly; but as long as we recognize that the ends do not justify the means, we cannot be satisfied with the goal being laudable: we must examine the chosen means to see if those are also laudable—or at least appropriate.

So on what grounds does the government have the right to tell its citizens what economic purchases they must make?

State governments command their citizens to purchase auto insurance. They make that a condition of driving legally. They enforce this mandate not through taxation, but through confiscating driver's licenses, and fines, and even incarceration. And a tax can be likened to a fine. Here, the justification is protecting people's property: requiring auto insurance protects property by making sure a financially-injured party gets compensated for their injury. But this justification does not so easily apply to the health insurance mandate, since a person's lack of health insurance does not threaten anybody else's property—unless you are counting a financially-indigent person's treatment in a hospital emergency room to be a threat to taxpayer money. However, the advocates of the tax penalty cannot honestly claim that this is their ethical justification, since they emphatically oppose holding an indigent person economically liable for their treatment.

Governments also require citizens to purchase certain licenses; here the justification is protecting people's safety. But only the people who choose certain businesses and actions have to pay for the required license—no government requires a license just for existing—so this justification is not so effective for the Obamacare tax penalty either.

Now advocates of the ACA, and of the individual mandate and the tax penalty, can simply say that the law is justified because it is good, or because it promotes the general welfare of the citizens. Except its goodness is debated, and we have already seen that it promotes the welfare of some individuals at the expense of others (which is often the case of "general welfare" arguments). Is it simple enough to say a thing is good when the majority of the voters—actually, the majority of Congress at a particular moment in time—say that it is good? And we must remember here that we are not debating if health care is good, or if health insurance is good, but whether a specific means of attaining that—specifically, fining/taxing people who don't wish to buy health insurance—is good. Why is it good to fine/tax a person for making a financial decision that other people would not make? And if it is good, what prevents us from extending that assertion to every other financial decision a person may make?

Perhaps if we separate the tax from the context of healthcare, we may be able to consider the means by itself, without the emotional and political baggage that comes with the healthcare debate. Except here we have another problem: no one is advocating any similar taxes on other financial decisions, and imagining scenarios that we might have a similar tax is difficult. We might tax/fine people [over a certain income level] who choose not to go to college, and use that penalty to fund college for poorer people. We might tax/fine people who choose not to buy a certain minimum of healthy foods. We might tax/fine people choose not to buy life insurance. Or we might tax/fine people who live in the city for not buying a bus pass. Yet all of these hypothetical taxes seem silly, if no one is actually advocating them. What is it about health insurance in particular that justifies this particular kind of tax, when we would not apply this kind of tax to any other policy?

If we cannot answer these questions (and I cannot), then we are left with a tax without any adequate ethical justification. We might stop here, and declare that the tax is flatly unethical; but supposing there is an ethical justification that I have not credited here, let us go ahead and examine the tax according to our common ethical principles, and discover how it fares.

To begin with, we must grant that it seems to pass the principle of Representation—as proven by the fact that taxpayers were able to respond to it by vote, and voted for representatives who repealed the tax. (Tellingly, only the tax was repealed; the bulk of the Affordable Care Act remained, after much debate regarding possible repeal.) But while it passes for Representation, we cannot say the same for the principle of Participation, since the tax did *not* apply to the whole of the population: for the tax penalty did not at all threaten those who already had health insurance (or those below a certain income threshold), so for them, the tax penalty was always a tax on Other People.

Evaluating the tax penalty on the criteria of Openness and Honesty is particularly instructive, thanks to some frank comments made by MIT Professor Jonathan Gruber, a health economist who worked on the Affordable Care Act. At a panel discussion at the University of Pennsylvania's Leonard Davis Institute of Health Economics, Gruber explained that the *lack* of transparency (honesty/openness) was instrumental to passing the bill and the tax:

> *"This bill was written in a tortured way to make sure CBO did not score the mandate as taxes. If CBO scored the mandate as taxes, the bill dies. Okay, so it's written to do that. In terms of risk-rated subsidies, if you had a law which said that healthy people are going to pay in—you made explicit that healthy people pay in and sick people get money, it would not have passed, okay... Lack of transparency is a huge political advantage. And basically, call it the stupidity of the American voter or whatever, but basically that was really, really critical for the thing to pass... Look, I wish Mark was right that we could make it all transparent, but I'd rather have this law than not."*

In the same month, Gruber spoke at another event at Washington University in St. Louis, where he also described how voter ignorance impacts taxes. There, he pointed out that a 40% tax on consumers wouldn't be able to pass, but the same tax on health insurance companies—which would subsequently be passed on to consumers in the form of higher prices—*could* pass, even though it would cost taxpayers the same. In fact, he had praised Senator John Kerry in a lecture at the University of Rhode Island the year before for the same thing, referring to him as a "hero" who was clever enough to tell voters "we're going to tax those evil insurance companies"—although it was "basically the same thing" as taxing the voters directly, since the cost would be passed along in higher prices. Gruber declared this to be a "very clever… basic exploitation of the lack of economic understanding of the American voter."

When these comments were discovered publicly, proponents of the ACA tried to downplay Gruber's involvement with the process, flat out lying about the extent of his involvement (more dishonesty) to distance themselves from these remarks. (Republicans, meanwhile, played up his involvement, dubbing him an "architect" of the bill—a label that news media organizations on both sides continued for years after.) But whatever the extent of his involvement, his comments remain a good description of the presentation of the bill and its taxes.

Other aspects of the passage of the bill and the tax are likewise problematic. For we can say that proponents of the ACA were open about the plan to require all Americans to purchase health insurance, and applying a financial penalty if they did not—but throughout the initial debate they insisted it was *not* a tax (perhaps because they were aware of the strong negative connotation voters attach to the word "tax"). When the Constitutional legality of the ACA was challenged, proponents of the law argued that Congress had the right to pass the law under the Constitution's Interstate Commerce Clause. Then the Supreme Court ruled that the Interstate Commerce Clause gave the Congress no such authority; but that the Congress could pass the law under its constitutional authority to levy taxes. At that point, everybody started calling it a tax. Now one might complain that this is more an example of dishonesty in the Supreme Court's ruling than it is in the authors of the fine/tax—debating the merits of that Supreme Court decision is beyond the scope of this text—but it is still telling that the use of the word "tax" was avoided when it was perceived to be politically harmful, and embraced when it was politically useful.

The law was by no means simple, producing over 10,000 pages of new regulations. However, this is a testimony of how complex the Affordable Care Act is, not an indication of the complexity of the tax penalty specifically. But as noted above, it is difficult to evaluate the tax penalty in isolation, because we have no other examples of this kind of tax, and therefore cannot compare this penalty to similar penalties to see if such a regulatory framework is common to them. Possibly there is a way to implement such a tax penalty without complex regulation; but it is also possible that any penalty so politically designed must have a great number of stipulations and caveats.

Such stipulations and caveats describe the population subject to the fine/tax, so this bring us naturally to our Appropriateness criterion: when raising revenue for a particular service, it is more ethical to tax the population being benefited, than to tax a separate population. Again, we must note that this fine/tax was not created for the purpose of raising revenue, but to change economic behavior—specifically, to change it in a way that benefits *other* people. Now the proponents of the fine/tax may argue that it benefits everybody, because a person with health insurance is better off than without it; but this argument assumes that nobody willingly chooses to go without health insurance (or that those who do choose to do this are making a mistake). This is suspect: if a healthy single adult in their 20's prefers to go without insurance that would cost them more than $10,000 annually, who are politicians to tell that adult they are making the wrong decision? But that was exactly what the fine/tax penalty did: it told this group of people, with low health risks, that they were required to spend upwards of $10,000 annually on health insurance with Minimum Essential Coverage (although the government would subsidize their purchase if they were income eligible), or they would be subject to a tax. This population was emphatically *not* benefited by having their economic options reduced; and this was done to combine low-risk and high-risk individuals in the same insurance pool, so that lower-risk individuals would pay the cost and higher-risk individuals would reap the benefits. This is emphatically *not* appropriate according to our criteria.

But at least it was considerate of the poor, right? Because people below a certain income threshold were not subject to the tax penalty, and those with little money who were liable to the tax penalty could receive subsidies to reduce the cost of health insurance. Except not everyone could receive the subsidies: for no subsidy was available to employed persons if their employer offered health insurance that met the federal government's definition of affordable (i.e. their cheapest plan for a single person would cost the employee no more than 9.5% of their gross income—which many people did *not* consider to be affordable, particularly when they had families and had to pay an even higher amount than that). So while the tax considered the very poor, it biggest impact fell on those who were only one step above poor.

This was only one of the harms resulting from tax and the larger ACA. Discussing additional economic harms brings us back to the problem of isolating the harms of the fine/tax penalty specifically from the harms resulting from the larger Affordable Care Act—harms which are vigorously debated, with differences of opinion largely split along party lines. Going back to the debate preceding the passage of the law and the tax penalty, we see that the arguments regarding costs and benefits were divided among party lines then, too, with one party touting the benefits and another party concerned about the harms. Given such a setting, can we truly say that the law and the tax were passed with consideration of economic harms, including ways to minimize those harms? Or is it more accurate to say that the majority with the power to pass the bill dismissed the claims of the minority party?

Such partisan division suggests that the tax would not fare well under the Peace criteria. But placing partisan politics entirely aside, it still does not pass the peace criteria: for it expressly creates a new method for coercing the economic behavior of some individuals, adding to the number of threats the government and the majority vote may deploy against citizens in the minority. This is quite an example of how a democratic form of government can turn neighbors into enemies: for here we have one neighbor with higher health insurance costs (and perhaps even a pre-existing condition) using the power of law to force another neighbor with less need for health insurance to part with some amount of their money, foregoing some amount of their own needs. When we remember that the law means men with guns will confiscate your property and/or your freedom if you do not comply with them, we must recognize that this is the opposite of peace.

It is the opposite of justice, too. Throughout the debate over health care insurance, the language of punishment is used: we must punish insurance companies for charging too much, and for denying people with pre-existing conditions insurance [at the same rate as other people without these conditions]; we must financially penalize (another word for punish) those who do not take up their "individual shared responsibility" to join a health insurance risk pool, taking on the burden of other peoples' risk. But refusing to buy health insurance is not an evil act (or evil inaction)—and we certainly don't want to send people to jail for this act/inaction; yet we will apply a tax penalty to take their money for the same reason (and then send them to jail and/or confiscate their property if they oppose the tax collection).

Fundamentally, the Individual Shared Responsibility Payment (aka the Obamacare tax penalty) is a tool of one faction of voters to require a second faction of voters to make economic decisions to benefit the first group. Anyone who refuses is failing their social "Responsibility" and must therefore be punished—not through criminal punishment, but through financial penalty. And this is supported on the dubious ethical grounds of pursuing a perceived Good (health care access for all) which turns out to be good for some and not for others, without ethical consideration of the means by which that good is attained.

Summary Report Card – the Obamacare Tax Penalty

Representation   **Pass**

As evidenced by the fact that the people did respond to this tax through the vote, and the tax was repealed.

Participation   **Fail**

The tax did not threaten those who already had the required product; but it quite threatened those who did not have (and/or did not want) the required product.

Honesty   **Flatly Unethical**

Proponents insisted it was *not* a tax, until of course it was. And the larger bill was specifically written in a way to confuse voters about the cost of taxes, and to prevent the CBO from scoring the new tax revenue as a tax.

Openness   **Debatable**

The larger ACA was written such that the taxes would not be transparent; however, the penalty tax rate was an advertised part of the larger law, and made visible to taxpayers through the IRS website.

Simplicity   *

The larger law that surrounded this particular tax was stupendously complex; it is difficult (possibly meaningless) to evaluate the simplicity/complexity of this tax apart from the context of the rest of the law.

Appropriateness   **Fail**

The specific purpose of this particular tax is to force people into a larger insurance risk pool, transferring costs from some people to others.

Consideration   **Problematic**

While the tax did not apply to the poorest of Americans, it particularly hit those next up, who were above the Medicaid threshold but who still could not afford to purchase the required health coverage.

Minimizing Harms   **Debated**

The benefits and harms of the larger Affordable Care Act that authored this tax are a much debated topic, largely divided along partisan political lines.

Justice   **Flatly Unethical**

The tax is explicitly designed to punish people (it's a penalty) for making an economic choice which the lawmakers don't like.

Peace   **Flatly Unethical**

This tax introduces a new method for some people to control the actions of other people: tell them to buy a particular product, or else you'll tax them.

Postscript: Elizabeth Warren's Employer Medicare Contribution

Health care is a highly emotionally charged issue for many; and for many, its importance is such that it often outranks many of the ethical criteria we have been considering. Consequently, even if a tax scores poorly on our criteria, some will accept the tax in the name of promoting their health care policy goals. For this reason, the ethical evaluation of the new Obamacare tax was simply irrelevant to many voters; and for the same reason, the taxes proposed by Elizabeth Warren in her 2019 presidential bid are also not given careful consideration, because they are proposed to fund Medicare for all. Most of these proposed taxes are of the kinds already discussed in this text; but one of them is a new kind of tax, which should arouse more intense ethical scrutiny. To fund Medicare for All, Elizabeth Warren proposed:

- a 6% wealth tax on net worth over $1 billion—touted as a tax on the wealthiest 1%, this would be one of the highest rates in the developed world—we discussed wealth taxes on page 195 and class warfare taxes on 205;
- a .1% financial transactions tax—discussed on page 162;
- a 35% tax on foreign earnings (expanding the United States' peculiar assertion of the right to tax income earned in other countries)—see page 124;
- raising the corporate income tax rate to 35% (bringing it back to one of the highest in the developed world)—discussed in chapter 8;
- taxing *unrealized* capital gains annually—a poor plan discussed on page 157;
- raising the capital gains tax to match the rates on labor income—see chapter 9;
- a new Employer Medicare Contribution, discussed below; and
- a new Supplemental Medicare Contribution targeting certain companies.

So what is this Employer Medicare Contribution? Elizabeth Warren tweeted on November 1, 2019, that they will be "taking the money that employers are currently paying in the form of premiums to private insurance companies and have them pay it to Medicare instead." Her published plan elaborates: "To calculate their new Employer Medicare Contribution, employers would determine what they spent on health care over the last few years… the Employer Medicare Contribution would be 98% of that amount—ensuring that every company paying for health care today will pay less than they would have if they were still offering their employees comparable private insurance."

This is an extraordinary new tax: it is a tax not levied on income, or consumption, or property; it is not quite a tax on an employer's purchase of health insurance for an employee, but rather a *forced replacement* of that expenditure. The employer would no longer be allowed to purchase private health insurance, instead being mandated to spend [98% of] that money on Medicare instead.

Immediately, you might note this will impact different employers very differently: those who spent larger amounts on employee health insurance actually start out by paying higher taxes than those who did not. Now Warren's plan included provisions for eventually equalizing those; but that would still be particularly hard on those companies which had negotiated pay/benefit packages that included higher employer contributions to the insurance premiums. Unless they are unionized employers—for Warren's plan specifically discounts the tax rate for employers who are unionized, and in the future non-union employers could "reduce their Employer Medicare Contribution by supporting unionization efforts." Thus the tax not only forcibly rewrites contracts between employers and employees by replacing their health insurance coverage, it compounds the contract violation by financially pressuring employers to enter into new union contracts.

Meanwhile some companies will have an additional Medicare tax: according to Warren's plan, "If we're falling short of the $8.8 trillion revenue target for the next ten years, we will make up lost revenue with a Supplemental Medicare Contribution requirement for big companies with extremely high executive compensation and stock buyback rates." The government will later decide what CEO and other management salaries qualify as "extremely high executive compensation;" and if Americans will already allow them to dictate the terms of employer/employee contracts on health care, what will stop them from also dictating terms on salary? Of course, a big company doing tens or hundreds or thousands of millions of dollars in business each year may still want to compete for the most capable CEOs (as getting the second-most capable can mean a financial cost of millions or tens or hundreds of millions of dollars), so we may expect that some companies will continue to pay salaries which Elizabeth Warren regards as "extremely high" (in common political rhetoric, these are often described as "outrageous" or "exorbitant," despite being negotiated by competitive businesses seeking to maximize profits), so the Supplemental Medicare Contribution may be extracted from a great number of large companies.

"Contribution" is, of course, another bit of rhetorical deception: it is a tax, and failing to pay it will result in prosecution.

Using Taxes to Promote Unions

Unions and unionization is also an emotionally-charged topic. The merits and demerits of unions are beyond the scope of this text; but this tax impact is not. If you are not a fan of unions, this tax is immediately appalling; but suppose you like unions—ask yourself: is it appropriate for the government to intervene in a negotiation between one party and another by *taxing the first party until they agree to the second party's demands*? Would Americans accept this arrangement in any other situation?

We noted that the Individual Shared Responsibility Payment created by the Affordable Care Act was a novel and significant tax, since it created a new kind of taxing power for the government, allowing the government to now tax *inactivity*, punishing ("penalizing") people for making economic decisions the lawmakers did not approve of. Elizabeth Warren's Employer Medicare Contribution is also novel and even more significant, for it would extend the government's taxing power even further, allowing it to alter the terms of individuals' freewill contracts. In doing so, it actually contravenes one of the most basic purposes of law and government.

Bad government is characterized by the arbitrary exercise of power, while good government is characterized by the Rule of Law—the restriction of the arbitrary exercise of power by subordinating it to established and well-defined laws. The legal apparatus of a government characterized by the Rule of Law has two fundamental functions: to protect property (people are punished for theft) and to enforce freewill contracts (people are held liable to do all they have agreed to do). Economic growth fundamentally depends on these two features: the entrepreneur must be confident their property is safe, and confident their business contracts will be reliable.

But the Employer Medicare Contribution does the opposite of enforcing freewill contracts: on the contrary, it negates them. Warren's plan would invalidate millions of employer/employee contracts by rewriting their healthcare provisions. It would invalidate all the contracts (about 150 million of them) between employers and private health insurance providers, terminating their freely negotiated business relationship (and putting many/all private insurance companies out of business, a fact Elizabeth Warren explicitly admits when she discusses what will become of about 600,000 displaced private health insurance workers (they'll "work in other parts of insurance," she answers, "life insurance, in auto insurance, in car insurance"). Then it further violates the freedom of contract by aiding one party (unions) against a competing party (nonunion employers).

Warren justifies all these violations of freedom of contract in the name of promoting universal health care, and in the name of promoting workers' well-being. She [says she] believes America will have a better health care system as a result of her plan, and [she says] she believes workers will have better wages and better lives; naturally, opponents disagree. Meanwhile she never even discusses whether or not it is appropriate to use taxing power to accomplish this—she just assumes that it is. And most journalists also neglect to question whether it is appropriate to use the taxing power to invalidate millions of contracts and take sides in millions of other contract negotiations—they just assume that the government may do what the voters will.

So my challenge to voters is this: will you make the same assumption? Or will you pause to evaluate the ethics of this expansion of the power to tax?

14

Further Ethical Considerations

We began our text lamenting the lack of frank and informed discussion about tax policy—or rather, about tax poli*cies*, since there are so many different types of taxes to consider. We noted that voters, as a whole, are not much aware of the economic differences between each kind of tax, and do not much consider the ethical differences between them. To help correct that, we have examined eleven major types of taxes, discussing their various economic effects and evaluating them according to some basic ethical principles that most Americans would agree upon. Except in doing so, we did discover some tensions between some of these ethical principles, and some of the other wants and values of the voting public. This is understandable: for the selected ethical framework was only a starting point, not an ending point, of discussion. Now let us revisit some of these criteria to consider these tensions, and then move on to consider some additional significant ethical issues that didn't fit inside the starting framework.

Tension within the Ethical Framework

The principles of Representation and Participation seem both natural and fundamental for a people in a democratic republic, for the whole of the government is founded on such principles. And as noted in the introduction, "no taxation without representation" was one of the earliest rallying cries of the American revolutionaries. But tension is inherent in Representative/Democratic government, since it has to find a balance between majority rule and minority rights. Hence many of the fiercest debates during the founding of this country were centered on this conflict: smaller, less populated states, for example, were afraid that larger, more populated states would be able to dictate terms to them.

The smaller states of the nascent republic were particularly worried about taxes. The nation was starting in debt from the war for independence; but if the taxes to pay off that debt were equally divided between the thirteen states, then the people of less populated states would have to pay much more in taxes than the citizens of more populated states. Thus the Constitution included a clause which required direct taxation to be apportioned among the states according to their population, equalizing the per capita tax burden. Surely, just about every American today would agree that the citizens of smaller states should not have to pay higher federal tax rates than the citizens of larger states; and they would also agree that the large population of New York should not have the right to extract greater taxes from the citizens of South Carolina, simply because the votes in New York outnumber the votes in South Carolina.

To virtually every American, this all makes sense so far—but then something extraordinary happens when we change the terms a little. Instead of talking about "more populated" and "less populated" states, talk about "richer" and "poorer" states—or just "the rich" and "the poor"—and suddenly things make less sense.

For some reason, many voters who would refuse to allow a majority group to impose taxes upon a minority group in one context are entirely okay with this arrangement when it comes to the rich and poor. Progressive tax rates and taxes targeted at "the wealthy" become acceptable by majority vote—although the same voters would *not* accept a majority vote from two foxes and one hen about what to have for dinner. Why is this?

It seems another value consideration is more important to these voters than the values of Representation, Participation, and Appropriateness. We might term this value/ethic Social Responsibility, Duty to Those in Need, Charity, or some other term, all of which describe the idea that those who are not in Want have not only the ability but also some obligation to assist those who are in Want. But while this might explain part of the situation, it cannot explain it entirely: for there is a significant moral difference between an ethical rule that states the rich person is under a personal obligation to help the poor, enforced by their own conscience, and a rule that states a rich person is under a *social* obligation to do this, enforced by men with guns who will confiscate the rich person's property or liberty (or life, if the person resists the confiscation of liberty) for noncompliance. Put another way, it is Good for me to help my fellow man by making a personal sacrifice; but it is a very different thing to say that it is Good to force my fellow man to make that sacrifice.

So what justifies the majority vote in this case? What value/ethic, in addition to Social Responsibility/Duty/Charity, justifies a tax policy which allows one group of people to dictate terms to another group of people? Perhaps some voters today subscribe to an ethic of Democracy which supports the right of the simple majority over the rights of the minority on a Utilitarian principle (the greatest good for the greatest number). It is worth noting that the founders of the United States of America carefully created a Republic, *not* a democracy, specifically because they rejected the right of untrammeled majority rule (the "tyranny of the majority"); but in more than two centuries since then, American values have shifted more towards democratic than republican values (the systems of government, *not* the political parties). Except this is not entirely the case: for the vast majority of Americans (and voters in other democratic nations) would absolutely reject the right of a majority vote to pass a tax on a minority for reasons of race or ethnicity. Only when the minority in question is the rich do we allow this. Why this exception?

Perhaps this is the Robin Hood ethic: it is right to steal from the rich to give to the poor? (Never mind that Robin Hood stole specifically from the tax collectors, to return the taxes to the people.) This returns us to the Class Warfare myth we considered earlier: if we imagine the rich to have obtained their riches by evil, then it is right to confiscate those ill-gotten gains. But we cannot call gains ill-gotten when they have been obtained through freewill economic interactions.

What about some version of Social Contract theory? The rich, by consenting to the social contract, also consent to paying a larger share of their own income to finance the [necessary] government. But this seems dubious to me. If a group of citizens all contribute to a common pool, and then votes about how to spend that money, that is supportable; but if the citizens then vote to demand a larger contribution from one [percent] of their number, simply because that one [percent] has more, this seems to me to be insupportable.

Of course, there is always the ethic of simple Pragmatism: the government needs money, and the rich have money, so the government takes it from the rich. Except, I rarely come across a voter who makes this explicit argument. (Do you?) Almost always, the ethical argument is based upon some conception of Fairness—of making the rich "pay their fair share." But "fair" in this discussion never means "equal," or even "just;" but rather something akin to "rich people must pay more because they have more," or sometimes, "it is fair to make rich people pay more because they benefit more." This last formulation makes some sense, if one is referring to the protection of property, the enforcement of contracts, maintenance of infrastructure, and other basic government services—and it surely applies to welfare for the rich, such as monopoly grants, business subsidies, and a host of other policies—but it does not make any sense when looking at redistribution and safety net programs. When considering welfare for the poor, we are explicitly considering an ethic of redistribution, *not* an ethic of "the rich pay more because they benefit more," and when considering handouts for the rich, if we agree that these are wrong and should be eliminated, then we can no longer use them to justify this tax conundrum.

Of course, it is possible that the ethical claims of Social Responsibility, Duty to the Poor, Charity, and Fairness are in fact just masks for a more fundamental claim— the pursuit of self-interest. Voters simply want other voters to pay the taxes. For if we really operated on the ethic that those who are not in Want should help support those who are in Want, then we must also demand more taxes from the middle class. Overall, there is more money available from the middle class on account of their sheer size; and they are certainly not in Want—indeed, the middle class in the developed world today enjoys an amount of wealth and luxury far exceeding what humanity has historically known. So, based upon the ethics above, shouldn't the middle classes also increase their contribution to the taxes? Indeed, in many countries in Europe, this has been accomplished, with VATs and payroll taxes and other taxes collecting significant taxes from the middle classes as well as the rich. In these countries, we might say they have resolved the Representation/Participation tension: if the majority of people are taxed, then we cannot say that voters are dictating terms to a minority. But in the United States at least, politicians do not gain popular support by promoting tax increases on the middle class; so we know there at least the voters are not being driven by Duty to the Poor.

To clarify here: I am NOT saying that Americans are not moved by Duty to the Poor; I am saying that this does not drive their tax policies. Outside of taxation, Americans are the most charitable people in the world, as evidenced by the fact they have the highest rate of charitable donations as a percentage of Gross Domestic Product. (New Zealand and Canada come next, followed by the United Kingdom, with the UK giving less than half the percentage of the USA.) Concern for the Poor definitely impacts private freewill economic decisions; but we cannot pretend that it is the driver of tax policies which push the responsibility for that concern upon the rich only.

Indeed, the principle of naked self-interest—guiding one's vote to shift any tax burden from oneself to others—is likely one of the reasons why voters *don't* examine tax policies from an ethical perspective: because from that perspective, the ethics are moot—and uncomfortable to consider, since it might reveal to us our actual state. The ethical principles of Representation, Participation, Appropriateness, and Peace make sense to us in the abstract; but they are very inconvenient for a people who want more services from the government and also want other people to pay for them.

A Potential (but Politically Impossible?) Resolution

The ethical criteria of Representation, Participation, Appropriateness, and Peace can all be satisfied, if we are willing. In fact, outside of tax policy, many people are very willing. Consider:

Almost everyone recognizes the evil (or potential evil) in allowing governors to pass laws that do not apply to them. Whenever the government exempts itself from a requirement laid upon the citizens, we rightfully object, and name that injustice. So... could we apply the same principle to creating tax policy?

This might be feasible in direct democracy: any citizen/governor who would not be subject to a tax may not vote on that tax. Those who pay no taxes would not be able to raise taxes on others; instead, every vote to increase taxes would be a vote to increase one's own taxes.

But in a representative government, this becomes less practicable: for the citizen does not vote directly upon tax policy, but instead votes for a representative who in turn votes upon tax policy—and on every other law brought before them. So while it would solve the Representation problem with regards to tax policy to prevent non-taxpayers from voting, disenfranchising them would create a bigger Representation problem for every other area of public policy. Such disenfranchisement would surely be intolerable to the vast majority of people.

Self-interest is often disguised as Consideration for others: we can say that we should not burden "the poor" with the expense of [necessary] government, while really meaning that we ourselves do not want to be burdened with this expense. Meanwhile, the Consideration principle itself becomes increasingly problematic the more we expand our conception of necessary government—as we demand more and more services from the government, beyond those which benefit everybody.

The people of democratic nations expect their governments to secure their liberty, their property, and their contracts. These are secured through the establishment of police forces (and on the national scale, the military, which protects the borders of the nation) and through the courts (as when we sue someone for breaking an agreement). Beyond these basic services, citizens expect many other common services, such as the maintenance of infrastructure, the regulation of business (the scope of regulation being very much debated, but with at least most voters desiring some amount of regulation to protect safety), and operation of public education. Now the poor have particular need of such functions (for example, crime rates tend to be higher in poorer areas, so they have a greater need for police to secure their property and safety), often beyond their ability to pay. Here is where the ethical principle of Consideration calls upon the larger population of a nation to pick up some of these costs, which support government benefits enjoyed by all.

But when we add to these government services additional services which are *not* enjoyed by all, then we are moving beyond Consideration (as described in this text) to an ethic of Redistribution (often called Charity, Social Responsibility, etc.)—an ethic we cannot say is shared by the vast majority of the population, for it is fiercely debated. Redistribution, being the seizure of some people's property for other people's benefit, inherently and unavoidably conflicts with the principles of Representation, Participation, Appropriateness, and Peace. All taxes [and spending programs] which serve the purpose of Redistribution fail these ethical criteria, and I cannot excuse them under the mantle of Consideration—especially when so many voters advocating Redistribution are not asking for consideration of the poor, so much as they are demanding consideration of themselves.

> ### Redistribution in Reality
>
> Most often, "redistribution" is assumed to mean transferring wealth from the more wealthy to the less wealthy; but alas, this is not always the case. For many policies redistribute wealth in other ways, such as when a tiny minority of well-connected farmers receive the bulk of farming subsidies, or jobs are "created" by government spending in one area after taxing economic activity in another, or when airline traffic to rural airports is subsidized—and thousands of other "essential" government projects.

Of course many voters support policies of Redistribution on other grounds (such as Equality), which they rank as superior to the principles we have been discussing. But not all voters; in fact, this is one of the more contested points in politics. Consequently, policies of Redistribution (like all contested policies in a democratic environment) are often advocated with some measure of deceit (violating Openness, Honesty, and Simplicity).

One of the simplest and more common forms of deceit is the disregard of costs: a tax policy is advanced based only upon consideration of its benefits ("this will raise x number of dollars over 10 years") without consideration of its costs (the same policy will result in 1.5x *fewer* freewill economic transactions, or restrict the available capital supply and depress wage growth, or other consequences). Such calculation also violates the Minimization of Harms criteria; and this is why it is so important for voters to develop a basic economic understanding, so they can anticipate these effects and see past the deceitful rhetoric. This also helps them with another common and similar trick, that of assuming that changes to policy do not affect economic behavior. For example, a politician may lament that the government "lost" x amount of revenue by lowering the capital gains tax rate, assuming that exactly the same number of economic transactions would have occurred under the old rate, although this is flagrantly bad economics.

Choice of words also contributes to the deceit. Notice that refundable tax credits—which are in fact transfer payments—given to the poor is called "tax relief" while indexing the capital gains tax for inflation is termed a "tax break" or "boon" to the rich. Here, the person is assuming the legitimacy or illegitimacy of the tax policy based upon the identity of the [assumed] beneficiary, rather than examining the policy itself. The phrase "boon to the rich" is used to stir up people's antipathy towards the rich; and any appeal to envy or class tribalism is a suspension of other critical faculties.

Of course anti-tax voters can and do use deceitful rhetoric also—and if both sides regularly employ deceit to win votes, can we really keep Honesty as one of our universally accepted ethical criteria? Here then is another significant tension within our ethical framework: for voters simultaneously want to be told the truth, and also want to make sure *their* policies prevail, even if that requires disguising the truth. We noted this strategy specifically in regards to how the Affordable Care Act was structured ("lack of transparency is a huge political advantage"), but the same strategy is always on the table for politicians, makers of campaign ads, and voters. So long as we are willing to "win" at any cost, then Openness and Honesty are not really governing values, but rather nice ideals we like to pretend we have. This same tension can be found in all our common ethical principles. We will forever be challenged to abandon any particular ethical restraint, or even all restraints together, in order to win the immediate political contest.

The Multiplicity of Taxes

We have looked at a dozen different kinds of taxes, and discovered that governments continue to invent new forms of taxation nonetheless. But why is this the case? Why the multiplicity of tax types, instead of a single, understandable, broad-based tax to pay for the government services that people want?

Our preceding discussion reveals one reason: Given that voters often want more government services, but also want others to pay for them, politicians/legislators (who also want to enlarge the scope of their own governments) face a continuous challenge to either defer or disguise the cost of government. The multiplicity of tax types allows governments to obfuscate the cost of government: for virtually no citizen is able to calculate how much of their money goes to the various taxes—both directly, and indirectly, through the passing along of taxes through higher prices. Even if a person knows that their top marginal rate of income tax is, say, 22%, and they recollect they pay some amount in payroll taxes (probably not cognizant that the amount the employer pays also reduces their income), they won't be able to add up all the additional costs of sales taxes, property taxes, Value-Added Taxes (for Europeans), excise taxes, and additional costs passed along to them from tariffs and taxes levied on businesses. Granted, some of the multiplicity of taxes is the result of multiple levels of government—for state and local governments need revenue streams apart from the federal government—but then you have a state government with income taxes, sales taxes, *and* property taxes, and you have to recognize that such a state has disguised the visible cost of living there by dividing that cost into separate parcels.

Of course, economists can estimate the total tax burden, if that matters to voters. Counting income taxes, payroll taxes, and Value-Added Taxes (VATs), the average American (who experiences no federal VAT) spends about 30% of their income on federal taxes (plus additional amounts on state and local sales taxes, which vary between state), while the average Swede spends more than 40% of their income and the average German about 50%. (Note: families with children spend less on taxes in all of these countries than do single individuals, on account of the exemptions built into the income tax codes). Yet all of these countries run budget deficits, and are ever looking for new revenue streams to fund the continually expanding array of government services (which the voters presumably demand). Now it is difficult to tell a person paying x% of their income for the cost of government that you want to raise their cost even further—particularly if those paying don't perceive that they will get any more benefit (which they won't, if the cost of government is increasing to serve other constituents). Hence there is a great advantage—from the government's point of view, if they are comfortable with the deceit—to disguise the total cost of government by dividing it among as many different kinds of taxes as possible.

Tax Policy as Social Control

While the multiplicity of taxes allows the government to disguise the full cost of government, and therefore promote revenue collection, it also helps to promote another purpose of tax policy: social and economic control. Since each tax type has different economic effects, the multiplicity of taxes gives legislators and prospective economic planners a variety of tools to tinker with different economic effects. (Note: planners and academics may consider "economic effects;" but it is useful for voters to remember that "economic effects" is another term for "the decisions and behavior of people.") Naturally, control over others' decisions and behavior is highly controversial and hotly debated—when this purpose is understood. Consequently, while politicians/legislators may advertise some social controls (such as when using excise taxes to reduce alcohol and tobacco consumption), they may labor to disguise other attempted controls (such as manipulation of wage rates, housing prices, retirement spending, etc.).

Now just as voters are ambivalent about tax rates—they don't like high rates applied to themselves, but often excuse high tax rates when applied to other people—they are similarly ambivalent about the use of taxes as social control: they don't like taxes which try to control their own behavior, but excuse taxes aimed at controlling the behavior of others. Of course taxes are not the only way of controlling other people's behavior: we can also pass laws flatly banning certain behaviors. But banning a behavior requires some enforcement—sending police with guns to take the lawbreaker to jail (we can also use fines; but fines themselves are enforced by men with guns who take the person refusing to pay the fine to jail). Taxes, however, provide people with the middle level of censure, for behaviors that people don't like, but don't dislike enough to punish with jail. They also provide a way to generalize a cost penalty that would be difficult to set in a lawsuit: we cannot ascertain the specific liability toward every individual for secondhand smoke, environmental pollution, increased risk when driving alongside inebriated motorists, etc., so we instead apply a general fine to such activity through a tax. However, there are significant differences between taxing a behavior because I do not like it, and taxing a behavior as a means of recovering costs imposed upon other people. At least, the differences are significant to those people who have separate conceptual categories for these two activities— but not perhaps to those who either cannot or do not bother to distinguish between the two.

For citizens in a representative government, this is highly problematic: for if we do not have these separate conceptual categories, we cannot have a fair discussion about how some behaviors impose real financial costs upon other people (costs borne both by individuals, and by the taxpayers collectively due to increases in government services like police and emergency hospital care). Once we establish these separate categories, we must then take care not to generalize our own personal dislikes to societal problems (for example, a person who does not like strip teases as an economic product arguing that strippers impose a cost on society through the deterioration of morals and an increase in suits for divorce). For the moment a voter is willing to exercise their vote for the purpose of altering their neighbors' behavior, they make themselves a threat and an enemy to their neighbor. Such a stance should be taken only after great deliberation: we may be willing to be the enemy of the thief, and a threat to the exploiter; but we may not want to become a threat and an enemy to the person who purchases medical marijuana (in a state where that is legal) to relieve their chronic pain. (Medical marijuana is an example of the category of things that Americans currently disagree about whether it should be legal or illegal. Where it is legal, it is invariably taxed—a source of revenue, sure, but also a kind of compromise between those who want to ban the behavior and those who want to allow it.)

Excise Taxation as Cost Recovery can be based upon an ethic that virtually all citizens can agree with—people should recompense others for the harms they inflict upon them—although citizens will continue to disagree about the exact extent of harms and appropriate level of compensation. But Excise [or any other] Taxation as Compromise Between Factions is not so universal: the taxation will be ethically justifiable to one faction, and ethically abhorrent to the other; and the two shall vie perpetually for the power to impose their will upon the other—or to at least prevent the other from imposing theirs.

Taxation of Firearms

While guns and ammunition are taxed in the United States to fund conservation efforts, some propose that we might also use taxation as a way to reduce gun violence. A higher tax would raise the price of gun ownership and gun use, theoretically reducing the amount of gun crime. However, taxation of firearms presents a special problem for the United States, since the right to bear arms is protected by the Second Amendment to the Constitution: a heavy enough tax on firearms would have the effect of denying that right to the less wealthy.

The debate over gun rights in the United States is highly contentious—and beyond the scope of a text looking to identify shared ethical principles for taxation. But as proposals to tax guns for the purpose of gun control become more frequent, it is important for voters to have the mental categories needed for such discussion. Would a tax on law-abiding gun owners be recovering any costs from criminal gun owners? Is it an appropriate Social Control to restrict the constitutional rights of the less wealthy? Or is this simply just a Compromise between Factions, without real resolution or common ground?

How Overspending Impacts the Ethics of Taxation

For most of this discussion, we have considered tax policy in a vacuum, excluding considerations of how the tax money is spent. However, we did note that spending interferes with our perception of taxes: for the more we perceive we *need* the funding, the less concerned we become with how the funding is obtained. Some people cannot contemplate a particular tax being unethical, because they are overwhelmed with the perceived disaster of losing needed funding. But while such perceived disaster interferes with our ability to reduce current taxes, we are a little more free in considering future taxes. Therefore we ought to give some consideration to how our spending patterns—and more specifically, our *over*spending patterns— drive the need for taxes, and how they can propel us toward tax policies which do not satisfy our ethical criteria.

In our attempt to stick to the most commonly held ethical principles, we will not debate most of the *content* of government spending, but instead focus upon the overspending only. The specific content of the budget (military spending, law enforcement, infrastructure, social security, health care, welfare, agriculture subsidies, and hundreds of other items) is subject to continual debate, with different portions of each country's citizenry hotly contesting each budget item. But putting aside the contests and controversies surrounding which kinds of spending to reduce, we can still identify the consequences and ethical implications of continuing to spend beyond our means.

Continual Budget Deficits

Individuals, businesses, and private organizations understand the consequences of a budget deficit: spending more money than they currently have requires them to pay back that amount at a higher cost using future income. Individuals, businesses, and private organizations may all run short-term deficits if lenders are willing to extend them credit—which they do so long as they believe the borrower will have the ability to pay in the future. But too many years of deficits inevitably result in bankruptcy, as lenders recognize they will not get their money back.

Similarly, a government may also run a deficit by borrowing money (such as through the sale of treasury bonds); and the government will likewise have to pay this amount back at a higher cost, using future tax revenues. But here governments have a superpower: they are able to run a deficit much longer—indefinitely even, so long as their borders are secure, for their future income comes from future tax revenues. However, this "superpower" brings with it moral hazard: for governments (that is, politicians and legislators), perceiving they can run a budget deficit indefinitely, do so, apparently heedless of the other costs involved.

A budget deficit for a single year, or for several years of need (such as during a war), can be paid back over the course of the following years. But a continuing deficit is never paid back—it just increases the national debt, which in turn increases the annual interest payments on that debt. The growing interest payments eat up a larger portion of the tax revenue each year, further exacerbating the annual deficit problem.

While many an economist will tell you a healthy economy can sustain a debt, that doesn't mean the nation bears no economic costs. A government's need to borrow money competes with the needs of private business to borrow money, reducing investment in the private sector and consequently impeding economic growth. Meanwhile a government with a less healthy economy incurs greater costs, as eventually investors refuse to lend to the government except at much higher interest rates, or on the expectation that another nation backs up the debt (it is not for no reason that we have the term "Greek-style bailout" in our lexicon). To attract more lenders, and/or to secure an international bailout, such debtor nations have to increase tax revenues: inevitably, the cost of borrowing in one year is borne by the taxpayers in a later year, with interest.

The United States of America may be in a *comparatively* healthy condition relative to some economies in Europe, and may be able to enjoy an influx of money as investors lose confidence in other governments/economies; but that is no help to the people of a less healthy economy now, nor to Americans in the future if present trends continue. (But as we have lamented earlier, future citizens have no votes, and cannot protect themselves from the costs their parents impose upon them.)

Assessing taxes from one generation in order to pay the debts of a prior generation violates the principles of Representation, Participation, and Appropriateness. Even if we had an otherwise perfectly ethical form of taxation, a pattern of continuous overspending forcibly transfers the costs from one group of people to another. Meanwhile the need to do so encourages us to pursue rather less than perfectly ethical forms of taxation, since any lesser evil will be excused in order to avoid the greater evil of economic collapse due to defaulting on the debt.

Automatic Budget Increases

One of the causes of continuous overspending is the addition of new government services without the collection of new tax revenues; but another common cause is the automatic increase in spending on established programs. In many countries, certain government programs and agencies automatically have their annual budget increased—which makes some amount of sense, if one assumes that that the need for that program or agency will grow in proportion to the nation's population growth (or if one assumes a certain level of inflation—see postscript below). However, it stops making sense if the amount of budget growth is greater than the amount of tax growth. For example, if the program or agency received an automatic budget increase of 5% each year, but the nation's economy only grew by 3%, then the increase would incrementally consume more of the nation's economic output, requiring a greater share of the economy in tax revenues (and borrowed funds) in order to be sustained. Again, one generation's demand for government services imposes an obligation upon a future generation to pay an increased cost.

In some areas, this could be easily enough avoided: simply restrict budget increases to be no more than the nation's economic growth. (In fact, if you restricted budget growth to be slightly less than the nation's economic growth, then economic growth alone would incrementally reduce budget deficits, and eventually pay off the outstanding debt.) However, this is not so simple a solution when the government has promised certain benefits to recipients. We discussed this in the chapter on payroll taxes and social security; and this same problem occurs at the state and local levels with pensions.

The problem with pensions (and social security) is that benefits are promised in excess of tax revenues. Politicians have every incentive to promise large benefits, because their re-election depends upon the present voters; whereas future costs are borne by future voters, who have no say in the current politicians' re-election. Throughout the United States, state and local governments face huge unfunded pension liabilities, because at some point in the past they made benefit promises which were not responsibly calculated in terms of future cost. Such governments end up in a situation where they must choose between two evils: they can either do evil to the pensioners by reducing benefits, violating the contracts they had with them; or they can do evil to their citizenry by increasing their taxes to pay for their bad math. Only raising taxes is not considered evil, but normal, expedient, and even perfectly acceptable. They then proceed to promise even greater pension benefits in the confidence that the next administration will be stuck with the problem (and be able to deal with it by raising taxes again).

Now many a voter may argue that government pensions are a good thing, and that it is entirely appropriate to offer such compensation to civil servants such as policemen and teachers and whatnot. But the problem I am pointing out is not pensions, but the *overpromising* of pensions, beyond the government's revenues. It may be 100% appropriate to offer a rewarding pension; but it is *not* appropriate to make patently unrealistic assumptions about future investment returns and revenues in order to pretend that the government can afford more than it really can. It is *not* appropriate to say, "we make this inviolate promise to you, which can only be kept by taking more money from other people (we haven't yet decided exactly whom), who will have no say in this negotiation whatsoever."

Unauthorized Expansion of Programs

With access to [apparently] perpetual deficit spending, governments throughout the world have a tendency to spend first, then seek funding afterwards. Politically, this makes a lot of sense: voters clamor for government services, but don't like paying for them; so the government provides and expands services without first asking how much the voters are willing to pay. Except we generally do not accept this arrangement in our other dealings: when we ask for a product in the market, we ask about the price, and then decide whether or not the product is worth that price.

But government agencies do not ask voters what prices they are willing to pay, and don't bother calculating marginal costs versus marginal benefits for each expansion of service. Instead, they just pursue their mandate (it's what the voters want), and they expand their mandate (presumably it's what the voters want, but we don't ask them)—and the taxes will just have to catch up. For example, California has a Welfare-to-Work program that pays for supportive services such as transportation and child care to help welfare recipients find and acquire work; this is part of their mandate. But then California adds a new supportive service, a stipend for diapers; this is an expansion of their mandate, an additional expense, requiring additional revenue—but they do not ask the taxpaying voters if they are willing to pay the cost of this additional expense. Instead, the expense is simply added to the existing program, the budget deficit increases, and then new taxes are pursued to catch up with the new spending. Now maybe the addition of a stipend for diapers was a good thing, and would have been approved by the voters—but we will never know, because we will never ask them.

We have discussed various kinds of taxes, and determined that some kinds of taxes are more ethical than others; but is *any* tax ethical when it is demanded to pay for something taxpayers have never given consent to? If the taxpayers ask for x, is it ever ethical to answer, "I gave you not only x, but also y and z; now you are obligated to pay for all of these, and for everything else I decide to provide you tomorrow."

The Reluctance of Taxpayers

Many people (particularly those in government) will argue that it is terrible policy to ask permission from the taxpayers first, because those greedy misers will invariably say no. But if we are afraid to ask the people if they are willing to pay for our very important and even necessary government program, then we have another kind of ethical problem altogether: for such a stance indicates we only pretend to want a representative government, when in fact we want a government that will have the power to do whatever we want it to do, despite the will of the governed.

The Assumption of Right

Continual deficit spending, automatic budget increases, and unauthorized expansion of government programs all are based on a more fundamental issue: the government's assumption of an unrestricted right to the wealth of the people. The key word here is "unrestricted;" for most people recognize that their government has a right to *some* amount of the people's wealth, in order to fund the specific functions of government as described by their country's constitution, and to fund those specific functions the people have delegated to their government through their votes. But unfortunately, the extent of the government's right to the people's wealth is not very clearly defined in the minds of many voters—and not very much acknowledged in the plans of many governors—so *some* right in theory easily becomes some greater right in practice.

This slip from some right to some greater right is particularly easy for those who believe they are promoting the good of other people. Since the government service helps people, *of course* they should expand such services, and *of course* they have a right to the people's money to make this possible. Meanwhile "the people's" money is a very different thing conceptually than a particular person's money; and this level of abstraction makes it even easier to justify using—taking—that money. Unfortunately, no one in this position can identify just how much money they are justified in taking; but the answer always appears to be, "more."

Does a government have a right to the entirety of the people's wealth? The vast majority of people would emphatically answer, no! It is not for nothing that we have a philosophy of *limited* government. Meanwhile those who would answer yes must consider that "the government" unavoidably means "the particular individuals who are in power at a particular time"—it is not a perfect and abstract "government" that would have authority over your money, but Bob, or Charlie, or another human being of errant judgment.

If a government does *not* have a right to the entirety of the people's wealth, then what portion of their wealth does it have a right to? Under the theory of representative government based upon the consent of the governed, it has a right to whatever amount the people consent to. In practice, it has the right to whatever amount it can get away with taking before the people revoke their consent through the removal of elected officials or through direct rebellion and revolution. But absent the threat of revolt, and absent a diligent populace ready to express their displeasure through the vote (which at times requires people voting against members of their own faction), those in power may well assume in practice that they have a right to spend the people's money however they wish. *It is a practical right/power that the voters cede to them through inaction.*

Taxation and Theft

The government's power to tax is ultimately backed up by force: if you do not pay your taxes, then the government can send men with guns to take away your freedom (and if you oppose them, your life). This naked reality is unpleasant to us; and we would much rather the government's power to tax be backed up by some moral claim, to which we all readily accede. But while most voters accept that the government, insofar as it is a duly constituted government representing the people and executing their will, has a moral right (or even duty) to collect taxes, not everyone does. Indeed, some people even go so far to assert that the government has *no* moral claim upon their property; they assert that taxation is simply theft of their property under a different name. This is a severe and highly provocative claim—so much so that it is beyond consideration for many people, and consequently dismissed as crazy. But dismissing a claim is not answering a claim; and if we are serious about considering tax policies from an ethical perspective, we must engage this claim seriously as well.

It is not so crazy—nor so new—as it might seem. For such a claim was advanced in the fifth century by Augustine of Hippo, discussing what a government is without justice:

> *Justice being taken away, then, what are kingdoms but great robberies? For what are robberies themselves, but little kingdoms? The band itself is made up of men; it is ruled by the authority of a prince, it is knit together by the pact of the confederacy; the booty is divided by the law agreed on. If, by the admittance of abandoned men, this evil increases to such a degree that it holds places, fixes abodes, takes possession of cities, and subdues peoples, it assumes the more plainly the name of a kingdom, because the reality is now manifestly conferred on it, not by the removal of covetousness, but by the addition of impunity. Indeed, that was an apt and true reply which was given to Alexander the Great by a pirate who had been seized. For when that king had asked the man what he meant by keeping hostile possession of the sea, he answered with bold pride, "What thou meanest by seizing the whole earth; but because I do it with a petty ship, I am called a robber, whilst thou who dost it with a great fleet art styled emperor."*

Augustine wrote in the context of the Roman Empire, and the history of all empires which acquired land through conquest, and subsequently collected taxes from conquered people. Of course, citizens of representative governments are not exactly in the same situation; but does the difference in situation make Augustine's observation any less relevant?

Historically, emperors, kings, and chiefs collected taxes to enrich themselves and wage wars. Taxes collected for the first purpose are certainly theft; and taxes collected for the purposes of conquering (stealing) other people's land would also be theft. But so long as the emperor, king, or chief was capable of violence against the taxpayer, the taxes would be collected. Yet raise the taxes too high, and the [less powerful, but more numerous] taxpayers will respond with violence of their own. Sometimes these rebellions were bloody, yet utterly ineffective. But other times, a rebellion could cause a change in tax policy—particularly when that rebellion was led by powerful nobles. The signing of the Magna Carta in 1215 was the product of one such noble rebellion, placing some limit upon the king's powers, including the power to tax. But wresting power from the king and placing it in the hands of a parliament of nobles did not by itself transform taxes into an ethical collection: for a parliament of nobles could also use tax powers to enrich themselves and to wage wars of conquest, if they chose.

Further rebellions took even more power away from emperors and kings. Republics were established, transferring taxing power to representatives of the people. But even this transfer did not automatically transform taxes, for as colonial Mather Byles asked, "Which is better—to be ruled by one tyrant three thousand miles away or by three thousand tyrants one mile away?" Voters in a representative government could also make evil decisions regarding taxes. Although here at least was a counterforce: one voter's evil wishes could be countermanded by another's, so it would be more difficult to use taxes as a method of plunder. Yet more significant than opposing votes was the establishment of constitutions limiting the governments— mandates that explicitly limited the government's power, including how it may tax and for what purposes it may employ the tax money.

The people who live in representative, constitutional governments live in a very different situation than an Augustine living under the power of a conquering emperor. But elected governors—and the people whom they represent—may yet choose to conquer and steal. They might wage war to enlarge their country; they may exact taxes from disenfranchised colonies; and a majority faction may demand tax monies from a minority faction, for their own personal enrichment. Taxes to fund conquest and personal enrichment remain theft, even if a majority of people agrees to them. So the moral difference between Augustine's situation and ours is not *who* has the power of taxation, but rather *how* the power of taxation is used, and for what purposes. Some purposes will always remain theft.

So what purposes are allowable? The citizens of representative governments throughout the world are by no means agreed upon this question. But the vast majority of them do agree to at least *some* common purposes, many of which have been explicitly established in their various constitutions. These include:

1. **Protection of property and enforcement of contracts**—or in other words, police and courts. People want their homes, their property, and their persons secure from theft and assault, and are willing to entrust this security to a common police force and set of courts they can appeal to. Of course people have plenty of room debate the *extent* of the police force and court system; but nevertheless agree that a common system of law is preferable to millions of individual systems, and are willing to pay for that.

   Police tend to be paid for and maintained at the local level. Courts may be maintained at both the local and national levels. The United States Constitution establishes a Supreme Court and delegates to the federal government the power to establish inferior courts, make uniform laws regarding naturalization and bankruptcy, and securing patents.

2. **National defense**. This is an extension of people's need for security. No one individual can mount a defense against an invading country, so people are willing to pay their government to maintain the armed forces necessary to protect them. And again, there is much room for debate regarding the extent of the armed forces—particularly when the phrase "national defense" can be so easily stretched to justify military actions abroad. But while citizens debate over how much of a military they want to maintain, and over what amount of military commitments they want to maintain, they still agree on the need for some amount of taxation to support the amount of military required to preserve their nation.

   The United States Constitution explicitly authorizes the federal government to establish a navy, punish piracy, declare war, provide for arming a militia, and to raise a [temporary] army (there was no expectation of a standing army at first, but afterwards Congress established a standing army—after President Washington requested it of them, twice).

3. **Basic infrastructure**. While some anarcho-capitalists argue that all infrastructure can be created and maintained privately, the vast majority of people believe that a common government is responsible for developing and maintaining the roads, bridges, streetlights, etc. needed for transportation and commerce. The specific types of infrastructure may be debated, but most people share a common willingness to pay some amount of taxes for it.

   The United States Constitution authorizes the national government to establish post offices and roads.

4. **Standardizing rules of commerce**. This is an extension of the protection of contracts and trade: for we need to have a common standard of coin and weights and measures in order to negotiate trade. Now *regulation* of commerce is a little more contentious, since the word "regulation" can encompass so many activities, some of which are amenable to voters (that is, they will gladly pay for these services), and others which are much disputed. Generally, most voters approve of some amount of safety regulation and consumer protection; but they will *not* want to pay for regulations designed to favor politically connected companies over newer companies without such political connections.

    The United States Constitution authorizes the national government to coin money and regulate its value, standardize weights and measures, and punish counterfeiting.

5. **Negotiation with foreign countries**. People want their liberty protected not only at home, but also abroad; but they have not the power to negotiate on their own behalf. Consequently, they will pay for a government that continues to secure their liberty, contracts, and commerce abroad—although again, there will be much debate regarding *how much* the citizens expect their governments to do for them, and how much they will allow it to do for the other countries being negotiated with.

The governmental functions listed above, having been confined to those functions which attract the near-unanimous consent of the governed, can legitimately be funded by taxes. However, these functions describe a minimal government, and no modern government in the world is so minimal: every one takes up a host of additional functions which enjoy varying degrees of approval/consent from the people—but all of which require the collection of taxes. Such functions include the provision of public goods (including parks, sanitation, funding for the arts and other public entertainments, etc.), the "management" of the economy (put in quotation marks on account of the diversity of definition for this concept), and the redistribution of wealth. What can we say about taxes collected to fund these additional services?

Here we return to one of the fundamental tensions of representative government—majority rule vs. minority rights. Knowing that no decision or rule can satisfy everybody, we defer to the right of the majority in most decisions; but we simultaneously seek to safeguard the rights and liberties of the minority, since it is possible for a majority of people to make an evil decision. Constitutional strictures and statements of rights throughout the world establish limits for majority rule. However, support for such limitations is ultimately impacted by majority opinion, so such limitations are ever subject to change, and erosion.

Suppose a majority want their government to provide certain public goods, like fine art, and public television, and a space program. The majority of voters are willing to pay for these public goods, even if they themselves do not consume fine art, or watch public television. But does the majority of willing taxpayers have a right to require others to pay for these services also? The majority argues that this is only fair, because those who do not pay would be "free riders," enjoying all the benefits of fine art production, and public television, and a space program. Meanwhile the minority may argue that it finds no benefit in particular productions of fine art, etc. How do we resolve this? Does a majority desire for a product give them the moral right to deploy violent force? (For the collection of taxes is always, inevitably, backed up with the threat of violent force to deprive people of their property and/or their liberty—and ultimately their life, if they resist.) Or does the minority have the right to say, no, you cannot deprive me of my money in order to fund your desire?

> ### The Locality of "Public" Goods
>
> Some public goods may truly extend to the entire taxpaying public. But others are necessarily restricted to a specific location, benefiting only a portion of the public. Parks, statures, theaters, and other physical objects must be located in a particular space. In light of this, is it ethical to collect taxes from the country to erect monuments in the city?

Now consider the majority's desire to redistribute wealth. If this purpose is just, then we must be able to demonstrate that it is just, *without* appeal to the majority; for certainly it cannot be just simply because the majority will it. If my two neighbors have a majority vote against me, have they the right to dispose of my property because their vote outnumbers mine? Do they have this right because their vote outnumbers mine, *and* I have more property than they do? Or perhaps they only have this right *if* I have obtained my property unjustly—but what then if we disagree about whether I have obtained it justly or not? Do they have a right to dispose of my property because they of the majority opinion *think* that I have obtained it unjustly, whether I agree with them or not?

Meanwhile the majority of voters can never know the circumstances of each individual's accumulation of wealth. They simply do not have this information. I can know that Bob has more money than I do; but do I have the means to determine *how* Bob acquired all his money? He acquired it through thousands of decisions, actions, and transactions—were they all unjust? Were some portion of those unjust? And if I can satisfactorily investigate all of the factors which led to Bob's current estate, can I do the same for everyone else with more wealth than I have? Certainly not! But if I cannot possibly know if Bob has obtained his wealth justly or unjustly, dare I confiscate it? On what grounds can I assume any right to any portion of it?

If we were truly attempting to redress individuals' unjust accumulation of wealth, we would pursue them in court. But taxes do not do that; instead, they avoid the demands of the court (demands for things like guilt, and proof), and they cast their net beyond the individual to a class of people. Or several classes of people, which overlap. For government redistribution of wealth is not merely the redistribution of wealth from the rich to the poor, but also redistribution from the young to the old, from the healthy to the sick, from the childless to the families with children, from the rural folk to the urban population, and from the disenfranchised to the politically connected.

Every government program designed to move wealth from a general source to a specific need is a redistribution with its own separate justification. In a representative government, all of these justifications depend upon the root justification of majority consent, so long as a majority of voters could theoretically end any particular program. Except in practice, that doesn't much happen. Many programs are structured such that the cost is distributed among the many, with the benefits concentrated among the few (which itself is in stark contrast to majority rule); and the rewards for lobbying are much greater for obtaining benefits from the government than they are for reducing their cost. Since not all voters exercise their vote, "majority vote" [most] often means a small faction (lobby) which is more active and effective than the complacent majority. Additionally, multiple factions can cooperate to combine their lobbying power, making them further effective at directing the redistribution of wealth among the less active populace.

In such a political culture, every faction knows that government is available for redistributing tax revenues, so it is in each person's individual interest to lobby for their own share of these distributions, instead of refraining. Since government redistribution of wealth is accepted as given, as normal, and as acceptable, all that remains is to compete for one's own portion of that redistribution. Thus the economist Frederic Bastiat observed: "Government is the great fiction, through which everybody endeavors to live at the expense of everybody else."

Here you may object that this may be an overly cynical description of the ugliness of political lobbying, but it is not a refutation of redistribution per se—we cannot dismiss the goal of meeting the needs of the needy by complaining about our imperfect processes for doing so. Yes, some people will be lobbying to live at the expense of others; but simultaneously good people (or at least well-intentioned people) will be lobbying to meet the needs of the needy. And while it is true that every person and every faction will have a different perception of needs (always with more awareness of their own needs), debate between these groups will resolve itself into some consensus regarding the allocation of monies to meet needs.

But it is prudent to remember that political consensus is not identical to consensus among the population. For political consensus is achieved by negotiating among the most active and powerful lobbies, making concessions and attempting compromises, to achieve a temporal majority of opinion among lawmakers. This majority opinion (which may be only a slight majority, and which may not even match the majority opinion of the population at large) is then given the power of law to make it effective amongst the whole population. And it is prudent to remember that the power of law is violence.

Redistribution through the government is accomplished through violence.

We pretend this is not the case, because we rarely have to encounter this violence, but it is there—just try to avoid the taxes, and you will discover it. Of course, we have more sophisticated means of enforcement, allowing us to disguise the violence: before we send men with guns to cart you away to jail, we will do other things, like confiscating your bank accounts. The banks allow the government to do this, because the banks know that the government can punish them if they do not. So no physical violence is perpetrated in most instances; but it is the threat of violence that makes the confiscation possible.

Now you may point out that the state of course has the right to enforce its laws; and I should agree with you that police force, including the threats of imprisonment and loss of life, is appropriate to enforce laws against murder, theft, and other harms. We legitimately use force/violence to oppose the evil use of force/violence. But I cannot say that it is equally justified to enforce laws which, instead of prohibiting harm, require action. *Do not murder; I will use force/violence to prevent you.* Good. *Give Bob money, for he is needy; I will use force/violence to make you do this.* This is not good.

Some will say that it is good—that it is necessary—in order to meet the people's needs. They say that voluntary charity is insufficient. Perhaps; but I would that we reason with people to encourage voluntary charity rather than recourse to the threat of violence. Impossible, say many: voluntary charity could never be sufficient to meet the peoples' needs! Very well, then: suppose then we could agree that some needs are severe enough, and the system of voluntary charity lacking enough, that some amount of force/violence/coercion is necessary. How much? Let us be very deliberate about *which* needs and about *what amount* of needs we are determined to meet through the threat of force—but let us never forget that we are using the threat of force to meet them. For we do forget—the voters forget (or have never recognized), the legislators forget (or refuse to recognize it)—for it is too unpleasant a thought to keep, and not at all helpful for convincing others to part with their money in order to meet your program of meeting needs.

Remembering this should make us hesitate with every new government expenditure, be it for a public good or for a redistribution program. The programs we design certainly seem good to us, for we can envision all the wonderful benefits—but we cannot so easily discern the costs. We're just collecting a little money from those who can afford it (and others who can't, as we discovered in our investigations of tax incidence), right? Well, no: we are not simply collecting money, but also threatening people with loss of liberty (and loss of life, if they resist—but no one will resist so far over small, incremental tax increases). The enforcement matters; but it is more pleasant to us to pretend that it does not, and so allow ourselves to reach for ever greater sums, always in the name of meeting needs and doing good.

For what purposes can we confiscate another person's money? If the answer is, "for whatever purposes the majority wants," then we have an ethical problem. If the answer is, "for whatever purposes the lawmakers want," then we have an even bigger problem.

Unfortunately, the cry "taxation is theft" is beyond the pale to many. This is an extraordinary change from a century ago, when Calvin Coolidge, the president of the United States, declared, "Collecting more taxes than is absolutely necessary is legalized robbery." Today, President Coolidge's statement is considered "radical;" and instead of being engaged in debate, it is often simply dismissed as unreasonable without debate. My challenge to voters today is: debate it. Justify your proposed taxes, instead of assuming that they are already justified. Do not be satisfied that government has a general right to confiscate property, liberty, and life in order to maintain itself, but investigate the limits of that right. Examining the possibility does not mean abandoning all claim of a government's right to tax its citizens—it may only mean discovering how much its claims are overstated.

Perhaps not *all* taxation is theft; but perhaps a great deal of it is.

Recalling the Common Ethical Framework

I began this text with a call for ethical examination of tax policies based upon common ethical principles. Clearly, the principle "taxation is theft" is not common as an absolute principle—but you may find common agreement that some *particular* taxes are theft (such as those that are hidden, disguised, overly complex, and/or have no basis in representation). My hope is a full and frank discussion of this issue will help voters to understand each other—and look for common ground, instead of simply competing for the political power to impose their will for the next electoral period.

Postscript: Inflation—an Effective Tax

An adequate description and discussion of inflation warrants an entire book all to itself; but we cannot properly conclude a discussion of tax policy—nor a discussion of government theft—without saying at least a few words about this here.

Unfortunately, the very term "inflation" is poorly understood (and debated between factions), with the average voter thinking it means only a general rise in prices. But this definition disguises what is actually going on, and the actual nature of prices; and our experience with inflation in the last century results in the uninformed imagining that it is simply normal for prices to continually go up—when in fact it is a normal consequence of the market economy that prices go down. Let us consider:

Why do prices go up at all? The simple answer is that sellers always seek the most profit, and the uninformed assume this translates into higher prices. But anyone who has actually engaged in selling knows that as prices go up, the demand for the product goes down, so a too-high price actually translates into lower profits. Furthermore, a seller's competitors in the market can offer the same or similar product for a lower price to attract customers—competition applies a strong downward pressure on prices. Meanwhile if all sellers throughout the market were to raise prices together (as the simple view of inflation suggests), we must wonder: where do buyers get the money to pay the higher prices? You can answer that the price of labor is also going up, so workers have more money to buy the things produced—and this is part of it, but it does not capture the whole of what is going on.

What's happening beneath the price changes is that the supply of money itself is growing: more dollars (or euros, pounds, or other fiat currency produced by the national government) are being circulated throughout the economy. Now if dollars/etc. were created at the same rate that the economy grew, then prices would not be so impacted; but whenever the money supply grows faster than the economy grows, then prices go up, as more dollars chase the same amount of products. Imagine, for example, that everybody woke up one morning to find their money had doubled. You see they would be no richer, if we did not also double the amount of food, clothes, houses, etc. available to buy: all of these things would simply cost twice as much, because twice as many dollars would be available to exchange the same amount of products available for trade.

But how is additional money created? In the days before paper currency, money was minted from gold and silver mined from the ground. Now gold and silver are not *just* money, but also desired for other purposes, so while new discoveries of gold or silver would reduce the price of gold and silver relative to other products, it wouldn't necessarily result in the overproduction of new coin, although it could. More commonly, governments (which had a monopoly on coining money) purposely inflated their coin supply by changing the coins' weights: the Roman government, for example, was particularly notorious for recalling old coins, melting them down, and then reissuing them at smaller weights but with the same nominal value. This theft produced more coins—more money—for the Roman government, but did not produce any more wheat, pottery, leather, or other goods in the Roman economy. Consequently, the Roman government got to purchase more things with its created money; but then prices went up for all the people in the empire.

Today, we use paper money and account balances instead of coin with intrinsic value. Money is created by both governments (which can print money, or accomplish the same effect through making purchases on credit and other obfuscated activities such as "quantitative easing") and banks (through fractional reserve banking, which allows a bank to make loans exceeding the amount of deposits they have available). Governments particularly leverage banks and central banking in order to create money at need (historically, the development of government-backed central banks has been instrumental in creating funds for waging war). Adjusting particular interest rates and changing the reserve requirement for lending are two of the major methods nations use to adjust the rate of expansion of their money supply (that is, the rate of inflation). Significantly, national governments and central banks use such tools to "manage" their inflation rates, as part of their overall goal of "managing" their economies.

**Across the developed world,
many nations specifically aim for a positive inflation rate of about 2%.**

You might wonder why nations do not aim for 0% inflation (keeping the expansion of the money supply roughly equal to the expansion of the economy, maintaining price stability). There are several reasons for this, with one of the most claimed reasons being the fear of deflation—the fear that a contraction of the money supply and the consequent reduction in prices would result in an economic recession. Historians of the 19th century would readily respond that such a fear is bunk: for they can site several decades of deflation in the United States and other countries coinciding with significant economic growth. However, the Great Depression of the 20th century is associated with deflation, and that specific association (along with the fallacious suppositions of the Keynesian economic theory) has led many to incorrectly assume that deflation and recession/depression must go together. In any case, the Fear of Deflation is the most commonly stated reason; but a consideration of some of the other impacts of inflation suggest some additional reasons.

As noted above, increasing the supply of money faster than the increase of economic products results in each unit of money having less purchasing power in the market—your dollars/euros/etc. simply don't buy as much now as they did in the past. Now, if *everyone's* supply of money increased at the same rate, no one would lose in this transaction: we would all pay more for goods and services (this includes employers paying their employees more for their labor), but because we had more money to pay with, we would all end up with the same result. However, such perfectly even inflation does not happen in reality, for in the real world, the increase in the money supply is *not* spread among all people equally; instead, *particular* people receive the new money first, which then gets spread throughout the economy as it is used to make purchases.

The person, business, or government entity which receives the new money first gets the full purchasing power of the new money, since prices have not yet been adjusted upward to account it. The new purchases increase the demand for the purchased products, which raises the price of those products; then the businesses which sold those products make their own new purchases, increasing the demand in another sector of the economy, increasing the prices there. Thus the prices in the economy don't go up all at once, but start where the money is first spent, and then gradually spread throughout the economy. The first people to get the new money pay the former/lower prices, while the last people to get the money pay the newer/higher prices. Overall, the process transfers purchasing power (and wealth) from those who receive the new money last to those who receive the new money first. The price of labor is one of the last prices to adjust (workers on fixed wages, for example, will receive no raise during the initial period of inflation), so lower-income workers particularly experience a real loss in purchasing power. A 2% inflation effectively transfers 2% of their purchasing power to other people. Put more bluntly, a targeted 2% inflation *steals* 2% of their income.

Inflation also transfers money from savers to borrowers. For the principle amount of a $100 loan made in one year can still be paid with $100 in a later year, even though that $100 has less purchasing power for new goods and services. Old debts get to be paid with money which is worth less; and whenever the rate of inflation exceeds the rate of interest, lenders end up losing money on their loans. Those with the most debt become significant beneficiaries of inflation, as their debt becomes relatively smaller (so long as their income has increased with inflation—again, lower-income workers on fixed wages will not experience the same benefit). Meanwhile those with the most savings (such as retirees who must live off their former savings) experience the opposite effect: their saved money has less purchasing power than it formerly did. A 2% inflation effectively shrinks a person's savings by 2% every year, effectively transferring that wealth to those who are in debt.

Now consider, who or what carries the largest amount of debt in the nation?

In many countries, the biggest holder of debt by far is the government (or governments, plural, since state and local governments carry debt in addition to the national government). Consequently, the national government with a large debt gains significantly from [a low to moderate rate of] inflation, for its income (tax revenues) continues to increase with the expansion of the money supply, allowing it to pay its prior debt with less-valuable dollars/euros/etc. Inflation effectively discounts the cost of the government's borrowing: for paying 3% interest on a government bond with money that has lost 2% of its value is equivalent to paying only 1% real interest on the debt. And maybe this is where the real Fear of Deflation comes from: for deflation would conversely increase the cost of the government debt by requiring them to use more valuable dollars to pay for yesterday's expenses. Thus the government is highly incentivized to maintain some positive rate of inflation—so long as it doesn't get so high as to cause greater economic problems, such as a recession or civil unrest.

Simplification Disclaimer

The account above simplifies several topics a great deal, so I must recommend to readers to pursue further reading for a full and fully accurate account of the topics of inflation, money creation, monetary policy, and central banking. Though if you undertake this, you will likely encounter texts that quite disagree with one another on many of these matters—particularly regarding the subjects of deflation and the role of government in "managing" an economy. But all of them shall agree regarding the conclusions that a positive rate of inflation tends to benefit borrowers while costing savers, and that fixed-wage earners bear significant costs.

It is also important for me to note that national governments do not have direct control over banks, and there may be tensions between an elected government's preferred fiscal and monetary policies, and the preferred policies of the central bankers. Central banking systems are generally established with some amount of independence from politics, so newly-elected officials cannot simply order them to do as they wish. The elected government may desire more inflation, but those who run the central banks may desire to reduce the inflation rate, if they believe that will stabilize or improve the larger economy. Thus we ought not imagine that a government has direct power to set the rate of inflation—it is much more complicated than that—but we can say that governments benefit from inflation, and that currently, the majority of central banks which do purposefully act to influence the inflation rate agree that a positive rate of inflation is desirable.

Another way governments benefit from inflation is through increased income tax collection. Consider, for example, the following progressive tax brackets (these are the 2020 rates in the USA for single individuals):

Taxable income	$0 - $9875	$9,876 - $40,125	$40,126 - $85,525
Tax rate	10%	12%	22%

An individual with $40,000 taxable income is going to pay $4,602.50 ($9,875 x 10% + $30,125 x 12%), an effective tax rate of 11.5%. Now fast-forward for five years of 2% inflation: the individual now has an income of $44,160 (no more purchasing power than before), and pays $5,505.20 ($9,875 x 10% + $30,250 x 12% + $4,035 x 22%), an effective tax rate of 12.5%. Inflation pushed this person into a higher tax bracket, increasing the proportion of his income he had to send to the government. Simultaneously, the value of any deductions and exemptions claimed decreases with every year of inflation—the nominal exemption values remain the same, but the dollars saved have less purchasing power, and represent a smaller share of the person's income. Multiply such [unvoted] tax increases across every taxpayer on the threshold of a new tax bracket, and you can begin to appreciate how advantageous such "bracket creep" is to the government tax revenues.

Fortunately, bracket creep is easier for voters to address—if they desire to—than the general problem of inflation. Solving bracket creep does not require debating any economic theory on inflation; all that need be done is to index tax brackets and exemption amounts to keep pace with inflation. Of course a government hungry for revenue will not advertise this solution; but an individual politician will, if they believe it will help them win election and/or re-election. Voters, if they choose, could start with this action; and then perhaps move on to address the larger problems of inflationary policy.

Inflation is not technically a tax; but it increases the effect of other taxes, and it transfers purchasing power from people to their government like a tax, with a rate that can be manipulated by government policy—so it is, effectively, a kind of tax. But it is a kind of tax invisible to much of the citizenry, who being ignorant of the purposeful expansion of the money supply, cannot express their opinion of the matter through their vote. Probably retirees would be unhappy to know that their governments were purposely reducing their retirement savings by 2% every year; and probably workers would be unhappy to know that their government was purposely reducing the value of their wages by 2% each year. But for the most part, these potential voting blocs are not much aware of the matter—which probably suits the indebted governments just fine. After all, according to the governments' preferred economic theory, this is not stealing, but simply "management" of the economy to promote economic growth.

15

Moving Forward
to a more Ethical Consideration of Tax Policies

We began this tax by noting that voters are generally apathetic toward the discussion of ethics as applied to taxation. Now, after reviewing more than a dozen different kinds of taxes, perhaps we have a better idea of why that is. No kind of tax seems to be perfectly satisfactory; and worse yet, many of the least satisfactory taxes seem quite indispensable to the government (and the people who benefit from the government's policies). The government needs money—government services that the [seeming] majority of voters desire need to be funded—can we really indulge a discussion of ethics if that means eliminating the needed funding?

Of course we can indulge it: For the very idea that certain government services are needful presupposes an ethical argument, and the moment one argues that it is "right" for the government to do a particular thing, or that people have "a right" to services that require other people's property and service, one is admitting an ethical debate. In theory, at least—in practice, we do not want to think too much about arguments that are inconvenient to us (and we certainly don't want other voters to think about such arguments, either). From a purely self-interested point of view, it is better to ignore all discussion of ethics and instead cultivate the assumption that all should be lobbying the government for the services that they want. But perhaps that is not the kind of society we want: perhaps we want something better than the eternal conflict of trying to force other people to pay for the government services we want.

I propose that we can do better—incrementally. Certainly we will not be able to accomplish a complete overhaul of all government policies regarding both taxation and spending, nor can we start over from scratch with a clean slate. We can only start with the real state of affairs, and take steps toward a better state of affairs, knowing that each step will only be a marginal improvement. But we must work at exactly this— lest every step lead us to a marginally worse outcome, with government policies becoming less and less encumbered by ethical concerns, with the citizens both accepting and perpetrating incrementally greater injustices.

So how might we be more careful about future tax proposals? And what can we possibly do to modify current taxes?

Representation / Participation

Ideally, taxes passed by a representative government reflect the will of the voters regarding the amount they are willing to pay for the government services they want. However, as we reviewed various kinds of taxes, we noticed that some taxes do this better than others, and we recognized that governments (and factions of voters lobbying the government) in pursuit of tax revenue will look for ways to increase taxes in spite of the will of the people—or to place the burden of new taxes upon a smaller voting bloc that cannot oppose them. What can we do to improve this?

Let us begin with the problem of geographic representation. Currently, centralized government services and tax collection can draw money away from less populated areas (which have fewer voters) to distribute that money among larger population centers (with more voters); these less populated areas do not have the voting power to oppose the majority's will to take and use their money. So one thing we need to do is promote the localization of taxes (for those government services which can be administered at a local level). We could also propose a budgeting rule requiring every new tax proposal to report on such anticipated flow of money, so that representatives could be made aware of and be held accountable for moving money from one geographic constituency to another.

Another thing we (I say "we," but this next point applies more to the citizens of European countries than it does to American voters) can do to support representation is promote/protect national sovereignty against the calls for international taxation and tax harmonization. Tax harmonization is the policy of making tax rates in different countries substantially the same, so that people and businesses pay the same tax rates wherever they do business. Significantly, calls for tax harmonization invariably call for harmonization at the higher rates among countries, rather than the lower rates. Tax harmonization deprives the voters in smaller countries representation, because larger countries become the ones who set the international tax rates. Moreover, people and businesses not only lose political representation regarding taxes, but also lose the ability to "vote with their feet" by moving to another tax jurisdiction. But governments gain revenue; so governments, and international agencies which support government, will continue to advocate for such policies so long as their voters allow them to do so.

The Best Tax Harmonization Argument

While tax harmonization is entirely bad from the point of view of Representation, I should note the best argument in its favor: it reduces economic efficiency (the amount of wealth that can be produced using a given set of economic inputs), because businesses will be incentivized to make investment decisions based upon tax advantage. This is quite true—if we are comparing the business decisions to the optimal decisions made in a zero-tax environment. But at any other percentage, we have to measure this loss in efficiency against the typically much greater loss in efficiency that results from diverting funds to from private entities (which must consider market constraints, and therefore allocate efficiently) to purposes established by governments (which do *not* have the same limitations, and therefore tend to allocate much less efficiently). So for this argument for tax harmonization to work, they really must argue in favor of harmonizing at lower rates, rather than higher ones.

Another important way to promote Representation in tax policy is to allow voters to consider tax policies directly, instead of having tax issues always folder into a package of larger decisions. For in any representative system, a voter does not get to choose a tax policy—they choose a representative, who in addition to promoting a particular set of tax policies also promotes a great variety of other economic and social policies. So long as those other policies are more important to voters, voters are required to accept whatever bad tax policies their representatives want. This is particularly problematic in a two-party system like in the United States: for voters on both sides will prefer to accept some disagreeable policies over the alternative of letting the other team win; so both parties can get away with unethical tax policies so long as other issues are more important to the voters. But there are ways out of this conundrum.

For example, Article 94 of the Constitution of the nation of Georgia (not to be confused with the state in the USA) requires new taxes to be approved by the vote of the people: "A new type of common-state tax, except for excise tax, may be adopted or the upper limit of the current rate may be increased by a type of common-state tax only through a referendum." Thus, the legislators in Georgia need to ask their citizens' permission to raise most taxes. Similarly, the state of Colorado in the United States has a Taxpayer Bill of Rights (TABOR) added to their constitution, which also requires legislators to get permission from the voters to raise taxes. And in Colorado, the state government isn't even allowed to spend surplus revenues, but must refund those to the voters. If voters in other jurisdictions advanced similar bills (perhaps through the initiative process, if their elected representatives were not interested), then all future taxes would become more Representative—and no one needs to sacrifice the interests of political party to promote this.

The nation of Georgia also provides us an example of good Participation: in their Organic Law (Article 1), they prohibit using the referendum from being used to implement a progressive tax system: "The tax progressivity principle or methodology/tax regime may not be the subject of a referendum." Thus income taxes must be applied to the whole of the population, rather to only a part of the population. (However, as noted in the preceding chapter, it does not appear that a majority of voters accept this particular application of the Participation principle, even if they support the principle in other contexts.)

Honesty / Openness

Why are taxes disguised, and why are politicians dishonest about questions of tax policy? Because politicians know that voters hate taxes (on themselves), and yet are pleased to be promised new government services. So they take the simplest way out, which is to give in to the voters' demands for goodies while trying to hide as much of the cost as possible. And we cannot simply blame the politicians for this—not so long as voters continue to vote for the ones who are successful at this, while voting against the ones who honestly tell the voters what government services will actually cost.

Therefore this is probably one criteria that will not be fixed by any structural change to government, voting, or how laws are made. It must be accomplished through an attitudinal change in the voters: voters need to *want* to know the cost of services, and *want* to hold politicians accountable for lying about that.

Or perhaps there is some structural change we can make—regarding Participation—which will have an impact on Openness. Currently, one successful political strategy for raising taxes is to promise voters that *other people* will pay the tax (which may be the actual policy, or it may be a lie, and the actual policy is simply to disguise who pays the tax). But if we adopted the policy of charging taxes to the whole of the population rather than applying them to smaller subsections—for example, through flat income tax rates, or flat consumption tax rates—then every voter would know that *they* would bear the cost of the government services they want.

Simplicity

The simplicity/complexity of a tax also affects politicians' ability to disguise or lie about a tax—the simpler the tax is, the harder it is to lie about. However, disguise is not the primary purpose of complexity. Tax complexity, as we have noted in the previous chapters, gives governments/legislators more options for wielding power: variations in the specifics of the tax code provide them with a great number of tools for influencing economic activity—and more options for rewarding allied lobbyists and punishing adversaries. For the government, tax complexity is a feature, not a bug.

Again, voters may feel compelled to accept this so long as they have to vote for the larger package of issues supported by their preferred candidate or political party. But just as requiring taxes to go through voter referendum solves for this problem, it would also tend to reduce the complexity of tax policies. For the voting electorate does not have the specialized training to attempt as much social and economic manipulation through specific tax provisions (and those voters who do wish to do this will find more opposition among their fellow voters than politicians find among their fellow legislators); and individual voters do not get the same benefits from lobbyists that politicians do. Tax proposals put to the voters would be tend to be simpler, not only so they could be more easily understood, but also to attract a broader base of support. (This is not to say that this would *remove* complexity—only that it is likely to reduce it.)

Minimizing Harms

Simpler tax codes would also reduce the cost of tax compliance, which is one of the economic harms of bad tax policy. Every year, millions of hours of labor are diverted from wealth-producing activity to reading, interpreting, and processing tax forms. But this cost is only one of great number of the economic harms/costs of bad tax policy, many of which we looked at in the preceding chapters. Unfortunately, many of these harms and costs are invisible to a large percentage of the electorate, who simply don't have enough knowledge of economics to identify the likely consequences of various tax policies.

Here is where economic education is paramount—but how do we address this difficulty? The natural proposal for correcting a lack of education is to suggest more education—but if we expect such education to be accomplished through a public—government-run—school system, then we have a conflict of interest, don't we? For a government that wants to increase tax revenues is not likely to promote an education that would tend to diminish tax revenues. Better for the government to promote Keynesian economic theory in their public schools, and publish textbooks which celebrate the great advantages of government in solving for all social ills. It may be that in some countries, good economic education will have to come from sources other than the public schools.

Fortunately, education outside the government-run schools continues to grow in both quality and availability, thanks to the internet. Therefore we do not have to lobby the government to change the way public schools teach economics; we can instead take action to learn and to teach economics without the government's help or permission.

Only after the larger voting electorate understands the significant harms of particular tax policies will we be able to effectively lobby elected officials to avoid these harms. For no elected official wants to be associated with harms and costs; but they will gladly be associated with benefits when the costs are unknown. But suppose voters, as a whole, understood the great harm/cost of having marginal high tax rates on productive activity, or layering extra taxes on savings and investment—imagine if working class voters perceived their own interest in these matters: then how would politicians attract their votes?

If we are to mitigate the economic harms of bad tax policy, we must make them known—and make them known not only to some educated population of economically successful individuals (who will be dismissed as "the rich" in pursuit of their own self-interest), but to *all* who bear the costs of bad policy.

Justice / Peace

This might be the most difficult to correct moving forward—at least it *seems* to be, in the world of highly polarized and emotionally-charged partisan politics. Except I do not think that the polarization of politics is the cause of the difficulty, but rather another effect of the root problem, which is that representative governments wield too much power. For the more power governments wield, the more they can harm me; and when this powerful entity is directed by my neighbor's votes, that means my neighbor can harm me. Political factions are the inevitable result of this, as people join together to be strong enough to protect themselves from their neighbors' decisions, and to ensure that the powerful government is their ally rather than their adversary, enabling them to enforce their own decisions upon their neighbors.

Some people purposely want to wield tax policy as a weapon against other people, whom they cannot confront in court. Others want to direct tax policy to ensure that other people pay for the services they want. And others simply want to take control of tax policy to protect themselves from other people having control of tax policy. These tensions and contentions are inevitable; but they will be made greater and more significant as the power of government—and the potential power one may wield over their neighbor—increases.

We can mitigate this by reducing the power of government—which would involve reducing both the extent of taxation *and the amount of government spending*. However, a full discussion of spending issues will require another book. To confine ourselves to questions of tax policy, we might note that the lower the tax rates in general, the less threatening those rates are to peace between different factions.

Ending the Assumption of Right

All of these changes, however, depend upon a more fundamental change to our [elected representatives'] perception of tax policy: we need to end the assumption that all taxes are acceptable. If the government has a right to *some* amount of tax revenue, it does not logically follow that it has the same right to *all* of the people's income and property. Similarly, we must abandon the notion that the government's right to any portion of one person's income and property is established by the votes of *other* people. The idea that two people have a right to a third person's property because their *vote* outnumbers them is substantially identical to the idea that they have a right because they can *physically* overpower him.

This is hard, because the assumption of right has been taken for granted for so long: governments have the power to tax; that is what they do. They tax income, and real property, and savings, and specific products, and particular market transactions, and market transactions generally, and now even the absence of preferred market transactions—governments tax. And representative governments tax according to the will of the people—that is, the will of the politically powerful factions that compete to get the greatest amount of government benefits while deferring the bulk of the taxes to less powerful factions. This is simply the nature of governments; so why not join in and compete for the same?

But perhaps we can make it better. Not absolutely perfect, but *incrementally* better. A little change here, a little restraint there—a little *more* respect for the income and property of other people. We do not have to abandon every government project at once in order to make our tax system a little more ethical than it is now; but we do have to abandon our determination to make it worse. And we can start with simply a judicious consideration of alternatives *that includes consideration of the ethical dimension*. Tax proposal A is expected to bring in so many dollars, while tax proposal B is expected to bring in a little bit less, but is ethically preferable—but perhaps the ethical advantage of B is superior to the dollar advantage of A. Yes, such a calculation is difficult to make—for how much is an ethical standard worth?—but perhaps we can at least convince enough legislators that $90 given freely is more valuable than $100 obtained through the threat of a gun. Incremental steps.

We start by educating ourselves and others about the alternatives. We become aware of tax policies, plural, as opposed to just tax policy, singular; we learn that different policies have significantly different economic effects beyond the mere generation of revenue. We share; we discuss.

We proceed by making these discussions more significant to our political debate. We make them an issue in primary elections, we recommend them to our elected representatives through grassroots lobbying and social media. We patronize news media which actually discusses these issues, and refuse to let a single source of news dictate to us what is important. And *we withdraw our support* from the officials and organizations which refuse to discuss them.

Not all voters will agree on every ethical conclusion—not all readers of this text agree about them, either—for you each have your own opinions about which taxes are preferable to others. But we do not have to agree to everything to start making incremental progress; we only need to agree that we *want* to make progress, and that it might be possible to make progress—that some policies are preferable to others, and we can have some reasonable discussion about why.

If you at least can agree to that—then go forth, and discuss it.